D0329210

Reinventing a Continent

By the same author

The Ambassador
Looking on Darkness
An Instant in the Wind
Rumours of Rain
A Dry White Season
A Chain of Voices
The Wall of the Plague
States of Emergency
An Act of Terror
The First Life of Adamastor
On the Contrary
Imaginings of Sand

Mapmakers (*essays*)
A Land Apart (A South African Reader, *with* J. M. Coetzee)

REINVENTING A CONTINENT

Writing and Politics in South Africa

André Brink

ZOLAND BOOKS
Cambridge, Massachusetts

First United States edition published in 1998 by
Zoland Books, Inc.
384 Huron Avenue
Cambridge, Massachusetts 02138

Printed in the United States of America

05 04 03 02 01 00 99 98 8 7 6 5 4 3 2 1

This book is printed on acid-free paper, and its binding materials have been chosen for strength and durability.

Library of Congress Cataloging-in-Publication Data

Brink, André, Philippus, 1935-
Reinventing a continent / André Brink : with an introduction by Nelson Mandela.
p. cm.
Originally published: London : Secker & Warburg, 1996.
Includes bibliographical references.
ISBN 0-944072-89-5 (alk. paper)
1. South Africa—Civilization—20th century. 2. South Africa—Race relations. I. Title.
DT1752.B75 1998
968—dc21 98-13859
CIP

Contents

Preface

by

President Nelson Mandela

The road this country and its people traversed in the long journey to the dawn of full nationhood and the beginnings of the freedom we are now celebrating, was built by the multitude of hands that cleared and levelled the terrain and broke and laid the paving stones. It is the confluence of countless tributary tracks and paths and spoors trodden by millions of feet marching, each in its own way, in pursuit of that nationhood and that freedom.

Central to our quest for nationhood is the search for unity and coherence, given the destructive divisiveness of our past. Our freedom is, also, the liberty to be *one*, emancipated from the tyranny of being *forced apart* on the basis of social differences. In the victorious convergence of the diverse contributions to the building of the road we have walked, lies our hope for a future path together as one nation. The struggle against apartheid — drawing on the rich sources of human courage and decency and the abhorrence of injustice that were to be found amongst all groups and in all sectors of our society — was simultaneously an act of opposition and an exercise in nation-building, opening us up to our common humanity and patriotism.

The imposition of silence was a powerful tool in the oppressive arsenal of apartheid. Through a myriad of measures it attempted to keep untold the story of the suffering it inflicted, throttle the cries of anguish emanating from the victims of its brutalities, mute and obliterate the voices of courageous protest and dissent, render unheard the words and telling deeds through which people reached out to one another, keep unsung the lyrics proclaiming our common humanity and our belief in a world better and more beautiful than the degraded one it sought to engineer. We were meant not to hear one another and ourselves, nor the world of us, except in the censored and sanitized terms it would determine and prescribe.

In countering and breaking the tyranny of silence, the writers and intellectuals of our society were key. Part of the tragic human wastage of the authoritarian and racially divided past we come from, has been that even such potentially free thinkers were often trapped into and compromised by their group affiliations and sympathies. That so many writers and intellectuals from all sectors of the population did in fact over the span of many decades join combat against that tyranny of silence, is certainly testimony to the indestructibility of the human spirit. They, the writers and intellectuals, documented and analyzed; proclaimed, protested and prophesied; narrated, dramatized and sang. The South African struggle for liberation and democracy was always and everywhere — in exile, in prison, in the internal mass movements and the underground — informed and inspired by the rich body of thought and creative work produced by our writers. Their work continued to demonstrate, even in the darkest years, that the South African voices of justice and reason would not be silenced.

A particular feature of our situation, in which history pitted white Afrikaner against the black majority in the latter's search for freedom and equality, has been the significant number of Afrikaner intellectuals who through their writings added their voices to those denouncing injustice and crying out for a society all of whose people would be equal citizens. That long road we have walked to where we are today carries indelibly the tracks and the footmarks of these courageous men and women who dared to challenge the powerful structures of their own ethnic group to proclaim allegiance to the ideal of a greater

South Africa. This collection of essays is one example of such beacons along that road.

These essays give an insight into the intellectual path walked and some of the problems that had to be grappled with on that road. At the same time they open a vista on the challenges and the rich possibilities ahead. The quality of our freedom in the future will depend on the creative and critical input of our writers and intellectuals, just as much as the attainment of the present conditions for that freedom was brought about by their contributions.

Cape Town, May 1996

Note on the American Edition

To most Americans South Africa is very far away indeed. It used to be associated with apartheid, which was a Bad Thing; and now it is associated with Nelson Mandela, which is a Good Thing. Beyond that, public interest tends to fade. Yet for all their differences, the parallels between the two countries run so deep that what happens in one inevitably implicates the other. In his introduction to *Loosing the Bonds,* a massive inquiry into the economic, political, and moral ripple-effects of apartheid and the disinvestment movement in the US, Robert Kinloch Massie cites Robert F. Kennedy's address to students of the University of Cape Town in June 1966: "I come here today because of my deep interest in and affection for a land settled by the Dutch in the seventeenth century, a land taken over by the British, and at last independent; a land in which the native inhabitants were at first subdued and relations with whom are a problem to this day; a land which defined itself on a hostile frontier; a land which was once an importer of slaves and now must struggle to wipe out the last traces of that form of bondage. I refer, of course, to the United States of America."

In the wake of the Second World War, just when the US, under increasing pressure from the civil rights movement, began to engage more urgently and constructively than before with the problem of race, South Africa began to implement its pernicious and all-pervasive system of racial separation in the form of apartheid. For a time, and on the surface, as South Africa spiralled ever more deeply into injustice and oppression, it appeared that the US had made a decisive move toward equity and social justice. Yet below that surface tensions continued to simmer, regularly breaking out in explosions of long-hot-summer violence which encouraged the South African rulers to pursue their own alternative. As Massie puts it, "Each country has served as a refuge for the imagination of the other." It may also be said that each country saw in the other what it most wished to avoid.

But the situation was never simple. Even when Washington denounced apartheid, it continued to have trade and other relations with South Africa which effectively bolstered the racist régime. And when, in the eighties, previously unfocused sentiments of indignation in the US began to be translated into demonstrations and processes of "divestment" on a vast scale, American action against South Africa served many purposes, not all of them noble or very honest. Many Americans did indeed commit themselves to the anti-apartheid movement from deep conviction. But in the distorted perceptions of the Cold War, and in the grip of the kind of paranoia presented by the McCarthys and Hoovers (enthusiastically emulated by the South African security establishment), many American leaders secretly, and often not even secretly, saw in the apartheid leadership a useful ally in the struggle against world communism. And many Americans who campaigned vociferously against the evils of racism in South Africa were actually covering up their inability to do something effective about the racial mess in their own country. It is always easier to jump on the bandwagon of faraway causes than to face the nasty reality at home.

But there is no need to indulge only the uncharitable view. In America's fascination with South Africa in the eighties, and in the gradual move toward democracy which forms the backdrop to the essays in this volume, one could also read a genuine concern, verging often on despair, about the worsening situation at home. Later events like the Rodney King outrage or the

O. J. Simpson circus revealed the fault lines of American society to resemble all too unnervingly those of South Africa. And it is particularly poignant to be reminded, as we are by Massie, that "the founders of both Afrikaner nationalism and the African National Congress, the two movements that would battle over the future of South Africa for most of the twentieth century, can be said to have been blessed by the same pair of American hands." (He is referring to the missionary David Lindley, who was appointed the official pastor of the Boers of the Great Trek, and also brought up a young black boy, James Dube, whose son John later studied in the US and returned to South Africa to be elected as the first president of what became the ANC.)

Even given the large and obvious differences between the two societies — a white ruling majority and a black minority in the US, a small white élite forcibly subjugating a vast black majority in South Africa; in the US a black population descended from slaves imported from elsewhere, in South Africa an indigenous black population subjected by colonizers from abroad — the problem of race as such designated South Africa and the US as uneasy laboratories where the racial tensions experienced by every society in the world would either explode (with dire consequences for all) or be solved (which might open up a new space of shared experience for the global village). Ultimately, no American, black or white, could avoid that conclusion; certainly no South African could.

And this is the context in which *Reinventing a Continent,* first published in England in 1996, is now offered to an American audience. It is a view filtered through a writer's conscience and consciousness. And if much of it was first shaped by authors like Camus in the time when I was a student in France, a large part of that shaping was also done by Americans: by the courage and the inspired eloquence of Martin Luther King, Jr.; by the pervasive rage, muted by sadness, of James Baldwin; by the fiery invective of Stokely Carmichael (who married South Africa's great singer Miriam Makeba, Mama Africa, as a result of which she was rejected by both societies); by Alex Haley's relentless pursuit and invention of roots; by the intellectual flame and emotional flood of Eldridge Cleaver, before he betrayed the cause; by the visionary humanity of Toni Morrison.

Beyond the scope of "political writing," American literature, born from that society's long groping toward definitions and redefinitions of justice, has come to embody the need for a larger moral vision. And now that the narrow system of apartheid has crumbled under the combined onslaught of international pressure and internal resistance, South African literature, too, may grow into new dimensions, even as it takes up the burden of normality — that daunting, multifaceted thing which in America has produced such a range of literary experience — from Melville's tussles with destiny to Twain's relentless comedy, from Hemingway's defiant despair to Faulkner's elegiac vision of a sinking world, from the delicate acupuncture of Carson McCullers to the rumbustious physic of John Barth, from Heller's shining darkness to Pynchon's dark lightning. These names may be read as randomly chosen signs of the reinvention of the American continent over many years; likewise the reinvention of Africa, most pertinently its southern tip, will hopefully be read, in due course, in its literature. And the processes of its reinvention cannot but concern, quite intimately, if not always comfortably, its startlingly similar sibling in the northern hemisphere.

Cape Town, November 1997

Introduction

Reinventing a Continent spans fifteen of the most turbulent years of South African history, beginning more or less where my previous collection of essays, *Mapmakers* (Summit, 1983), left off. Covering the last, and probably darkest, years of apartheid and the transition toward democracy, it ends three years after the first free elections of April 1994, at a time when the euphoria of freedom has begun to give way to a more realistic assessment of where we have come from, where we are now, and where we may be heading for.

The essays in this volume have been selected from a wide range of reflections accompanying my novels from this period.* Representing a variety of impulses, and of reactions to a constantly changing set of circumstances, they were not intended to form a single line of argument. But in the process of selection they almost naturally began to cluster around a specific nub of questions and problems, at the heart of which lies not politics in the narrower sense but culture, and more specifically the relationship between writers and their society.

But inevitably, through the whole of the collection, runs the river of contemporary history in South Africa, so a brief retrac-

***A Chain of Voices* (Morrow, 1982; Penguin, 1983), *The Wall of the Plague* (Summit, 1984), *States of Emergency* (Summit, 1988), *An Act of Terror* (Simon & Schuster, 1991; Vintage 1993), *Cape of Storms* (Simon & Schuster, 1993), *On the Contrary* (Little, Brown, 1993), and *Imaginings of Sand* (Harcourt Brace, 1996).

ing of its course appears necessary. It begins with the continuing ripple-effect of the shock of the Soweto uprising in 1976, when a young black generation rebelled against their continued oppression in general and the imposition of the Afrikaans language as a medium of instruction in schools in particular. This event heralded the last series of convulsions in the racial conflict that had marked more than three centuries of colonial rule to culminate in the system the world came to know as apartheid.

In the years before 1976 many people on both sides of the divide (including writers) had persisted in believing that peaceful resistance might in the long run yield the same result Gandhi's *satyagraha* had produced in India, but the massive revolt of the young in 1976 irrevocably polarized all positions. By 1982, when this volume opens, a mindset that had come into being as a characteristic of a slave-owning society had evolved into its more pernicious shape. The result was twofold. On the one hand, it invited more and more militant resistance within the country, aided by growing international pressure through sanctions and overt support for liberation movements like the ANC. On the other, there were increasingly draconian laws and security clampdowns, paradoxically linked to too-little-too-late attempts by the régime of P. W. Botha to contain the situation through a show of "reform." The latter included, notably, an all-white referendum in November 1983 which approved the introduction of a tricameral parliament. This brought Asian and so-called "colored" (mixed-blood) voters into some of the processes of power while still excluding the vast majority of South Africans, the blacks.

In August 1984 Botha delivered his notorious "Rubicon" speech, widely rumored beforehand to introduce far-reaching political reform; when at the last moment, under pressure from his right wing, he rewrote the speech to dash all hopes of radical change, it dealt a crushing blow to the economy and provoked the final irrepressible groundswell of resistance which, ten years later, was to sweep Mandela to power.

While the ANC remained in exile, with most of its leaders still imprisoned on Robben Island, the United Democratic Front orchestrated internal resistance. This came at a time when the régime's resources were already severely taxed by South African involvement in the Angolan civil war and in Namibia, where the South-West African People's Organization (SWAPO) was fighting its war of liberation. In June 1985, unable to cope with the mounting pressure in any other way, Botha declared a national State of Emergency which was to be renewed annually. In spite of this, and also because of this, the situation grew steadily worse.

A turning point came when a delegation of prominent Afrikaners left the country in July 1987 for secret discussions with the banned ANC leadership in Dakar, Senegal, soon to be followed by a cavalcade of similar missions, including one by a group of writers and academics who met their counterparts in the ANC at Victoria Falls in Zimbabwe, in 1989. This movement toward change was accelerated by the perception that South Africa was beginning to lose its war against SWAPO and Angola; early in 1990 Namibia became independent, which brought the northern and western frontiers alarmingly close to Pretoria.

At the same time a decisive change in the international alignment of opposing forces had taken place with the fall of the Berlin Wall in November 1989 and the crumbling of the Soviet empire. Previously the threat (real or imagined) of international communism had been seen lurking everywhere, but particularly in the so-called frontline states of Mozambique, Angola, Zambia, Zimbabwe, and ultimately Namibia; and of course most insidiously within liberation movements like SWAPO and the ANC. But after the Wall came down, the old threat could no longer be used to impose on the nation a semblance of unity in the face of a common enemy. All of a sudden the most convenient rationalization of apartheid as a last stand against the Red Peril had fallen away. Even the Afrikaans churches, which for so long had bolstered apartheid with religious conviction and moral justification, were showing signs of balking.

The decisive blow came when in 1989 Botha was incapacitated by a stroke. After continuing to cling for several months to the last vestiges of his once terrifying power, the Big Crocodile, as he'd become universally known, was forced to abdicate by some less-than-honorable swordsmanship by F. W. de Klerk and Foreign Minister Pik Botha; and before the end of the year de Klerk was himself in power.

Deep down, there was little difference between the mad old king and the new leader of the pack, and de Klerk's record in politics prior to 1989 is an ignominious display of rightist moves and expedient, self-serving maneuvers. But de Klerk had one faculty his predecessors lacked: he was not a slave to ideology and, endowed with a canny instinct for political survival, he had no illusions about the situation into which history, with more than a little nudge from himself, had thrust him. Also, and this is important, de Klerk liked to be liked. And in the dead-end into which apartheid had forced South Africa internationally, he discovered that he could indeed win the hearts and minds of the West by playing his bad cards in the best possible way. In this endeavor he was aided in no small measure by the eagerness of the Bush and Major governments to support any move by a white South African leader toward liberalizing an odious situation. It suited to a T the promotion of their own economic and political interests.

There is really no need to be ambiguous about the situation in which de Klerk found himself: he had little, if any, choice about the cards he could play. His skill lay in playing them in such a way that he actually persuaded the world it *was* through choice, and clairvoyance and his own inclination, that he did what, in fact, any other political leader with a modicum of common sense and intelligence would have done in those circumstances to save South Africa, and his own skin. His heart was never in it, as his petulance since the elections of 1994 has demonstrated only too clearly; but in the process he salvaged for himself and his party the possibility of keeping a finger in the future power-pie. (If the metaphors are getting mixed, it is no more than a reflection of the prestidigitation the situation invited.)

The first notable act of his rule came with the famous speech at the opening of parliament on February 2, 1990: this was the one moment when indeed de Klerk reached beyond political shrewdness to statesmanship. Within days, Nelson Rolihlahla Mandela was free. After having fired the imagination of the oppressed masses in South Africa, and increasingly of the rest of the planet, the most famous prisoner in the world stepped from the region of myth into the limelight of actuality. And perhaps it was unfair to de Klerk that history should have lumped him together with a man like this. For after a somewhat stumbling beginning (Mandela's first public address in Cape Town after his release was a disappointing jumble of clichés and party-political rhetoric that came nowhere near the soaring expectations the world had cherished of him), he soon took charge of a country in a state of turbulence, anger, and uncertainty; and long before he was officially elected, first to the presidency of the ANC and later to that of the country, his name became a symbol of hope in a cynical and confused late-twentieth-century world.

In private the humblest and most generous of persons, with an ever-ready sense of humor, and a gentleness and inner serenity which enthrals whoever is privileged to share an intimate moment with him, he is also a formidable and visionary statesman, ennobled by suffering to deal with the power-mongers of East and West while retaining his ability to understand, from the inside, the plight of the poor naked wretches who inhabit so much of our world.

His qualities were sorely tested during the difficult years of transition to the elections of 1994. Several times negotiations between de Klerk's National Party and the ANC (and a number of smaller constellations) broke down; on a few occasions it came close to civil war. Even as the negotiations were taking place, there were massacres of black civilians, mainly ANC supporters, with the active participation of a Third Force recruited from, and orchestrated by, the old power establishment of de Klerk's own party. Place names like Boipatong, Pholla Park, Bisho, and others became markers along a *via dolorosa* that could so easily have ended in a wasteland of despair and destruction — especially after the murder, by white extremists, of the charismatic black leader Chris Hani during Easter in 1993, when the country came to the brink of disaster. As de Klerk withdrew in impotent bewilderment, two individuals stepped into the breach. They were the Transvaal ANC leader Tokyo Sexwale (later elected as premier of Gauteng Province) and Nelson Mandela. The country was saved from the kind of devastation that had followed the assassination of Gandhi, or of Martin Luther King, Jr.; and once again the negotiations became committed to a successful conclusion.

At last came the watershed experience of the elections. For a brief moment all the divisions of centuries of conflict, suspicion, and misunderstanding were resolved; and Mandela's installation as president on May 10, 1994 marked the celebration of the first taste of democracy South Africa had ever known.

The inauguration program itself made it quite clear that a page had been turned. There was no lack of the weighty oratory the world had come to associate with such occasions; but in addition there was the theatrical exuberance of a Xhosa praise-singer. More pertinently, the program involved a broad range of artists: musicians, poets, dancers, writers — in marked contrast with the dour and narrow-focussed patriotism of public occasions during the sad half-century of Nationalist rule. (Even at the inauguration of the Afrikaans Language Monument, twenty years earlier, not a single Afrikaans poet or writer of note had been invited to take part.) Suddenly, the whole spectrum of culture was swept into a domain previously reserved for politics. And at long last South African public life had room for humor and celebration and a full-fledged sense of fun.

Since then, inevitably, the course of events has not always run smoothly. Afrikaners, spoiled by the experience of near-absolute power after they themselves had suffered the humiliation of colonial subjugation and the trauma of two wars of liberation against Britain, now have to reassess both their history and their future as they try to readapt to a situation devoid of special privilege. With hindsight, as a kind of afterthought to what I wrote about Afrikaners in 1988, it would seem that the great reward of the liberation of South Africa and the elections of 1994 has been the opportunity at long last to "come home to Africa." (In a very literal way this has been demonstrated by the emigration, since 1996, of a number of Afrikaner farmers to settle in African countries like Mozambique, Zambia, or Zaïre, now the Democratic Republic of Congo.)

This may account for the apparent demise of the militant extreme right-wing after the tragicomedy of a last, disastrous attempt, just before the 1994 elections, to occupy the black homeland of Bophuthatswana. As happened in Namibia after its independence a few years earlier, Afrikaners can now reconcile themselves to the long-repressed positive side of their collective personality and their history, to take their place alongside all their compatriots in what Archbishop Desmond Tutu has called, not without a touch of wistful wishful thinking, the "Rainbow Nation." For we can no longer devise ways out of the new reality: the moment of our accountability to history has arrived, and it is up to us to make the choice. Sadly, though, as the memory of the elections fades, increasing numbers of Afrikaners appear to resort to the old, easy way out by blaming everybody but themselves for their present misfortunes; or to turn their sudden loss of power into the negativism of trying to opt out of responsibility for everything that is happening in the country.

At least something of this reaction may also be read into the decision of F. W. de Klerk, in 1996, to lead his party out of the government of national unity which took power after the elections of 1994, and to resign as leader of the National Party a year later. While one can understand the frustrations of having to adapt to an inferior position within the structures of power once dominated by his own group, de Klerk's moves gave rise to suspicions of, first, placing the interest of his own party above that of the country as a whole and, subsequently, piqued by what more and more people, including his own supporters, construed as failure, getting out while it was still possible, and leaving the shambles for others to clear up.

But not only Afrikaners have had to adapt to radically changed circumstances. The disappearance of a common enemy and the nefarious activities of *agents provocateurs* from the previous régime, notably in the province of KwaZulu-Natal, have undermined the erstwhile solidarity of the black majority and encouraged new divisions and internecine strife. At the same time, with the disappearance of a strongly repressive police force, crime has escalated, and — as in Russia and other recently liberated countries — an extremely violent and volatile society has taken shape. Taking advantage of the social instability that inevitably accompanies change, criminals have begun to swamp the cities; among the once deprived and dispossessed, now propelled into positions of power, some have succumbed to the temptations of corruption, nepotism, and exploitation; the frustration of unrealistic expectations has erupted in ugly confrontations, making it all too obvious that racism is not yet dead.

In the midst of increasing turmoil one beacon of hope has continued to shine, albeit surrounded by more and more controversy: the Truth and Reconciliation Commission, and its attempts to bring to light the most painful and shameful memories of the past in order to pave the way toward a new understanding. Deliberately turning against the example of retribution presented by Nuremberg, and daring to go beyond the safer parameters set by its predecessors in Chile and elsewhere, the commission led by Archbishop Tutu attempts to do the near-impossible: bringing together the perpetrators and the victims of the apartheid atrocities and abuses in the hope of resolving the impasses of the past. It has been said that post-apartheid South Africans, collectively, represent an abused child who must now learn to work through its past torment; it would be truer to say that we represent *both* the abuser and the abused, trapped in the same body. The TRC has become a stage where a national drama is being performed — except that Sartre's distinction between *act* and *gesture* has fallen away: the actors are acting out their own lives, and past, present, and future are all at stake. Just as the years of apartheid highlighted the problem of racism in *all* societies in the world, the experiment in peaceful transition concerns every single society where conflict reigns and where, historically, a recourse to violence has been the "normal" reflex. The workings of the TRC involve the sanity not only of one country but, in a real sense, of the global society at the end of our millennium. Of course it does not preclude other approaches or other solutions elsewhere; but if it fails, a tendency to failure in humanity may be endorsed, while if it succeeds, it would introduce at least the *possibility* of success into the global mix.

Because of the contrast between the present turmoil and the hope and joy of only a few years ago, the situation might well be interpreted as yet another failure of democracy. But I believe that it can also be read to mean the opposite. Sometimes, when one watches on television a crowd of demonstrators clamoring for wage increases the country simply cannot afford, trashing streets and campuses and factories in their blind excess, one may be tempted, for a fleeting second, to wonder: *Is this the face of democracy?* But, of course, a truer response would be, *This is the face of democracy denied.* For centuries the have-nots in the country have had no opportunity whatsoever of engaging in dialogue with the haves; increasingly, in such a closed situation, violence became the only articulation available to them. It takes time for a whole society to work its way into the new structures for dialogue and discussion made available by democracy. The concept itself, like so many others, has to be redefined in startlingly new terms. It is part of a difficult yet exhilarating reinvention of a continent which we once thought we knew, but in which we have to rediscover, as if from scratch, our places and the range of our possibilities.

Against this changing backdrop, what primarily concerns me in these essays is the functioning of literature, and of the writer. Which doesn't mean for one moment that I would presume to assign any preordained "role" to the writer. Of course writers fulfill functions in the world, but this should be seen as a purely practical consequence of their existence, not as any kind of metaphysical or philosophical or prophetic burden they are "required" to assume. And even within a single historical juncture, different writers may, and do, react differently to the same circumstances.

At a seminar in Salzburg in July 1993, I had the privilege of interacting very closely, for two remarkable weeks, with some sixty other writers and academics, mainly from the recently liberated countries of Central Europe and elsewhere, to discuss the possibilities available to literature as a political force in the not-so-brave new world following the collapse of totalitarian régimes. Almost every evening, when the formal discussions of the day were over, we found ourselves confessing that we actually missed the good-bad old days of repression and censorship, dictatorships and closed societies and *samizdat*. Those had been the days, terrible as they may have been in many respects, when writers and writing still appeared to "mean something," when the relationship between reader and writer was electrified with expectation and mutual reward. Now, released from the old constraints, we were faced with the prospect of a freedom in which anything goes — with the result that nothing goes anymore. A widespread gloom is settling over many writers from recently liberated countries, in the curious perception that, suddenly, "there is nothing to write about anymore."

But one should not take this in too absolute a sense. It is a reaction normal to prisoners who, after their release, suffer for shorter or longer periods from dizziness and agoraphobia, and even miss at times the reassurance of restricted space. (There is also the consideration that the imagination is never so free as when the body is behind bars. Shakespeare's Richard II knew this, and so did Cervantes, and John Bunyan, and Andrei Sinyavsky, and innumerable others.) But there is another aspect to the new experience: the discovery of a near-miraculous opening up of the horizons of the possible, where after decades of mental and emotional conditioning, we can now engage more deeply with the various dimensions of our craft than ever before. Among many other possibilities, it involves the management of memory, repressed or not. The functioning of the Truth Commission is replicated in many ways in the challenges posed to literature in the new dispensation. And central to the process is the need to discover, or rediscover, the truism that with freedom comes responsibility — especially in the domain of literature, where the very notion of the "aesthetic" has so often, and so deeply, been enmeshed with the "moral."

It is never easy to assume moral responsibility in a state of repression, where to acquiesce (or, alternatively, to move out) is such a natural response; on the other hand, the attraction of the "moral high ground" can all too readily result in pontificating or sloganeering, or even in profiteering. But in a sense all of this pales in comparison to the problems of moral responsibility in a situation where all is acceptable — a restatement of Ivan Karamazov's problem with evil in a world from which God has withdrawn.

It was not to answer these questions that this collection was compiled, but to make sure that they were stated, and to try to define the terms — and then perhaps to refine the definitions — in which to state them.

The individual texts, written initially in a wide variety of forms — newspaper articles, research papers, public talks, academic lectures, or whatever — have been revised for this publication in more permanent form; but the editing has been restricted to a minimum, involving mainly a pruning of trimmings and adjectives, a clarifying of the sense where necessary, the addition of brief explanatory phrases. But each text still bears the signs of its first context, sometimes formal, sometimes popular, as the case may be.

Much of what I wrote at a given moment may not accord at all with what I would think about the same subject today. In a few instances, where I believed present perceptions might illuminate more clearly, or develop further, a point of view put forward a number of years ago, a brief reflective or retrospective postscript has been added without disturbing the original. It seems to me part of the contract with the reader in a volume of this kind that arguments be allowed to unfold, to develop, at certain moments to retrace the same territory, even to explore their own contradictions; in order to signal, within a constantly evolving and changing environment, the vicissitudes of literature as writers attempt to explore the options available to them, or the openings they themselves may try to pierce into the fabric of society.

I did not attempt to avoid repetition too rigorously, apart from weeding out some passages which appeared to me *mere* repetition. There are, for example, several references to my interaction with historical documents used in the writing of *A Chain of Voices,* but such repetition as remains addresses, I trust, different aspects of the situation: in "Speaking in Voices" the focus is on the need to allow, as far as possible, the "authentic voices" of slaves from the past to speak within the apartheid world in which I wrote; in "Reflections of Literature and History" slavery itself, as a phenomenon, is discussed; in "Literature as Cultural Opposition" the argument involves the leap from historical fact to the imaginings of fiction; and in "Reinventing A Continent" my concern is primarily the textual nature of history and of the world. Here, quite clearly, my early views are not exactly consonant with the later ones. But I am prepared, for the sake of interior dialogue and of respect for chronology, to run the risk of discrepancy. *Tempora mutantur, et nos mutamur in illis.*

Cape Town, 1997

JUNE 1982

Speaking in Voices

"You have no right," says my WASP acquaintance in New York à propos of my novel *A Chain of Voices,* "*no* white writer has either the right or the ability to appropriate a black character's voice in a novel for the purpose of interpreting the Black Experience. It is an imposition. It is a presumption and an obscenity. Imagine," he insists in a tone of horror, "a white writer from the American South writing *Roots* . . ." I turn my thoughts inward before he can embark on his own interpretation of the White Experience of the Deep South (he is a Northerner).

Variations of the same accusation are common. A male writer cannot/dare not write about the female experience. The upper-class writer should avoid the peasant in fiction. The non-Jew can never fathom the Holocaust. (By extension, and in flippant mood: a younger man cannot write about an older one, a myopic person about one with normal vision, a hirsute man about a bald, a thin woman about a fat one . . .?)

The argument is not, of course, without a certain validity. What White Protestant Male could have written the books of Ngugi wa Thiong'o, or Toni Morrison, or Elie Wiesel? Who but Virginia Woolf could have written Virginia Woolf? It required André Schwarz Bart and Isaac Bashevis Singer to write what they have written, as it required Maxim Gorky to imagine

First published in *Le Matin*, Paris, June 1982.

The Lower Depths or Madame de Lafayette *La Princesse de Clèves.* None but a Frenchman could have written *La Comédie humaine,* none but a German *Buddenbrooks* or *The Tin Drum,* no one but a Spaniard *Yerma.*

And yet, to argue thus is to approach the problem from one side only, revealing more than just a passing glimpse of chauvinism. There is a formidable gallery of convincing male characters in George Eliot or George Sand; and a Tolstoy was necessary to create Anna Karenina. Dostoevsky imagined not only Prince Mishkin but also Nastasya Filippovna. And William Styron's Sophie — a Pole, a Jew, and a woman — has become a quintessential figure in the fiction of our time. It took a Nabokov to interpret a vital part of the modern American consciousness, and a white man, Athol Fugard, to give a voice to the fate of being colored in South Africa today. Racine turned Greeks and Romans into Frenchmen, and Shakespeare transformed the whole world, ancient and contemporary, into an extension of Elizabethan England: yet humanity's knowledge of itself would have been immeasurably poorer but for them.

Presumption? Perhaps the writer is by nature a creature of presumption: at least of that initial presumption that is a condition for every act of the imagination. Without that, writing would be narrowed down to the small, rational task of recording what, in the strictest sense of the word, one has "personally experienced": not only would it deny that basic and stimulating part of experience which involves confrontation with, and exploration of, and even immersion in, the Other, but it would intolerably restrict the meaning of "experience" itself. In short, it would impose on the writer the literary and existential equivalent of the politics of apartheid: *thou shalt not consort with the Other. Thou shalt not trust thine own experience of the Other. Thou shalt deny the Other, even that part of the Other which thou findest within thyself, and that of thyself which thou seest in the Other.*

It may be more presumptuous to exclude all exploration of the Other than to attempt the hazardous act of discovering in the Other the humanity you share with him or her.

★

At least two very important issues are at stake here: the writer as an individual, and the writer as part of humanity.

As individuals, writers have a primary responsibility to their "own experience," which in the final analysis is the only valid store from which they can draw, and on which they may rely in writing—that is, if writing is not a simple diversion but a quest for truth and a testing of values (a quest and a testing directed and defined by language as a system of signs in which the social need for communication and the personal urge for expression coincide). But what does this private experience comprise? Browning's Andrea del Sarto offers a suggestion:

> I can do with my pencil what I know,
> What I see, what at the bottom of my heart
> I wish for . . .

All "valid" writing derives from an experience so intensely and profoundly lived by the individual, so much "part of oneself," of one's consciousness, one's emotional make-up, one's perception of the world, one's sense of self, that one's very identity comes to be defined by it. Which is why the stereotyped distinction between the novel of the "private ache" and the "political" or "social" novel is made so often. And yet I find the distinction misleading. Even social and political experience can become so thoroughly absorbed by the writer that it constitutes part of what is usually perceived as a "private ache." In fact, it seems to me that *unless* one's "public" experience becomes fully integrated with one's most private awareness, writing about this experience can never transcend the level of the obvious or the propagandistic. What is required, in other words, is that confluence of "external" and "internal" circumstances where coercion and whimsy are subsumed in the perfect harmony attained by the Zen archer who spontaneously lets fly his arrow at exactly the moment the tension of the bowstring "demands" of him to do so. I find it strange if people ask me whether I do not sometimes yearn for an occasion to write a "private" story with no political overtones to it: as if what I wrote were dictated solely by the external "South African situation" in which I find myself and to which I feel an obligation. The question simply does not arise. Should I feel the urge at any stage of my life to write a love story set on a remote island in the Pacific (remote even from the Falklands), I shall have no hesitation to write it — provided the story itself demands urgently enough to be written. A "political dimension" is not something I feel obliged to add to or impose on a story: it is there, as part of what matters to me, part of my experience of the world, part of myself — even if, invariably, it is for me a point of departure only, from which to explore a condition that transcends the *faits divers* of sociopolitics. Human solitude, and the urge to reach out and touch the Other, will remain long after its political metaphor, apartheid, has disappeared.

An integral part of my experience is the existence of black and white in a variety of relationships — as masters and servants; as antagonists; as rivals; as collaborators; as friends; as human beings. Some of it derives from my earliest youth when, during holidays spent on the farms of friends, black and white boys grew up together, played together, ate and quarrelled and laughed together. What differences there were — of class more than of race: relative affluence as opposed to dire poverty — could be bridged by the unquestioning togetherness of youth: we were all children, all excluded from the grown-up world; we shared the race memory of peasants in a rural existence, we spoke in every sense of the word the same language. Then came the divergence and the gulf created by a society in which whiteness and blackness were identified with having and not-having, with oppressor and oppressed; at best with foster-parent and child. Still later came a period of renewed contact, now as students and equals in Europe, linked by a deeply rewarding sense of allegiance to the same continent (a mystique which the children of Mother Russia can readily appreciate). And finally there was a situation which still endures: of contact within a racist society itself — people reaching out and touching across all artificially imposed barriers, as colleagues or acquaintances, in a few precious cases as real and lasting friends. This is what makes it possible for me to perceive, in and through an association with individuals, some essential ingredients of the specific conditions termed by others the "black" or the "white" experience. Much of this experience is vicarious. Much of it is direct and real. And through the closeness of the contact it enters into my personal world and becomes part of it: a part that requires exploration and interpretation as much as any other part.

Even in these circumstances it is obvious that "exploration" should never be allowed to degenerate into "exploitation." And the line separating the two can be very tenuous indeed. It is a matter of instinct more than of rational decision. At the time of writing *A Dry White Season* I was tempted to approach a major portion of the material through the eyes of the black victims of apartheid, Gordon Ngubane and his son Jonathan. Had Steve Biko not died in the custody of the security police shortly after I'd started writing, I might have gone through with my original project. But his death changed it all. Pursuing the *via dolorosa* of a fictitious black man in the wake of the real death of a real man (and what a man!), appeared to me obscene. And when, after several months, I resumed writing, the whole angle had changed to that of a white man investigating the death of a black acquaintance, and the exploration of the devastating gulf between their worlds. With *A Chain of Voices* it was different. In the hundreds of handwritten documents from the Cape Archives I encountered the *procès-verbaux* and the first-person depositions of all the witnesses and accused involved in the slave revolt of 1825, white and black alike, slaves and masters. And although much of it was filtered through the stale officialese of the Court secretary transcribing the interrogations and statements, there remained the impression of being in touch with the stark reality and individuality of all the lives urging toward self-expression in those documents. They were *there,* speaking to me: speaking, indeed, across a divide of a hundred and fifty years, but speaking in their own voices, telling their own stories, exposing whatever truth of their tortured lives they could grope at: and in this case, to have ignored their voices in favour of either silence or a *Whites Only* interpretation of the event, would have been as much of an obscenity as riding on Steve Biko's back would have been. It would have meant betrayal (yet another betrayal!) of their cause and of the dark reality of their lives.

One South African white liberal accused me of "manipulating" history in favour of romantic existentialism by offering a view of slaves accepting the full horror of their condition and provoked into revolt only by the frustrated promise of liberation, which the critic saw as a reinforcement of the rightist attitude to withhold reform for fear that "if you give them the little finger they'll grab the whole arm." This person ignored the fact that the argument about a freedom promised and then denied runs like a refrain through the original testimonies themselves, notably those of the revolt leaders Galant and Abel. This rage informed the very timbre of the "voices" speaking from the mute documents which the critic had not bothered to consult: to have suppressed it would have been yet another form of betrayal — that of history itself.

Speaking in "voices" like these imposes on the writer, at the very least, the need to be as faithful as possible to the lives embodied in those utterances — even if their views and their truth run counter to contemporary expediency or personal preference. The act of faith, the act of the imagination, is a paradoxical one: if it leads as deeply as possible into the self, it also probes as far as possible into the Other. Which brings about the inevitable rediscovery of what is the starting point of all fiction: the need to make strange the wholly familiar; the need to find in the wholly strange the spark that causes the flame of recognition to jump from the self.

And so the pursuit of the writer's individual experience has led to the restatement of the writer's allegiance to humanity: *Homo sum . . .*

A critic of *Looking on Darkness* once objected to the portrayal of the main character, Joseph Malan, a "colored" man, on the grounds that he is portrayed "as if he felt and acted and reasoned just like a white person." Which was, of course, exactly what I had set out to do. Shylock: "I am a Jew. Hath not a Jew eyes? Hath not a Jew hands, organs, dimensions, senses, affections, passions, fed with the same food, hurt with the same weapons, subject to the same diseases, healed by the same means, warmed and cooled by the same winter and summer, as a Christian is? If you prick us, do we not bleed? If you tickle us, do we not laugh? If you poison us, do we not die? And if you wrong us, shall we not revenge?"

It is the intensity of private experience that drives a person to take up the pen; but it is the measure by which the expression of this experience transcends the personal that determines the quality of the writer. To discover the Other in the self; to imagine the self in the Other: this is the cliché to which both reader and writer are referred for their interaction to be validated. Voices may speak: but unless they are informed by tongues of fire they can only babble. *This* is the real issue — not whether the writer chooses, through an act of the imagination, to speak in one voice rather than another. If that remains our only concern, we shall all remain victims of an apartheid of the mind greater than the political system practised in one particular corner of the world.

Quite understandably, more and more black readers and writers have in recent years objected against exploitation by white liberals. But there is a considerable difference between, on the one hand, a solidarity which is both real and existential; and on the other, a "sympathy" bestowed from above. The writer who presumes to act as "spokesperson" for blacks may well be guilty of the same totalitarianism as the oppressor he or she professes to attack. The man who presumes to speak "on behalf of" women may be committing an obscenity worse than those overt ones perpetrated on women by other men. The writer who exploits

Babi Yar for a nice literary effect may be betraying the most profound moral principles of literature itself.

I cannot "take it upon me" to interpret to black people the nature of their suffering: they know it more urgently than I could ever hope, they are *living* it, every blood-warm instant of their lives. And even if they should feel a need for an interpreter there is any number of eloquent and inspired writers within their own community who can fulfil that function.

But does that mean that I should remain silent? If the suffering of even one black person has entered into my life to become part of my own most profound experience, would it not be an act of self-betrayal to write about trees and flowers and love on a desert island, pretending that that portion of myself is invalid or does not exist? Precisely because I *am* white, I may feel a responsibility to express my solidarity with others, black, whose lives have touched my own.

How precarious the ledge between exploitation and perversity on the one hand, indulgence and self-gratification on the other. Yet the very danger inherent in the situation makes it important to go on trying, because of the imperative to explore the full consequences of whatever particle of truth one finds in one's experience. Presumptuous? Yes, alas, and thank God. Provided it is that peculiar form of creative presumption that is always tempered by profound humility: the humility derived from an acute awareness of the awful nature of the challenge, and the ever-present likelihood of faltering and failure.

Andrea del Sarto again: "Ah, but a man's reach should exceed his grasp,/ Or what's a heaven for?"

Postscript 1997: The crucial question concerns *power relations.* As Morgan (1994: 3) points out, there is a difference between men's appropriation of feminity in order to strengthen their own authority and their attempt to question masculinity through adopting a feminine position in the system of sexual difference; and the same would apply to a white writer speaking, in a racist society, in the voice of a black.

JUNE 1986

A State of Emergency

Mr. State President

In this country torn apart by violence your white minority régime and its agents have, through their arrogance, intransigence and organized campaigns of terror against the oppressed, created the circumstances you required for the declaration of a State of Emergency.

Annoyed, no doubt, by the courts, by interference from concerned bodies and individuals, parliamentary investigators, enterprising journalists and others who persisted to bring to light the truths about your embattled régime, you have now succeeded in establishing a deadly silence surrounding yourselves: now no one can report on what you are planning or doing, no one can expose your lies and evil, no one can speak up for those oppressed, hounded, turned out of their burning homes, tortured or even killed by the latest incarnations of the Gestapo. Not even the names of those who are "disappearing" around us daily may be divulged.

You assure us that you have good reason. "I have the facts," you have been shouting since last August when, believing you could walk on water, you first tried to cross the Rubicon and

Open letter to State President P. W. Botha on the declaration of the State of Emergency in June 1986; first published in the *Guardian* in that month.

floundered. You require us to take your word, no matter how many times your régime has lied to us in the past.

We have seen the quality of your "facts" exposed before. Your Minister of Police offered the world your facts at the time your courageous and beleaguered forces tamed a violent mob at Uitenhage last year: when public pressure forced you to institute a commission of enquiry, we learned that men, women, children and babies in a peaceful procession had been shot in the back.

Is that why you have been so adamant in refusing to institute another enquiry into the violent confrontation between vigilantes and squatters at Crossroads and the KTC squatter camp outside Cape Town, an event described by an Afrikaans commentator as, "in terms of human suffering and deprivation . . . the greatest disaster that has struck the country" (Willem Steenkamp in *The Cape Times,* June 17, 1986)? At least 50,000 people were left homeless through violence in which, to say the least, your "security forces" (sic!) appeared to have played a dubious role. Numerous affidavits by priests, medical doctors and others suggest that your own agents took part in the violence and the burning, to the point of allegedly firing at refugees and burning their shelters in order to "persuade" them to move to a place you had previously designated for their resettlement.

If you deny such allegations, why do you refuse to appoint a judge to investigate what "really" happened? You cannot blame me, or innumerable others, for believing the worst: we have only your record to go by, ever since the time you had a hand in laying waste District Six, the traditional home of generations of colored people in Cape Town.

You try to convince gullible Western leaders like Reagan and Thatcher that you are in fact a Great Reformer. So you scrap the Mixed Marriages Act, but then forbid married people from different races to live together where they choose. You end the forced removal of whole communities; then unfortunate incidents like Crossroads happen to "encourage" the homeless to move voluntarily. You abolish the pass laws, then set about arresting countless blacks for "trespassing" in white-owned areas.

You bring a handful of colored and Indian people into parliament and offer them an illusion of power-sharing, but the moment they hesitate to collaborate in passing some of the most draconian legislation this country has ever seen, you treat them like schoolboys — and then press on with the legislation regardless. You announce that you will discuss constitutional reform with black leaders, while ensuring that the true leaders of the people are kept in jail or detention. You assure the world that this is a free country, yet since long before the State of Emergency the meekest peaceful protests have been brutally broken up. You tell us you are a Christian, yet you send in your forces to fire tear-gas at funeral processions, forcing the mourners to drop their coffins in the road. And when we profess we cannot believe you, you try to end all criticism by imposing the Big Silence.

Where do I stand as a writer in this State of Emergency?

I know very well where I stand: the very act of committing to paper this open letter to you is a crime. I can be arrested for this. And if it happens, you may do your best to ensure that people in South Africa will not even know that I am among those innumerable nameless ones who disappear every day. But I also know that I cannot submit to being silenced forcibly as long as I have a conscience to live with, and as long as I have breath enough, not just to say, "*J'accuse!*" but to plead, "For God's sake, let this end before it is too late."

I have no illusions about what a writer can do, physically. But neither should you have illusions about a writer's impotence.

You are confident that you have finally reduced us to silence. But you have not. There may be some temporary silence in the land: the silence of prison walls so thick that you cannot see the blood on the insides or hear the muffled screams. But that blood, those screams, have a way of filtering through into the pens of writers.

I appeal to the writers of my land to bear witness. We shall not be silent for ever. We have history on our side. We have truth on our side.

You have muzzled journalists. The "facts" may not be reported, except in the bland or mutilated forms of your choice. But *fiction* has a way of recording a truth deeper than fact. What cannot be stated directly, we must record in other ways: that is what makes us writers. And if we are not allowed to publish, we must find other ways to disseminate what conscience impels us to write. If need be, we must now emulate our Russian colleagues and resort to *samizdat*.

You may well fly into another of your rages at the thought of our following, of all things, Russian examples. But how many times has your own régime allowed itself to be inspired by the Kremlin in your state control of the economy, in your interference with production and marketing, in your restrictions on free expression, in your police-state methods?

Recently, in Argentina, a commission of enquiry reported on the atrocities of the previous military régime in its attempts to stay in power. The report makes chilling reading, especially in South Africa, where one recognises so many signs of heading in the same direction.

The Argentinian report is titled *Nunca mas:* "Never again." What a sad and terrible plea, in this broken world. But there may be some small solace, too, in knowing that certain historical patterns *do* recur. Not only the darknesses, but the light as well. Nuremberg may indeed come round again.

Sieg heil!

André Brink

OCTOBER 1986

The Hour of the Idiots

I am not, have never been, one of those who think that "Germany" means only one thing, one episode, one nightmare, one name.

My awareness of the country began when as a first-year student I came across Goethe in translation and decided that I had to learn the language in order to read him in the original, even if it had to be a fumbling, stumbling way, looking through a glass darkly. And having mastered *Faust,* I proceeded to the work of others — Schiller, Heine, Kleist; and, unforgettably, Büchner; and then Rilke; and later Mann and Brecht and Böll and Grass. (George Eliot: "How can the life of nations be understood without the inward life of poetry — that is, of emotion blending with thought?")

And yet, travelling through Germany recently, as a South African, I suppose it was inevitable that a morbid and only half-conscious urge drove me toward a meeting with destiny — a meeting with a self I had to face sometime in my life, a reaffirmation of Henry Miller's profound truth: "There is only one journey that is truly worth while, and that is inward, toward the self." It was not to indict Germany, but to confront the dark side of the moon in humanity, in my own people, in myself,

Essay based on a journey through West Germany; commissioned by, and first published in slightly shortened form, in *Der Stern*, October 1986.

that I was driven along the route I eventually chose. And I know now that on this journey I was really travelling toward my own history and a vision of my own future: South Africa's Third Reich has just begun (and how depressing to think that the friendship shown to South Africa by Chancellor Kohl should find a response in the fond recollections some South Africans still have of the war years, when they admired Hitler: in embracing Mr. Kohl, they are reaching back to Herr Schickelgrüber . . .) and in today's Germany one might acknowledge something which may still lie in South Africa's future.

"Why not explore," suggested *Der Stern,* "German attitudes toward your country today?"

Yes, I thought, I might just do that.

But it turned into something infinitely more complex. Because German attitudes to my country proved to be inextricably linked to German attitudes toward themselves: their affluent and streamlined present; and, more subtly, more darkly, more unsettling, toward their yesterday.

In the barren Little Karoo in the interior of the Cape Province, the "ostrich town" of Oudtshoorn, which owed its first burst of prosperity at the turn of the century to the international demand for feathers, still boasts a few so-called "ostrich palaces," weird and wonderful gothic monstrosities built by the *nouveaux riches* who had more money than they could handle. Rumor has it that there were only a few of these ostrich barons at the time and that they were jealous to keep their fortunes intact. Looking down on their inferior neighbours, they only associated among themselves; and their sons and daughters, not allowed to stray beyond those few select bloodlines, embarked on a process of intermarriage which very soon resulted in the birth of idiots in each of these families.

According to the Afrikaans writer Abraham de Vries, who first told the story, the families concerned did all they could to keep the existence of these children secret from the God-fearing community in which they lived. And so the idiots, with "colored" nannies to tend to all their needs, were relegated to the cellars of the extravagant mansions. In order to keep the houses cool during the ferocious summers of the Karoo, the foundations were built very high, so that each room in the house had a kind of "double" below it, a dark complement, a secret subconscious built to exactly the same dimensions and contours as the room above. Here the idiots were kept, in darkness, for the span of their natural lives.

Only once a week were they allowed out: on a Sunday afternoon between two and three, when all good Christians were safely asleep in their beds after the midday meal at which huge quantities of beef, mutton, fowl, saffron rice with raisins, brown beans, potatoes, pumpkin and dumplings had been consumed. During this one hour every week, with the conscience of the town at rest, the idiots came out and walked the blazing dusty streets, accompanied by their nannies. "The hour of the idiots," it was called. And at three, when the pious people rose from their stupor to have coffee and milk tart and *koeksisters* and cream cakes and rusks, the idiots were led back into their subterranean cellars like evil or lascivious thoughts restored to the Id.

In the prosperous and regimented Germany of today (is there another nation in Europe where *everybody* still obediently waits on the kerb for traffic lights to turn green before they cross the street?) I stumbled across some wandering idiots and followed them back into the uneasy recesses of the mind in which they normally lurk; and I discovered, with dismay, that they were familiar to me.

In a men's clothing shop in Munich the charming young man wrapping up my handmade shirt enquires: "What is the language you are speaking? Where do you come from?"

"It is Afrikaans. I'm from South Africa."

"Really? You must be glad to be here. Isn't there a war going on there?"

The first crystallisation of my thoughts took place in Dachau.

I know, I know: Dachau has become a cliché. Who doesn't know about it? Who still wants to be reminded of it? Hasn't everything that could possibly be said about it, already been said?

Yes.

No.

All has been said. Nothing has been said. The mere fact that so many millions of words have been spoken and written about it suggests that something must forever remain unsayable. Dachau is a confrontation with the inadequacies, the impotence, of language. There are regions of the mind, aspects of experience, so far beyond the reach of language — and yet so achingly familiar to humanity — that words cannot grasp them. (It may sound blasphemous, but the castles of Ludwig of Bavaria represent another of these excesses, at a different end of the spectrum — or not so different after all? — where language becomes opaque and dissolves.)

What struck me — among so much horror, so much darkness — was the terrible punishment with which any inmate of Dachau was threatened who dared to leave the slightest scratch or mark or inscription on a wall, a table, a bunk, a floor, a utensil. What a blow struck at the core of humanity, to deprive people of signs when signs are what make them human. The need to say: *I am. I am here. I was here.* The need to exist beyond the limits of the I.

But it is understandable, of course. The SS *dared* not permit the making of signs. The whole organization was aimed at silencing the word, keeping language at bay. A South African film maker, Manie van Rensburg, not allowed to make the film he wants to make on the life of activist leader Steve Biko, recently said, "You have to kill all the things you cannot speak about."

Yet today there is the obscenity, in spite of a proliferation of warnings on the walls, of contemporary graffiti appearing like dark blotches on the skin of a victim of the Plague. Why this sickening need, in contemporary visitors, to proclaim with a signature on a wall: *I have been to Dachau?* (Or is that, too, a sign of the frustrations of a language feeling the urge to grasp something, yet forced to acknowledge its own limits?)

The worst sign of all: a swastika engraved on a table in one of the restored bunkers. Below it, a date: 28.6.86.

One wonders whether perhaps the earth itself in this place — the small grey pebbles, the gravel, the patches of smoothly raked soil — has not become a photographic plate registering all the agony which language could not grasp?

There is a terrible purity about these extreme territories of experience, an amazing simplicity. From all the records which have been compiled it is obvious that one of the worst aspects of life in Dachau must have been the abundance of bodies, the suffocating lack of space, the inescapability of the "other." One building shutting out all light from the other; one bunk on top of another; bodies, bodies, breathing, excrement, vermin, filth. Yet the overwhelming impression left by Dachau today is one of space: the most empty emptiness I have ever experienced. The serenity of a Buddhist garden in greys and greyish whites; with low grey clouds above. In this emptiness each individual is doomed to solitude, one's footsteps separate and aching, impressed on the silence of crushed stone.

But the very space makes it impossible to escape from it; no hand, no word, can reach to touch what lies beyond; what lies *there.* One wanders, inside the museum, from one phase of experience to the next: the "innocent" beginnings; the increasing severity; then the atrocities. The photographs and relics and instruments of torture become unbearable. But there is no escape: when you turn away to a window to control your tears or your urge to vomit, the thing, the place itself lies there: the experience called Dachau. This immensity of space, this silence which language cannot penetrate. It is there: you are there, in the midst of it. Living in the heart of a scream no one can hear.

All the more of a scream because the place is so neat, so ordered, so hygienic, so well-planned, so organized, so structured. In the crematorium, the ovens stand like pottery kilns (the glaze of eternal silence); and behind them an ordinary white washbasin for rinsing and cleaning one's hands. Afterwards. Tonight the hands cleansed here may caress the breast or vulva of the butcher's wife. Nothing is quite as obscene as the banal, nothing as true as a cliché.

At the entrance to Dachau a foreign visitor has written, in English: *Are you not ashamed?*

He missed the point. Totally. Below it, a German visitor has written in reply: *Nein*. He, too, missed the point.

"Oh," says the lady who sells me the delightful little netsuke, "I have relatives in South Africa, you know, in Johannesburg. I had a letter from them only last week. They assured me things were not nearly as bad as we think over here."

One of the most haunting photographs in Dachau shows a condemned man on his way to the gallows, escorted by prisoners who are forced to play music as they go — fiddles, concertinas, whatever. The kind of happy group one would expect on any German town square on a Sunday afternoon. One is compelled to remember the role of music in spreading the gospel of the Third Reich. All those hundreds of thousands of people singing, singing. Children breaking into song. A screen of sound to mask the silent horrors, to evacuate the mind. In South Africa the government has just spent the equivalent of more than a million Deutschmarks of taxpayers money on a "Song of Peace" to be sung by a mixed choir to inspire the masses. Music by command. Sing for our execution.

"What is it like to live in South Africa?" asks the friendly lady in the Bremen hotel.

"It's a beautiful country, but spoilt by politics."

"Ah yes, of course." A brief frown of concentration. "I think I've heard about it." She brightens. "But don't worry. I'm sure it will all be over in a few weeks. These things never last long."

The German word for a place like Dachau is "Lager." In South Africa the "laager," traditionally the circle of ox-wagons within which Boers secured themselves in battles against black attackers, has now become the spiritual enclosure in which the mind entrenches itself against a hostile world.

But even in the literal sense of the word South Africa has had its version of concentration camps in the form of the resettlement camps used to "process" the nearly four million blacks uprooted from their traditional places of abode in order to put into practice the doctrine of apartheid, based on the ideological need to safeguard the purity of the white race. And not only the terms "European" or "white" have been used to distinguish between the elected and the negative existence of *non*-whites, *non*-Europeans, etc: within the last few months a tendency has come to light in some Afrikaans cultural circles to distinguish specifically between "Germanic" and "non-Germanic" speakers of the language. What is frightening is that this new terminology does not arise from the extreme right but from moderate, so-called "enlightened" sections of the establishment.

Compared to the inmates of Dachau, the people forcibly removed from their homes and resettled (either temporarily or in semi-permanence) in camps, experience more freedom: those capable of finding work are allowed to come and go as they require. (The notion of work remains paramount. *Arbeit macht frei.*) The settlers are often destitute and without adequate means of sustenance. But they are not, in the traditional sense of the word, "prisoners." Even so, the barbed-wire fences are often in evidence. And the armed guards, some of them as young and blond and clean-shaven as the guards of Dachau; and the dogs, and the guns, and the military vehicles that patrol the area.

Even as I am writing this article news is breaking about a new Gulag system of secret "reabsorption camps" established in South Africa in recent months, allegedly to cope with at least some of the almost four thousand children detained in terms of the State of Emergency. The Government insists that all the children selected for "processing" in these camps are there with the written permission of their parents; but of course in Dachau, too, prisoners had to sign that they agreed to their incarceration. And the South African government fails to explain how it comes about that so many of these children whose presence in the camps are "voluntary" insist on escaping. Not even the whereabouts of the camps have been divulged officially; and how many citizens of the Third Reich knew exactly where the camps of the Final Solution were situated?

"No, I'm sorry," says the man in the post office in Nürnberg. "I really know nothing about South Africa. And I must say that, frankly, I don't care. We have enough problems of our own to worry about. Nuclear weapons, pollution, Chernobyl, the Turks. South Africa is very far away, you must admit. What happens there cannot possibly concern us."

We retire to our hotel in Munich, the Vier Jahreszeiten (splendid place, provided you have a room in the old part; the more recent additions have nondescript rooms for which you pay the same as for the better ones; and there seem to be communication gaps between some sections in the administration), to study at more leisure some of the documentation obtained at Dachau. It comes as a shock to discover that this very hotel was the seat of the Germanic Order established in 1918, camouflaged as the "Thule Society" — an apt name, in view of the Götterdämmerung which lay ahead. Any South African would immediately recognise the parallel between this order (based on the conviction that "everything non-German must be fought against") and the secret "cultural" society, the Broederbond, established by Afrikaners in the thirties to protect and promote their tribal interests and which still continues as a think-tank for the government. Its influence remains pervasive. When I left South Africa in early August to undertake this trip, I was editor of the Afrikaans literary magazine *Standpunte* ("Points of View") which had been in existence for forty years. It was an independent magazine, but financed by a publishing firm controlled by the government. Presumably because of my conviction that the present State of Emergency threatens writers and literature and my stated intention to confront the situation in *Standpunte,* the sponsor withdrew its support; but the magazine had enough money to carry on for another year or so. Yet, upon my return to the country I was informed that the magazine had been closed down behind my back. And when I approached a newspaper with an article to state my case I learned that prominent members of the Broederbond had instructed Afrikaans newspapers in the country not to allow me any opportunity whatsoever to comment publicly on the fate of *Standpunte.* So much for points of view in a society where the signs of a new Third Reich are too clear to ignore.

These signs are, of course, masked under the noble pretences of "state security"; of "law and order." In November 1918 the then Reichskanzler in Germany made a famous appeal for "Ruhe und Ordnung" — based on the argument that "socialist subversive activities" were a stab in the back of national morale and had to be eliminated. (How familiar, the appeal by the Reichskommissar in 1933, to "all Bavarians who love their nation and homeland to support me in my struggle against the undermining of the nation by the Marxists and their sympathisers"!) The next step is inevitable: "for the protection of the state and people" the *Legal Bulletin of the Reich* suspends, on February 28, 1933, the freedom of the individual, the right to free speech, including freedom of the press and the right of assembly and to form groups, and authorises the interception of mail, the tapping of telephones, house searches, even the confiscation of property.

In South Africa in recent years, and at an accelerating tempo, the courts have been denied the right to question legislation curtailing individual freedoms, in the name of "state security" people have been detained without trial, political and cultural organisations have been banned or persecuted, black trade unions legalized in the name of "reform" have been relentlessly harassed and have experienced the "disappearance" of their leaders, all of which — under the pretext of acting against "Marxist-inspired unrest" in the country — culminated in the State of Emergency declared on June 12, this year. This step was justified by President P. W. Botha in terms which could have been Hitler's own: "Because I am thus of the opinion that the ordinary laws of the land are inadequate to enable the Government to ensure the security of the public and to maintain public order, I have decided to declare a national state of emergency."

Among the regulations which have already become part of the everyday lives of South Africans, is the prohibition on the "making, possession or dissemination of subversive statements," which stipulates that any person who:

> (a) makes, writes, prints or records or causes to be made written, printed or recorded any subversive statement
> (b) possesses any subversive statement
> (c) disseminates, distributes or circulates or causes to be disseminated, distributed or circulated any subversive state
> ment among the public or any section of the public or who . . . dispatches, supplies or offers or causes to be dispatched, supplied, or offered any subversive statement to any person
> (d) displays or causes to be displayed any subversive statement in such a position that it is visible from any place to which the public has access, or
> (e) utters, or by means of any apparatus, plays or causes to be played, any subversive statement within the hearing of any other person, shall be guilty of an offence.

And "subversive statement" includes the promotion of any object or organization declared unlawful; or inciting anyone to take part in unlawful strikes or to impose any boycott action or to take part in any unlawful demonstration, gathering or procession (most demonstrations, gatherings and processions are "unlawful" in South Africa, including peaceful and purely academic ones); or discrediting or undermining the system of compulsory military service . . .

It is even an offence, without the written consent of the minister, to disclose "the name or identity of any person arrested in terms of any provision of the Act or of these regulations."

The aim is secrecy at all costs. (In Dachau: the cartoon by A. Paul Weber, from *Resistance,* depicting a skeletal newspaper tied to the stake and bearing the subtitle: "Speak up now if you can.") Which has most recently led to the absurd and frightening new additions to the Emergency Regulations, in terms of which no journalist may even find himself "within sight" of any action performed by the security forces.

One is reminded of a directive issued in 1941 about the transport of Russian prisoners to Dachau. The order is based, not on humanitarian reasons, but on the need to keep reality out of sight of the public:

> Especially during the march from the railway station to the camp . . . a considerable number of prisoners have been seen to collapse dead or half dead from exhaustion and have to be picked up by a car following behind.
>
> It is inevitable that the German people notice these incidents. Although these transports are usually escorted by members of the army, the general public will blame the SS for these incidents.
>
> To avoid such incidents in future I hereby order that from now on all Soviet Russians . . . who are obviously dying [e.g. from hunger, typhus] and therefore not capable of any exertion, especially marching even short distances, are to be excluded from execution transports to the concentration camps.

The blanket of secrecy imposed by the South African authorities, to prevent the general public from knowing the extent of the arrests, the harassment, the persecution, the beatings, the torture and the murders committed by the so-called "security forces," is a precondition for the development of a situation comparable to that of the Third Reich. South Africa may not yet be there: but all the groundwork has been done in preparation for it; and we are heading in that direction at an alarming rate.

The man at Frankfurt airport: "South Africa? Oh yes, a friend of mine went there once. To Rio de Janeiro."

Nürnberg: a city of water, stone, wood. The name is like the title of a poem, recalling instantly a magic evening on the square below the ancient walls, opposite the Dürer house, with timbered houses and pointed roofs and green foliage against a dark blue sky, for all the world like a theater set in which we play roles shaped for us by history, although we do not yet know the words and have to improvise as we go along. A quartet of musicians playing Mozart. This will remain an abiding memory of Germany: the sudden bursts of music from squares and streets and alleys, day and night. (And only in Bremen did the law intervene when an enchanting flautist was thrown off the Böttcherstrasse and forbidden to continue with his playing.) Wagner. Beethoven, Mozart, Bach. Incorruptible and timeless, they had all been here before Herr Hitler. And they are still with us. He has become an episode and an agony.

Nürnberg: ancient city of the emperors, raped in the name of the banality of power that wore the mask of "culture." Forced to pay the price of its hospitality to Hitler. (On a column in the church of St Sebaldus a reference to the "evils" of Nazism has been obliterated by an angry pen.)

We go in search of the depressing relics of the Third Reich: the Rally Grounds with Congress Halls, Luitpold Arena, Zeppelin Field and Stadium. But they are not easy to find. A conspiracy of silence seems to surround the whereabouts of the notorious grounds: people approached in the street, deny all knowledge of them; hotel concierges gesture vaguely "somewhere in that direction"; a policeman merely shrugs. Even at the tourist office specific directions are hard to come by, and the attractive Fräulein in charge appears to blame me for my questions as if I had made an obscene proposal. The inhabitants seem ashamed of the idiots in their cellars; perhaps they are on promenade only on Sundays, when the arena roars with the sound of racing cars and cycles.

But we do find the place in the end, in strange silence; defined by space. The current exhibition on the Nazi era is closed in the mornings, as if the organizers prefer to let it go unobserved as much as possible. (Nowhere in the whole city did we find a single poster advertising the exhibition.) And in the visitors' book over 90% of the German inscriptions condemn the exhibition:

> *Why single out Hitler? Why no exhibition on Stalin or Napoleon?*
> *Hitler is still alive.*
> *Nothing can destroy the Nazi ideal.*
> *Why no reference to the atrocities of the Allied Forces?*

The buildings, gangrenous with time, seem singularly exposed in their ridiculous volume: stupendous, colossal, magnificent, in the Cecil B. de Mille tradition. Power as show-business. Lugubrious, oppressive, devoid of inspiration or authenticity. I cannot help thinking of the building programs in South Africa in recent years, in spite of economic recessions, increasing unemployment (up to 70% of blacks in the district where I live are out of work), famine, persecution and misery: vast sports stadiums, imposing theatres and opera houses have been constructed in most of the main centres. Culture, culture *ueber alles.* No matter that the costs of running some of those theatres are so staggering that most of the available money goes into maintenance, with hardly anything left to mount performances! The masses must be entertained; must be impressed. The Berlin Olympiad in 1936: the millions wasted on the South African Games of 1986. The idea is the same. *Panem et circenses.* Only, in South Africa, it is often "culture" *instead* of bread. When furbedecked whites emerge from their opera houses and slide into their limousines, black children line the street begging for bread.

I try to imagine the crowds on this Zeppelin Field. The swarming Party gatherings and parades. In South Africa, too, P. W. Botha has begun to introduce these annual rallies. In South Africa, too, the regular police force has been supplemented by reservists. In South Africa, too, huge indoctrination programs have been introduced in all government schools under the slogan of *Jeugweerbaarheid* ("Youth Preparedness"). From a German Reader of 1926: ". . . all hope for our Fatherland depends upon the education of our youth toward a self-sacrificing love for their home and Fatherland. This is the aim of the new reader." In South Africa, too, history has been taught from an exclusively white perspective for many years, although it is true that a new historiography is emerging, much to the dismay of those in power.

Hitler's popularity: the meticulously prepared histrionics, the attention to the "personal touch," in order to persuade the masses that he really cared about them individually. This has also been characterising P. W. Botha's style more and more markedly in recent times. Apart from his appearances in parliament or at party rallies or public functions, he has launched a campaign of "personal" advertisements in newspapers, bearing his own signature, addressing South Africans intimately and persuasively. Herr Schickelgrüber rides again.

In the Western Transvaal, during the War years, a farmer painted two huge swastikas on his barn to scare off the Jewish pedlars who used to visit the place and sell their wares. The pedlars informed the military authorities, who ordered the farmer to paint over the swastikas. This was done. But today, more than forty years later, and after hundreds of coats of paint, the swastikas still reappear, like stigmata, every time it rains. Some things can never be obliterated. Some experiences are constantly reborn to haunt the human mind. The idiots are always with us, awaiting their hour.

We drive back into the old city of Nürnberg. The excursion to the stadium has cast a gloom over the delights and the bustle of the lovely town. It is, after all, we remember, the place where the Nürnberg Laws were promulgated. "*Eheschiessungen zwischen Juden und Staatsangehörigen deutschen und artverwandten Blutes sind verboten . . .*" ("Marriages between Jews and German citizens and others of similar blood are prohibited.") Likewise, all sexual relations between members of different races in South Africa were forbidden for many years. It is true, of course, that in 1985 those laws were repealed: it is part of the grand "reform program." A movement away from the Third Reich? Hardly, alas. White and black may now marry, but they may still not live together where they wish. The Group Areas act, maintaining ghettoes for the "inferior" races, prevents it. In October 1985, when a white man and a colored woman returned to his home after their wedding in the small village of Villiersdorp, they were informed by police that she could stay in his house only if she was his servant; not if she was married to him.

And where, apart from South Africa today or Germany half a century ago, could a mere kiss be interpreted as a crime? Here is a report from the *Eastern Province Herald* dated November 30, 1984:

> A Black boy aged 13 was yesterday acquitted in the Grahamstown Magistrate's Court of assaulting a white baby by kissing her in October this year.
>
> The boy pleaded not guilty to the charge.
>
> He was found not guilty by the presiding magistrate, Mr. J. A. Terblanche, who said he could not reject the boy's evidence as false beyond any reasonable doubt.
>
> Mr. Terblanche said a kiss could be construed as an assault, but added that a State witness could possibly be mistaken about the kiss as he was some distance away.
>
> Mr. David de la Harpe, appearing for the boy, said the boy baby-sat regularly at a neighbouring house and was therefore well acquainted with the white child.
>
> He said that on the day in question, the boy was playing outside his employer's yard with his charge when the child, accompanied by a domestic, came walking down the street.

The boy then ran forward, fell to his knees and threw open his arms, Mr. De la Harpe said.

He added that the child ran into the boy's arms, and was hugged. The boy denied kissing the child.

"When we travel abroad," says my journalist friend, "we are actually relieved to be taken for Hollanders or Swedes rather than Germans. I'm sure it is the same with South Africans?"

We leave Nürnberg again, this time in search of the courthouse of the post-war trials, on the road to Fürth. Once again we are led astray by a proliferation of (deliberately?) false indications; but at last we arrive at the towering late-nineteenth-century building. From then onwards it is pure Kafka.

In the main building I enquire about the location of the historical Room 600 and am told to go to Room 625. The same bit of information is repeated by the armed guard in the Eastern wing. We go upstairs and follow the room numbers: 620, 621, 622 . . . then, suddenly, there is a single door marked 624/626. No sign of 625. Fortunately one member of our little group ventures further along the echoing passage and discovers the missing number 625, completely out of sequence. It is locked and deserted.

While we are standing about disconsolately, a small grey man with a large bunch of keys makes his appearance and unlocks 625. We hurry toward him and enquire about 600. This is indeed the place, he says; but we will have to wait. Without giving any indication about the duration of our wait he slips into the room, closes the door and turns the key from the inside.

Fifteen minutes or so later another small grey man with another large bunch of keys comes down the passage and also lets himself into the mysterious Room 625 immediately followed by a great eruption of voices inside.

After a while the second man reappears.

May we go to Room 600, we ask.

Yes. It's upstairs.

But when we got there the imposing carved door is solidly locked. Back to 625, where we venture to knock. Not a sound.

We are on the point of giving up when the door is suddenly flung open, the first small grey man comes out, and motions us to follow him.

All courtrooms are essentially alike. As a child I used to spend many afternoons crouched on a bench in the hall where my father presided as magistrate; it was my first intimation of Right and Wrong, my first discovery of that peculiar smell which defines justice. Something dusty. Musty. A hint of tobacco, stale sweat, fear perhaps. Old papers, black ink. And the buzzing of flies against high windows. Even that sound is translated into a smell.

Above the entrance, a louring sculpture including a head of Medusa.

So this is where they sat together for the last time. Goering, Von Ribbentrop, Kaltenbrunner, Frank, Frick and the others.

Perhaps, I think, it is not all gloom. If Nürnberg hosted the Rallies it also assisted in the conclusion. If the Third Reich is being reborn in a distant southern land today, then perhaps its predestined doom is also forecast by this room. Nürnberg may indeed come round again.

At least it is reassuring to remember that if Nürnberg witnessed the awesome parades in honor of the Fuehrer, it was also a town which provided a home to some of the most courageous people of the resistance to that régime. And I know that resistance is growing in South Africa too. The new Himmlers are doing their best, with their prisons and their torturers and the formidable machinery of the Party organization and the increasing militarisation of the country, to discourage and destroy all signs of opposition, arresting journalists, silencing criticism, incarcerating and eliminating opponents: but in the long run repression cannot succeed. One day the idiots will break out of their cellars and openly confront their captors in the full light of day. And there is one major difference between the Third Reich and South Africa today: Hitler did not have to contend with a great majority of citizens who opposed him.

But in order to oppose evil one has to recognise it first. And inevitably this aspect was also underscored by Nürnberg:

"We did not know," was the sickening refrain surrounding the trial. "We really did not know what was going on."

Apartheid in South Africa has been so diabolically effective in keeping different communities apart that the majority of whites — good God-fearing citizens — do not know what is happening in the black townships. South African television does not report it. The newspapers are muzzled. The only news disseminated in the country is the version put out every day by a State Bureau "to maintain the free flow of information," as they put it. On days when in one township alone five or six people are killed, the Bureau reports that all has been quiet; the State of Emergency is working well, unrest is diminishing. And South African whites can spend a lifetime believing they are living in one of the stablest, most prosperous and peaceful countries in the world.

They do not know.

They do not want to know.

"We are doing what we can," says the Lutheran pastor in Hamburg. "Our church is deeply involved, especially in Namibia. Our priests are arrested and deported all the time, but they cannot be discouraged. Only, there is so much to be done. And the public over here shows so little concern. As long as they can buy their Krugerrands from the Dresdner Bank, they are content."

"But Germans who have already lived through the horrors of Hitler, all those who have sworn: 'Never again': can't they see that what is happening in South Africa today threatens to repeat their own history?"

"I am afraid they don't. You must remember that West Germany is South Africa's most important trading partner in Europe. As long as they can make money out of trade links, why should they concern themselves with the internal policies of another country?"

There were other Germanies too, I discovered on this all too brief journey through the Federal Republic: and however different they were from each other, they shared something profoundly positive. First there was the ancient, timeless Germany which nothing, not even Hitler, not even the War, could destroy. The Germany of the small villages and of the rolling hills of the countryside (even if these are spoilt, for kilometers on end, by the stench of fertiliser): a timeless peasant world wise with the knowledge of the earth. The picturesque villages and towns of the Bavarian Alps (not the kitsch of Oberammergau, but the homeliness and warmth, the legendary *Gemütlichkeit,* of Füssen and Partenkirchen and Bayrischzell where, like Alice through her looking-glass, one is transferred from the everyday into a living postcard) or the Romantische Strasse, or the environs of Bremen (where the work of Paula Modersohn-Becker came as one of the profound artistic discoveries of my life, illuminating as it did the humane and compassionate reverse side of the early years of the century which paved the way for the Third Reich). Or, in a slightly different key, the sad yet noble remains of a Roman past, the dour Carolingian splendour of Aachen, the gothic rapture of Cologne's cathedral. It was this confirmation of human perseverance, the persistence of memory, which added a dimension in which the Third Reich became but a nightmarish moment.

And, in yet another different key, there was the aggressive bustle of the new cities, of Frankfurt and Hamburg, confirming the post-war "German miracle," even if not without dangerous overtones of the corruption of wealth, the cynicism of commerce, the arrogance of prosperity (for how precarious is human achievement, how easy to destroy, how vulnerable to hubris). Time and time again there were the inscriptions:

Built in 1825 (or 1725 or 1625. Or 1525 . . .)
Totally destroyed in 1945
Rebuilt in 1949

A nation which could survive the catastrophe of 1933–1945, which could start again from nothing but ruins and ashes and rebuild its own brave new world, offers hope and faith — but also a warning — to the world. Hope in regeneration; faith in the indomitable nature of the human mind; warning about the pretences of material achievement. And if the shadow of a Fourth Reich is already beginning to lengthen across South Africa (where a new variant of the swastika has appeared and where Eugène Terreblanche, leader of the growing Right, has adopted the Hitler salute and has embarked on a program of giving children military training), then, who knows, the resurgence of life in Germany may yet be an example for the future. If the stubbornness and stupidity of the present South African government precipitates the cataclysm, as Hitler's did half a century ago, then Germany's present may also offer some hope for my country's future.

"I must admit quite honestly," says my academic friend in Cologne, "that even five years ago I neither knew nor cared about your country. Then I began to read some of your authors and my eyes were opened. Now there are more and more of us who are deeply concerned. We try to find out as much as we can. We try to persuade those in power to see the folly of their support for the apartheid régime, which means support for everything Germany tried to eradicate after the war. We are still a small minority. But hopefully our awareness is spreading."

Rothenburg ob der Tauber. A German variant of Les Baux, overrun by tourists; the miracle is that in spite of this it has retained an atmosphere of authenticity. There is genuine vitality in the streets, the color and music burst spontaneously from buildings and people alike; at night the city gates look like a cottage from *Hänsel und Gretel*. It is like dreaming while you are awake. And a stay in the Eisenhut Hotel, a meal on its terrace at night, is the kind of experience which in itself makes the journey worth while. Which makes it all the more shocking to spend a few hours in the Mittelalterliches Kriminalmuseum, apparently the only one of its kind in Europe. With infinite — almost loving! — attention to detail the extensive floors of the museum unfold the darker recesses of the European mind (even if great care is taken to warn the visitor that the inclination to torture had not been Germanic in origin, but that the practice had been introduced by the Church . . .!). Stakes, gallows, whips, iron maidens, spikes, branding-irons, thumbscrews, pliers for pulling out tongues or nails, pincers, racks, cages are exhibited in sickening profusion, accompanied by detailed commentaries in several languages.

This, unexpectedly, adds a dimension to Dachau. And not necessarily a German dimension: suddenly cruelty itself is revealed as an essential territory of the human experience. Perhaps it is part of our condition, a prerequisite for the loftier soarings of the mind. In South Africa, a year ago, a courageous young doctor filed an affidavit with the Supreme Court in Port Elizabeth: "What disturbs me most is that detainees are taken out of my care for the purposes of interrogation and, during the course of this interrogation, brutally assaulted."

The "meaning" of torture lies, inevitably, in the denial of the humanity of the other: without fulfilling that condition, it would be impossible to proceed. Which is why torture demands a moral mask: this man or woman is a criminal, is an offence to society, is an outcast, a non-Christian, a deviant, a Jew, a black: not an *alter ego.* (Heinrich Himmler, 1943: "Whether or not ten thousand Russian women collapse from exhaustion while digging an anti-tank ditch only interests me in so far as the ditch must be finished for Germany." Jimmy Kruger, South Africa's Minister of Justice, after the death of Steve Biko in 1977: "It leaves me cold.")

And yet there is this terrifying irony in torture that by perpetrating what is inhuman on someone else, on a dehumanized "other," one confirms one's own humanity. It is because *I* know the meaning of pain that I dare torture the other, in order to celebrate the fact that it is not happening to *me.* There is always some vicarious, outrageous celebration in the suffering caused to a victim.

What makes it even worse is that it is invariably accompanied by a sense and a ritual of catharsis, an ideal of purity. The wash-basin in the crematorium at Dachau; the spotless condition of the floors; the immaculate cleanliness of the Aryan mind. Torture only fulfils its own conditions when it is performed in the name of an absolute: Justice, Christianity, Aryan purity, Civilization, Whiteness.

Münich again: just off the Marienplatz, in the green shimmering shadows of trees protecting us from the generous midday sun. "Afrikaans, you said? So you're from South Africa? Welcome, my good friend. My very good friend. Here, take my hand." A vigorous handshake. "You people are doing a wonderful job over there. Keep it up. We're right behind Mr. Botha. I want you to know, my friend: all of us at this table are real Germans. Real, good, old-fashioned Germans. Know what I mean?" He winks, and drains his huge tankard of beer. "We understand you. Even if the rest of the world doesn't. We'll keep your country going even if the rest of Europe imposes sanctions. Heil!"

In front of the Alte Pinakothek, where the late afternoon shadows are lengthening across the uncompromising green of the grass, a little girl is squatting on her haunches, picking small white flowers, her back turned on the great Moore sculpture behind her. Once, losing her balance, she topples over on her back, her left hand outstretched to keep her bunch of flowers intact. Deadly serious, she sits up again, grave blue eyes fixed intently on the sprinkling of flowers still waiting to be picked. Blonde hair spread across her hunched shoulders, gleaming in the sun. Such archetypal innocence it could almost be kitsch.

But it isn't. She is alive, unnervingly real, as she sits there, picking her flowers, a minute moment of blonde truth.

I shall take this small fierce memory back with me to South Africa.

I shall remember Germany when the idiots are out on their Sunday stroll. The darkness of Dachau. But also this quintessential little girl.

JULY 1987

The Arts in Society

At the beginning of a stimulating winter school program and festival of the arts centred in a splendid monument dedicated to the cultural heritage of the British in South Africa, we overlook the town of Grahamstown with its twelve-or-so thousand of more or less affluent white citizens, most of them avidly devoted to the pursuit of money or, at the least, the beating of inflation; but also the sprawling black townships on the adjacent hills where at least fifty thousand people, the majority of them jobless and subsisting below the poverty datum line, are so urgently involved in the business of physical survival that they have no time to think of the arts: and looking in the opposite direction we can see, or imagine seeing, the local prison bursting at the seams. Many would regard these observations as inappropriate for a festive occasion like this, where we celebrate the artistic achievements of our variegated culture. Yet unless one takes cognisance of, at the very least, this immediate geographic, physical context within which we find ourselves, it would be impossible to explore what has been announced as the theme of the Winter School program: the arts in society.

Both terms comprised in this key phrase demand closer scrutiny.

★

Keynote lecture at the Winter School, Grahamstown Arts Festival, July 1987.

To begin with: *the arts.* For obvious reasons my view is primarily that of a writer, but even though writers" peculiar relationship with language, and the peculiar involvement of language with meaning, may distinguish them in some respects from other artists, it seems to me that all the arts, and the culture of which they form a definitive part, are essentially related in terms of the function they fulfil in society.

Of course, "culture" can be defined so narrowly ("the Great Masterpieces of the race") or so widely ("all the distinctive spiritual and material, intellectual and emotional features distinguishing one society from another") as to be almost meaningless. Yet we are all aware not only of its existence but of the precariousness of that existence: aware not only of the need to foster it and to include it in our projections for the future of humanity, but of the paradox inherent in this aim — since conscious "protection" and "encouragement," by governments or the large organs and organisations of society, often has the opposite effect and instead of liberating individuals and nations merely succeeds in enslaving them by shaping them to preconceived moulds. Almost inevitably, a "cultural program" forms part of the grand design of any totalitarian régime: by controlling the creation of art, the structures of education, the scope of ethics, the direction and application of scientific and religious enquiry, even a well-intentioned government or its extensions may inhibit rather than stimulate culture. The most one can hope for is to help, as circumspectly as possible, to encourage, or simply to *allow,* the conditions and climate in which culture can come into its own.

It may be useful to define this "own" by thinking of culture, not as a content or a series or cluster of contents, but most especially as a constantly developing cluster of *structures* and *relationships.* And even this should be defined more specifically. What we are confronted with in culture, is not a set of "things," of "events," of "actions," of "products," of "processes" as such — but with things, events, actions, products and processes which *produce meaning.* This, to me, is the distinguishing mark of culture: it occupies that territory or dimension of existence in which meaning emerges — more precisely, that experience of meaning in which the individual is creatively related to the collective.

It follows that, approached in this manner, meaning can never be merely affirmative, but must necessarily be open-ended toward whatever lies beyond. The arts do not endorse or condone: they produce meanings more fully articulated than those that went before.

In order to articulate, they must proceed from a context, a framework of reference within which the private and the public can meet and interact. Which explains why the glorious periods of "high culture" in Western history — the Athens of Pericles, the Florence of the Medici, the Spain of the Moors, Elizabethan England — almost invariably turned out to be those in which the "culturally active," the "meaning-producing," segment of society shared a system of values and references (at the expense of a deprived, exploited and suppressed minority — or, sometimes, majority?).

This explains why, in our tumultuous times, and especially in the Third World, the arts are so often regarded with suspicion, as the prerogative of an élite or, since the French Revolution, of the bourgeoisie.

In a world threatened on an ever more stupefying scale by famine and disease, violence and war, refugees, tyrannies and oppressed multitudes, "art" may indeed threaten to become a dirty word. But only if we persist in thinking of culture as the preserve of the idle and privileged few, not if art is seen as the indispensable generator of meaning within society as a whole.

If art has over many centuries become identified with "those who can afford it," then indeed it has little to offer to those struggling for survival on a physical level. What reply is a musical masterpiece to the hunger pangs of a child? What "immortal" work of literature can break the chains of a slave? What comfort is a Rembrandt self-portrait to an abused woman?

But of course these are unfair equations. In fact, they are no equations at all. Hunger exists, and can only be overcome if the hungry are nourished with bread, not music. Bondage exists, and can be eradicated only by breaking all the innumerable chains, material and spiritual, that shackle the unfree. The acknowledgement of the full humanity of a woman is not dependent upon painting. But not for a moment does this imply that humanity as such — as a whole, as a collection of societies, or as a host of individuals — does not *need* music, or literature, or theater, or painting. To acknowledge our need of art is not to underrate the basic needs of human beings to survive, to be free, to improve their lot: it is only to acknowledge that humanity *also* requires meaning, or at least the opportunity to search for meaning. This does not replace the need to be fed, to be free, to be able to work: but it ranges itself with those needs which peculiarly identify humanity as a form of life on earth.

If there is — and there is — resistance and animosity in the minds of many to the arts of the few, it often results from the very efforts "to bring art to the masses": a symptom of a certain kind of missionary spirit that has done so much harm to so many people in so many ways.

Would it be more appropriate to propose starting from the opposite end and "take the masses to art"? In the light of my initial proposition this, too, would miss the point. "The masses" (deliberately to use an objectionable term) do not find themselves "over here" — and art "over there." Art is not a Promised Land to be aspired to. If, as I have argued, it is part of our faculty (and the expression of our need) to produce meaning, it inheres in the human situation. What needs to be done is to identify the circumstances within which, as it were, meaning can emerge most meaningfully.

Now one set of circumstances generally regarded as pernicious to the creation of art is violence. Yet it seems to me not only dangerous but wrong to see the relationship between them as one of simple antithesis. Particularly in a world of crumbling values violence itself produces a kind of meaning: it is society's way of saying *No.* It is meaning at its most emphatic — but also, of course, at its most destructive. Violence is the language culture speaks when no other valid articulation is left open to it. Once we have defined the true nature of violence within each context, a beginning may be made toward turning this destructive expression of meaning into a positive current. If violence is the only utterance possible in a given context, if murder and pillage are the only language conceivable in a given situation, the problem lies not with violence but with the suspension of other possibilities of human articulation. Understanding violence may well be the first step toward an understanding of culture, and of the arts.

It is not a territory to be ventured into with preconceptions and prejudgements. The pressure of violence may, by itself, stimulate counterforms of meaning: during the seventies South Africa experienced an increase in artistic creativity among all sections of the population — although the reasons for the sudden explosion of poetry might have been vastly different in black and white communities (and, within the latter, in Afrikaner and English communities). For many Afrikaans writers poetry became, in the face of censorship, a safe retreat from the much more exposed territory of fiction; white English-speakers, having lost their political power and much of their economic power after a century and a half of uncontested domination, found in poetry a — relatively — harmless domain within which the old muscles might be flexed in a literary manner, in order at least to sustain an illusion of power. For black writers poetry was exactly the opposite: an instrument of liberation, a new language which exhilaratingly gave shape and meaning to black aspirations and awareness, and an experience of solidarity that transcends all ethnic divisions: it is a means not of finding sanctuary from political power or a surrogate for it, but of *confronting* it. This is art at its most affirmative: and by no means limited to an exclusive élite.

In fact, what has been happening in South Africa in recent years also serves to confirm the paradoxical and vital nature of the arts: literature produced by black and white authors used to run in several more or less separate streams through South African history, a separation aggravated by apartheid. But more recently, although each has maintained an unmistakable identity, all three currents seem to converge in a singular expression of resistance to oppression. What individual writers express is obviously determined first of all by private experience temperament, hope or the frustration of hope: yet essentially all are involved in the same activity — not simply of opposing a political régime but of affirming, in the process, lasting human values in the face of it, and providing the openings through which these can expand and continue to grow.

The second term contained in our title is *society.* And this has to be defined in very precise terms, because there are many kinds of human society in the world, ranging from the most "open" and "democratic" (Sweden, France, the US, Britain . . .) to those we can only define as "closed," i.e. those in which expression and communication — the territory of politics, of the media, of education, and of the arts — are severely inhibited (countries behind the Iron Curtain, some countries in South America, some countries in Africa, including South Africa).

The kind of society we have in South Africa — that is, the particular society within which we are to explore the functioning of the arts, which concerns us at this Festival — is not only closed, but a society of siege.

Less than a month ago the General State of Emergency was officially extended. This merely served to give official recognition to a condition which has been developing steadily over many years. A whole generation of South Africans have never known any other régime than the present, any other policy or way of life than that of apartheid. And even as the situation grows steadily worse, people are adapting to it, accepting as "normal" with the dawning of each new day what would have been deemed "abnormal" only yesterday. A few months ago a friend of mine took her black charlady and this woman's two-year-old son to the beach for the day. It was the first time the boy had ever seen the sea, yet he didn't enjoy the outing at all: everything seemed strange and frightening to him, and he spent most of the day sitting on my friend's lap eating ice-cream. No matter how much he was prodded and cajoled, he didn't speak a single word all day. In the late afternoon they drove back the sixty kilometers to Grahamstown. As they turned toward the black township, the boy's eyes lit up, and he smiled, pointing at a yellow police vehicle: for the first time that day he spoke. "Casspir," he said. To him the armoured truck meant: home. It was the sign of the familiar, the first thing he had seen all day with which he could identify. How much easier, in the well-protected white suburbs of South Africa, for people to adapt to the shifting and diminishing territory of a land in a state of siege.

Certainly, our situation today is gloomier than ever before — even though (and perhaps because?) the country no longer finds itself in the focus and on the front page of the world's news media. Probing it is like a descent into a particular kind of hell. The State of Emergency, set to become a permanent feature of the South African Third Reich, has succeeded, we are told, in drastically lowering the number of deaths, injuries and "incidents" that have characterized the civil war raging unofficially in the country since September 1984. The "unrest," we are told, has now been contained: and the increased majority of President Botha's party in the recent all-white parliamentary elections appears to indicate support for the need of drastic security measures and also for the sophisticated humbug which masquerades as "reform" on the Botha agenda, while serving only to entrench ethnicity and racism more effectively than before.

The key to the situation lies in the words *we are told*. For the depressing fact is that the State of Emergency has *not* succeeded in easing tension or diminishing unrest, but only in repressing violent contestation and inhibiting the dissemination of information about it. Apartheid has always been diabolically effective in preventing each racial community in South Africa from natural access to or understanding of others; but the State of

Emergency has almost wholly blocked up the access to the most basic kinds of information. *We are told* that the unrest has diminished, but those who are aware of what is really happening in the black townships know how the security forces continue to provoke and terrorise the helpless: if there is a measure of silence, it is the silence of repression and of mounting anger, not of peace. *We are told* that the government intends to negotiate with black leaders, while behind the scenes it is increasing the kind of action which will prevent any self-respecting leaders from coming forward for discussion. *We are told* that South Africa wishes to live in peace with its neighbours, while the military (the real rulers of the country) continue to destabilise the whole Southern African region through unprovoked raids on neighbouring territories. *We are told* that ANC guerillas are killed when women and children are shot down in their sleep. *We are told* that the ANC is a Communist-dominated organization of terrorists who refuse to renounce the armed struggle, while the government itself has institutionalised violence.

How does all this affect the artist?

One feature of the present situation which never ceases to surprise outsiders is the apparent "liberalization" of official censorship (certainly as far as literature is concerned). Usually the relaxation of censorship can be seen as a sign of a society in the process of "opening up" (cf. Spain and Portugal in the seventies). But in South Africa it amounts to a mere façade. By appearing to allow artists more freedom — and this includes black artists, some of them unequivocally radical — the régime can attempt to gain credibility for its "reform" program in the countries whose commercial support is most urgently required. This appearance of liberalization enables the government to become *more* repressive in other areas.

But it goes further than this. Essentially, the government has been able to dispense with strict literary censorship *because it no longer regards writing as dangerous.* It believes it can shrug off the writer.

The real target of the South African censor today is the journalist. Literature, and art in general, is regarded as expendable, because it is viewed as an élitist preoccupation which cannot affect or influence the masses; what *is* feared is the dissemination of factual information by the media. Because whatever happens, people must not be allowed to find out. And, sadly, this may well be effective. Most people are confused or worried by reports about the unstable situation in which they find themselves: knowledge and awareness raise questions about action. So if the press is curtailed, it makes it easier to relax in the belief that unpleasant events happen only when they are reported to have happened. Few individuals will deliberately go in search of suppressed truth. And if they do, the government may find means to deal with them.

It is also relevant to our enquiry today to note *how* such "dealings" take place: the center of government action is no longer vested in parliament (which makes the recent white elections even more peripheral to the overall situation in the country): even committed supporters of the Party have little say in decisions taken or implemented. Parliament has become no more than a rubber stamp for decisions taken outside of it, by the State President and his "security advisers" who rule more and more by decree, making more and more sure that the courts of the land are either muzzled or turned into subservient handmaidens.

This means that the only effective opposition to the political power of the régime must also be sought outside parliament. The real future of the country is shaped by the ANC — in exile abroad, in innumerable cells throughout the country, even in the prisons where the true leaders of the people are incarcerated — or by the United Democratic Front, the trade unions, the youth organizations, even by the "street committees" who effectively run the black townships ever since the government's official bodies were largely rendered impotent in black communities.

This is the real territory where the battle for power is taking place. No wonder the authorities have come to regard artists as irrelevant.

But the question must be asked again: Does this really render the artist impotent, irrelevant? I must confess that recent events have driven me closer to pessimism than ever before. In Germany, in the thirties, there came a time when writers — Brecht, the Manns and a host of others — had to acknowledge that the only way to continue functioning as writers was to go into exile. Such a moment may well be awaiting South African artists too. And yet I believe it would be wrong to despair too soon.

Even if the government ignores artists I am convinced that this in itself need not mean that they *are* expendable. I have said earlier that an important part of the evil in the present South African situation resides in the régime's exploitation and misuse of language: that is, employing language not as a means of information but of disinformation; as a means not of creation but of destruction. And if this is the case, then surely artists whose life-blood is their commitment to *meaning* should become even more intensely involved in using language as a means to counter the lie by unmasking, revealing, bringing to light, and disseminating knowledge. (I am using "language" here in the widest sense of the world to include every kind of articulation employed in literature, in the theater, in painting or sculpture or music or dance or film or photography.)

In a society where people are no longer allowed to find out what is happening from day to day, the artist may even — at least temporarily, or up to a point — assume some of the functions of the purveyor of information, in the way illiterate washerwomen in Chile began to embroider cloths to communicate what was happening in the prisons when newspapers were not allowed to print it.

But it goes beyond such preliminary actions. Far beyond. Because quite obviously it is not enough to state that one is against violence or evil. Some act of transformation, perhaps of redemption, is required. If artists have come to be regarded by the authorities as irrelevant, perhaps it is because they have not yet grasped the full extent of their possible functioning within society. Certainly black artists in South Africa have been a vital force in the developing revolutionary climate where they fulfil a function of conscientisation; if white artists are regarded by the authorities as expendable, it may well be that they have not lived up to the demands of their time. Within the power strategies of South Africa today the artist can hardly continue to function within the framework of nineteenth-century individualism. A much more urgent identification with the organisations and strategies mustered against apartheid may be necessary: at least on the level of the artist-as-citizen.

Even so, I cannot demand of the artist only, and simply, to be the mouthpiece of a cause, however noble. We all have a real need of the *discoveries* of art: we all crave for *meaning* in our lives. But meaning transcends political causes, treatises, pamphlets, however indispensable these may be in themselves. Meaning has to do not only with the rights and wrongs of a given system or a struggle but with the good and evil of being alive, being human. Without this concern, which to me is the primary concern of the artist, no short-term struggle can amount to much. Perhaps it is part of the hell of being an artist to learn to accept that you may be branded as redundant within the immediacies and urgencies of a political debate: your concern is not a power game, but the larger and more abiding ideals of truth, of freedom, of justice.

I have sometimes been accused of being "old-fashioned" in my belief in the word, in my dedication to the values which can be discovered through literature. But in a country where the word has become employed more and more to distort and to destroy, I am committed to the faith that only the word can be used to correct and to create.

I do not claim any special dispensation for the artist. If the violent forces let loose in South Africa today are allowed to be polarized utterly into a struggle between black and white, I accept that those of us with white skins may be obliterated in the cataclysm which seems to be drawing closer every day through the obstinacy and arrogance of those in power. One cannot create art to "promote a cause" or, worse, to "feather one's nest" or to curry favour with whoever may be in power in South Africa today or tomorrow. One can commit oneself to art only in terms of what one sees, what one lives, what one totally believes in. It is something of a destiny. If the work proves worthless, or tainted, or insufficient, it will be rejected by history, and the artist with it. But one cannot allow such fears and doubts to inhibit or silence one.

Certainly, artists can never presume. They are always cut back to size. To tackle politicians or the military head-on is quixotic: the challenge to artists is of another kind, their territory of another order. They are not agents of power, but campaigners for invisible values no human being can live without. This takes place through ceaseless questioning. Perhaps, in the final analysis, all art can really do is to help us formulate those questions on which our true survival as human beings depends. Only through questions can one hope to gain access to truth.

Not one of us stands guardian to that access: not one of us knows the truth, the whole truth, and nothing but the truth. All of us blunder in lies and gropings and fears and hopes. But if we can keep the *access* to truth open through ceaselessly posing questions about everything that happens, about everything that touches our humanity, something is salvaged in the long run. And that "something" includes the possibility of justice, and of freedom, and hopefully of truth.

In such a situation art can exercise its most ample function, in terms of that quiet revolution of the mind and the senses without which no political or social revolution can ultimately succeed.

OCTOBER 1988

Visions of the Future

I imagine it happening on an April day, in early autumn, when the Cape is at its most beautiful: vineyards turning the color of burgundy, the oaks and poplars a blazing yellow, the sky translucent. From the top of Table Mountain one would overlook the rugged spine of the mountains jutting into the cold ink-blue waters where Atlantic and Indian oceans meet. Below would be the sweep of Table Bay, and perched in its embrace, a mere smudge on the surface of the sea, that notorious island, Robben Island, which has been, through the centuries, a leper colony, an asylum for the insane, a dour prison, South Africa's Alcatraz: a prison with possibly the most beautiful view in the world, dramatising the contrast with the lugubrious interior. One might well imagine, above the main entrance, that awesome inscription:

Lasciate ogni speranza, voi ch'entrata . . .

Except, on that day I am thinking about, that day in the near or distant future (yet I hope it will be in my lifetime), there will be a commotion on the island. The prison gates, unlocked recently, will be ceremoniously opened and a symbolic procession will move from them to the jetty, where an open boat, a joy-

First published in *Der Spiegel* (Germany), October 1988.

ously decorated, festive boat, will be waiting, with others bobbing on the water behind it. The procession will go on board. From high up there, from the top of Table Mountain, one would be able to follow, through binoculars, the progress of the flotilla to Cape Town harbor, a bright white spray in their wake. All the boats and ships in the harbor will be blowing their horns in bleating, booming, roaring homage, and on that remarkable day even that normally mournful noise will sound exuberant. From the harbor, along the Heerengracht, on the territory reclaimed from the sea, past the statues of the Dutch founder of the first refreshment post at the Cape of Good Hope, Jan van Riebeeck and his wife, up along Adderley Street, into the shaded avenue of the Company Gardens leading to the Houses of Parliament, the streets will be lined with hundreds of thousands, perhaps with millions of people of all ages, all colors, waving the green-and-yellow-and-black flags of the African National Congress. And as the procession passes them — on foot, perhaps, the way de Gaulle led his people from the Arc de Triomphe to Notre Dame on that Liberation day — a great roar will erupt: a roar not resembling human voices at all, but a sound breaking from the very earth, from the rockbed and molten lava and swirling gasses in its core, a roar that gives voice to the entire continent of Africa: the endless barren deserts of Sahara and Namib and Kalahari, the great plains and savannah prairies of the interior, the burnt-out craters of Ngorongoro, the snow-capped peaks of Kilimanjaro and the Atlas Mountains, the primordial jungles of the equator: the voice of a continent celebrating, finally, its ultimate liberation: a voice echoing down through the centuries, the combined voice of all the millions upon millions of slaves who were dragged in chains from the Isle of Gorée on the coast of Senegal, from Angola, from Mozambique, to toil in the service of whites on distant continents: the voice of all the poor, the rejected, the oppressed, the sick and suffering, the famished — rejoicing in a moment which, for all of Africa, will mean the final acknowledgement of its dignity and humanity: that moment when the racist régime of South Africa finally cedes power to the people.

In that great throng, that yellow-and-green-and-black ocean, that booming roar of jubilation, a small group of people, men and women, will march, heads erect, toward the Houses of Parliament, waiting to receive them. In their midst, at their head, will be a man already stooped by age, but on that day his stride will be youthful and his grey head erect; and beside him will be the tall beautiful woman who, through all the years of his imprisonment, never flagged or flinched in carrying for her people the torch of hope, faith and nobility: Nelson Mandela and his wife.

This, invariably, is the image conjured up in my mind whenever I try to visualise the "New South Africa" which must inevitably emerge from the gloom and the ashes and despair created by the evil Botha régime which at this moment is still clinging to absolute power in the face of the whole civilized world. The desperation demonstrated by the way these men manipulate the country's judicial system makes nonsense of democratic institutions (including parliament itself). Their resort to terrorism and murder to silence opponents (the attack on the lawyer Albie Sachs in Maputo earlier this year, the assassination of Dulcie September, the ANC representative in Paris . . .) has all the overtones of the Apocalypse: and often the only relief is to try and visualise what will come *after* the Götterdämmerung they are preparing.

What is more difficult to visualise, is the sequel to that day of exuberant liberation. Two different visions impose themselves:

In a flight by airplane over the country I look down at the towns and cities below. They are clearly visible in the stunning lucidity of the African light: the clouds of smoke that used to obscure the cities and vast stretches of the countryside, especially in the Eastern Transvaal, have disappeared: people have learned to respect their environment, now that they have learned to respect their neighbours. The waste and effluvium of factories and power stations are controlled; pollution is less obvious. The wonderful natural resources of the Eastern Cape — forests and lakes, a coast teeming with marine life — have been restored, no longer disfigured by P. W. Botha's highways which once threatened to lay waste a luxuriant stretch of land. Down in Cape Town, the hideous open scar on the lower slopes of Devil's Peak, left when P. W. Botha (then Minister of Colored Affairs) bulldozed the legendary District Six, heartland of "colored" people for many generations, like a latterday Lidice, has been rebuilt. People of all colors are living there, happily, side by side, relaxed in the knowledge that they are all South Africans; that no statute book makes any distinction any more between "white" and "black" and "colored" and "Asian." Flying over the towns, one sees them sprawling over the brown, scorched African *veld,* the suburbs of the rich, the densely populated areas of the poor . . . but the very visibility of apartheid has disappeared: "rich" no longer automatically means "white," "poor" is no longer the inescapable synonym of "black." Previously, flying from Johannesburg to Cape Town, there used to be that startling contrast between the affluent white towns and their depressing shoebox satellites which housed the black workforce on which the vast riches of the country depended: now people can live where they wish; and there is no ceiling to the upward mobility of the poor, because they are no longer restricted by the color of the skin. Many of the vast estates previously run by syndicates or by wealthy white farmers who lived a jet-set life commuting between Johannesburg and New York, Frankfurt or Taipeh, have now been taken over by the state and redistributed among the poor who have been driven from the land by the greed of a small élite. I alight from the plane at Mandela Airport in Johannesburg (the flight from Tambo Airport in Cape Town has taken barely eighty minutes). It is election day. I still have time to vote. I join a queue of blacks and whites, chatting and joking among themselves. I see staunch Afrikaners voting for a black candidate. In another constituency, blacks are throwing in their weight behind a white candidate whose visions for the future they appreciate and trust. Scanning a list of the candidates all over the country, I notice that almost half of them are women. Years ago, when white Afrikaners travelled to Dakar to meet the ANC, they had not a single woman delegate among them, while the ANC had women in top positions. This, it seems, has become infectious.

But sometimes, at this point, my vision changes. Instead, I watch television on the night before the election and listen in a state of shock as a minister announces that an insurrection of white Afrikaner extremists has launched terrorist attacks all over the country: many people have been killed, and bloody battles are raging in many parts of South Africa. In the circumstances, the elections have to be suspended, and the State of Emergency, previously decreed by P. W. Botha to salvage his régime, has had to be reinstated. The president appears on the screen. What he says reminds me of Mugabe, years ago: he is the bringer of sad tidings. Massive aid programs, promised by Western countries on the day of liberation, have been cancelled unilaterally. Urgent appeals from the Azanian government have met with shrugs of refusal, or blank, bored stares. The world is no longer interested in South Africa. It has lost its news value. The white régime has been crushed: why should the United States, or Britain, or West Germany or France care about the fate of blacks in a black country? If it goes down the drain, just too bad: what else can you expect of Africa? As long as those precious strategic minerals can still be obtained, as cheaply and as advantageously as possible of course, why should Europe or the US care about the rest? If everything, sadly, grimly, grinds to a standstill in the grip of famine, disease or economic decline, *tant pis:* they wanted to be independent, didn't they? Well, then let them save themselves . . .

Visions of the future often depart from a false base, as if the future were some mythical country or promised land which already existed, a place where, if one travels long enough, one will inevitably arrive. But the whole point about the future is *that it does not yet exist,* except in the measure in which it is created, permitted, made possible, by what exists *now.* Which is why the Greeks had a very different way, compared to ours, of assessing progress in time: we tend to think of time as a river running between its banks, carrying us with it, on a boat or a raft perhaps, looking forward, the past behind our backs. But precisely this image presupposes that the future already exists, that we face it as we move toward it. Whereas the Greeks, using the same river image, suggested that we find ourselves on our little raft facing the past as the present sweeps past us and becomes visible, intelligible; while we move backward into the future which does not exist yet. This means that South Africa's future, too, does not yet exist as a place of unavoidable arrival: it is being brought into existence by what we are doing right now.

This means that, if the visions I suggested above have any chance of being realised, one has to evaluate them in terms of the present. *What makes those alternatives possible?*

Walking through the streets of Hillbrow, Johannesburg's most cosmopolitan district, where blacks and whites and so-called "coloreds" and Indians, Afrikaners and English, Portuguese, Taiwanese, Germans, Greeks, Poles, Hungarians and others work and shop together, and in fact live in the same flat buildings, it is indeed possible to visualize a shared future. Oh, occasionally there are eruptions, brawls, arguments, as happens in any community on earth; but by and large the easy cosmopolitan atmosphere of Hillbrow allows everybody space to do whatever they want, to be whatever they feel like. The same goes for suburbs like Woodstock or Salt River in Cape Town, where — as in the District Six of old — whites and Malays and others live peacefully side by side. Some go their private ways, others have become house friends: few of them even think in terms of "color" any more. They are all, quite simply, South Africans. Over the years, the lure of work in the cities has created this influx of all races and nationalities: the needs of a modern world have eroded apartheid, preparing people on the most mundane, and at the same time the most intimate and homely levels of their existence, to accept one another, to share, to work and shop and dream together. Left to themselves, most communities in the country may well develop along similar lines.

Inevitably, in some areas whites will tend to create a more or less exclusive community to themselves; in others blacks will do the same. There are ex-colonial English-speaking whites who still look down on Afrikaners as an inferior peasant breed and who would like to keep their posh suburbs to themselves. And in many places, especially in the small villages of the deep interior of the Orange Free State or Transvaal — the old Boer republics of the nineteenth century who rose up against the full might of the British Empire and won the admiration of the world in the course of their doomed war of liberation — Afrikaners may continue to close ranks and keep strangers and "enemies" out. Many black communities may do the same. It happens all over the world. *But this need not be enforced by law.* If people are allowed to decide for themselves, communities will evolve naturally, some more exclusivist than others, some more tolerant than others. It is already happening in South Africa.

Or rather: it has been happening in the recent past. But at the moment, in a shocking reversal of the natural evolutionary processes in the country, and in a denial of the policy of "reform" P. W. Botha has been using to fool the world, the South African government is now threatening to close in on these "open" communities and force them to segregate. A few may be allowed to continue as "grey areas," but there are so many restrictions and regulations to comply with, and the authorities are invested with such awesome powers to intervene in the most private areas of individual lives, that a natural impulse toward the sharing of the future by different races has now been frustrated.

"We fear Africa," wrote a British author recently, "because when we leave it alone, it works." This is what also characterizes the Botha régime in South Africa: it has discovered that South Africa can "work" if it is left to the people themselves to devise the patterns of their existence: but the government's power is vested in continuing to control individual and group destinies. Too much power and money has been invested in apartheid by the small clique in control to consider relinquishing it.

In many other respects, too, economic and social forces have been creating a climate from which might evolve the kind of South Africa I described at the beginning of this essay. In sport, in the universities (at Rhodes University, where I teach, 30% of the students are black: a larger percentage than on almost any campus in the United States), in business, South Africans of all colors have been discovering the opportunities — and the adventure — offered by acting and living together, rather than segregated: but government policy forces them to stay apart. Which means that "white interests" must be safeguarded, even if it requires that a massive — and increasing — majority of people must be subjugated into a modernised state of slavery so that a few chosen whites may prosper precariously. If only they knew how many young whites there are in the schools and universities — not a week goes by without my encountering some of them — who plead with great urgency: "Please, we want to meet young black people of our own age, but the government (or the education system) makes it impossible: just tell us what we can *do* to make contact!" I know of few more revealing indictments of the kind of country apartheid has created: a country in which two different realities, one black, one white, exist side by side, occupying the same physical space, and yet giving the impression that they are on different planets, neither as yet discovered by the other.

There are black organisations in South Africa, supported by increasing numbers of the young generation who, since 1976, have taken to the streets in open and violent confrontation with the government forces: their attitude is that black patience has only increased black suffering, and that the time for patience is past. They see themselves as having nothing to lose: what is the value of a life of humiliation and severely restricted chances anyway? And yet, at the same time, there are organisations still willing to consider a future in which whites will have a share. This is, most especially, characteristic of the ANC, whose long history as a non-racial organization, and whose present composition, in which people of all races in the South African spectrum are in leadership positions, *demonstrate* its openness, its generosity, and its commitment to a future in which not color or race, but loyalty to South Africa, will be the decisive test. More and more South African whites, especially Afrikaners, are travelling to other parts of the world to meet representatives of the ANC: and each time the discovery of their mutual South African heritage and of the non-racial nature of the ANC are the greatest surprises the travellers take back home with them. Of course, the government keeps these facts about the ANC secret, as they would undermine the government's own vicious portrayal of the ANC as purely a terrorist organization. (It is so useful to call your adversary "terrorist" if that is the characteristic of your own methods.) With more and more desperation, and increasingly violent threats, the government is trying to discourage such contacts, as they unmask the government's own hypocrisy and lies. But more and more white South Africans *are* becoming aware of the truth, and are changing their conceptions of the ANC. And as the ANC is still, undoubtedly, the leading liberation movement in the South African context, its policy of racial openness is a major factor at the present time which makes it possible for the kind of future I personally dream about to be realised.

Among the many questions constantly asked about the possible future of South Africa, two return with particular frequency, one from the Left, the other from the Right.

Sceptics on the Left want to know: "Will the Afrikaner ever accept profound change? Isn't he so obsessed with the Masada complex that he'd rather follow a scorched-earth policy, the way many whites did in Zimbabwe, and destroy everything (and even sacrifice his own life) rather than share the country with Blacks?"

I must confess that there are many Afrikaners of that kind; and the growth of the parties on the extreme Right, embodying more and more of the attitudes and even the insignia of the Third Reich, indicates that their numbers are increasing as the situation grows more desperate. They cannot be discounted. To them, the quality of life is dependent upon a white skin. (How ironical that many of these Afrikaners have, in fact, darker complexions than so-called "coloreds"! A guilty conscience is a powerful factor in any movement toward "racial purity.") To them, God had a purpose with the Afrikaner: he had to conquer southern Africa and impose his brand of Old Testament "civilisation" on it, built on the blood and sweat of black laborers who, as the descendants of Ham, were cursed by God to remain forever the slaves of their (white) brothers. Even Afrikaners like P. W. Botha, who try to present an "enlightened" or "reformist" image, seem secretly to rely on this conviction. Yet I believe that, in spite of their growing numbers, these anachronistic people are a lunatic fringe. At the very least, one should remember that another brand of Afrikaner exists. From a very early stage of white colonization this strain of Afrikaner began to identify with the continent of Africa, often entering into alliances with indigenous black peoples against foreign imperialist invaders. For obvious reasons apartheid has come to obscure the existence of these people, but the phenomenon of dissent in Afrikaner ranks has persisted. Today there is a whole generation of young Afrikaners who have begun to question the values their own parents took for granted, and who openly voice their discomfort and resentment. To them, black majority rule poses no fundamental problems, the chauvinism of their parents has changed, in them, to a broader sense of belonging to a New South Africa already discernible on the horizon. The tragedy at the moment is that not enough of them are as yet ready to prepare actively for that situation. Perhaps they are still hesitant about the true extent of their Africanness? The ancient dichotomy between Europe and Africa is still not resolved.

The other question, asked from the Right, comes down to this: "But are blacks ready to govern?" I don't think it is necessary to dwell on this, as the mentality behind the question is so repugnant (or, at best, so ignorant). Even if one were to approach the situation in purely Western terms, it should be obvious that in South Africa more Africans have been exposed to "white civilisation" over a longer period than anywhere else in Africa. Even if black education is of an abysmally low standard, and even if much is still done from above to "keep the blacks down," there are more than enough leading black figures in most fields of public life available to ensure sound administration, a concern for education, and above all an awareness of human dignity. Certainly I would feel much more at ease with my life ruled by present leaders from the ANC than by any single member of Botha's troglodyte government.

Above all, once again, the point is that there is no need for an extremist white nationalism to be replaced by an equally extremist and racist black nationalism. The choice is *not* between one or the other, but between fascism and exclusivism on the one hand, and openness and non-racialism on the other.

Lest the tone of my argument sound too optimistic, I must append a very sombre warning. There is, in fact, very little reason for any optimism at all in South Africa today. P. W. Botha, ruled by his temper and his whims like any of the less stable emperors in the declining years of the Roman Empire, lacks both the intelligence and the knowledge to cope with an increasingly complex and violent situation. The true rulers of the country are the security police, who have proved themselves worthy successors of the SS and the Gestapo. What matters to them is not the possibility of a New South Africa, or even a smooth transition in that direction, but simply the maintenance of white power. And they are all the more dangerous for pretending to be concerned with civilized values and human dignity and even with a policy of "reform." If South Africa appears calmer on the surface today than two years ago, the tensions below that surface are worse than ever, the chances for peaceful settlement fewer than ever: at least while the present régime is in power.

And for every day that the government persists in its present intransigence, the chances for a relatively peaceful, negotiated transition toward the happy South Africa of my first vision are diminished and the possibility of the second is increased. Which is tragic, precisely because the *potential* for negotiation and harmony exists.

This, too, should be said: as long as the rest of the world hides behind hypocritical protestations about not wanting to impose sanctions "because it hurts the blacks" (while the protesters are only concerned about continuing their lucrative trade with South Africa, and living off the fruits of apartheid and human exploitation), the possibility of a peaceful changeover is frustrated. Blacks themselves have announced that only through sanctions can the world demonstrate its moral solidarity with their cause. Only recently South Africa was represented in West Berlin at the session of the International Monetary Fund. Will German money once again be made available to help foot the bills generated by the staggering economic and human cost of apartheid? Or will the German people, who themselves have suffered so much through the delusions and power-madness of the Nazi régime, at last recognise that the present South African régime is moving in that same direction — and be prepared, in the name of humanity, to help put an end to it?

Then, perhaps, we can draw a step closer to the realization of that vision of a shared future for all South Africans, which may in due course become something of a model for the rest of the world.

OCTOBER 1988

Afrikaners

The old man was quaking with rage. But his stooped shoulders, whose usual squareness suggested the confidence of a man who knows that God is on his side, betrayed the underlying pain. On a chair against the wall his wife was slumped, sobbing quietly, a motherly hen disturbed in her brooding; and on the edge of the small bed sat a young man, pale, his blond head bowed, but with a body rigid in defiance. "It would have been easier for me today," said the father, his voice trembling, "to have been told that my son was dead. Rather than *this*." I felt like an intruder in that intimate and agonising scene. What I was witnessing was more than the gulf which separates generations: it was, in a family context, the breakdown of one system of values and the affirmation of another; the shattering of an image the world had long taken for granted, that of the Afrikaner monolith. Half an hour earlier the young man, a postgraduate student in my department, had telephoned me and asked me to come to his digs. He had just informed his parents that he was in love with a girl who, like himself, was the child of an Afrikaans-speaking church minister — except that, in terms of the South African

This is the full text of a project commissioned by the *National Geographic Magazine* and published in shortened form in October 1988. Where necessary, the names of people interviewed have been changed to protect their identity. Names of persons who are widely known, and/or are in public positions, have been retained.

racial laws, he was white while she was classified as "colored." "What will become of us?" asked the old man in horror. "I shall lose my job in the church. Not one of our friends will speak to us again." This, to him, was more important than whatever might happen to his son. "He is still our child," the mother whispered in quiet desperation; her husband did not even seem to hear.

Much of the disturbing quality of the scene lies in the fact that *all* the participants are Afrikaners. Which wreaks havoc with stereotypes. Indeed, having spent the more than fifty years of my own life among Afrikaners, I embarked on the many journeys undertaken in preparation of this essay as a voyage of discovery and rediscovery, finding myself forced, as I progressed, to revise and adapt many of my own conceptions about this "people on the wrong side of history," as the philosopher Martin Walser so poignantly described them.

Haphazard recollections from my journeys over the past year confirm the confusion. On a farm in the lush subtropical Eastern Transvaal I encountered an irascible man known to his black workers as *Makahlane,* "He who kicks," which refers to the crude manner in which he asserts his near-absolute authority over them. On the adjacent farm, a young man has just completed building an impressive row of new houses for his laborers, and over several weekends he has even constructed a soccer field for them and sponsored all the gear and equipment their team requires for its games. The managing director of one of the major banks in South Africa is a portly, urbane man in Pretoria responsible for the handling of billions of rands every day, while close to the main road in the Swartland wheat area near the Cape one finds the home of a wizened sun-scorched man who never ventures out of sight of his little hovel, as his deep-seated suspicion of banks prompted him many years ago to keep all his life's savings in a trunk under his bed. On the covers of many glossy magazines around the world one regularly encounters the immaculately groomed face of a blonde beauty who, in 1974, was elected Miss World. Outside a village off the Cape West Coast lives a surly old man who does not have a single magazine or newspaper in his house and who has on the walls of his ill-furnished house only two fly-bespeckled pictures as adornment: a photograph of his crayfish packaging factory, and another of two of the tractors ploughing on his farm.

At first sight it would seem preposterous to suggest that these people can have anything at all in common. But they do. They are all Afrikaners. And an encounter with them, or with an endless variety of others of their species, can but confirm what was so succinctly stated by Willem de Klerk, sometime editor of the leading Afrikaans Sunday newspaper *Rapport,* until he was forced to resign when the government became annoyed by his criticism: "The Afrikaner is bursting out of his definitions of himself as well as those of others."

There were no problems with these definitions in my childhood, spent in a succession of small villages in the arid interior of the country, where English was an almost unspeakable foreign language, where the only black people one encountered were servants or laborers, where God was a daily reality and visions of Apocalypse pervaded one's dreams at night. Some of my earliest memories — images which persist as archetypes in the collective Afrikaner mind — derive from a feeling of snugness and security, as I stared out at the world from a brightly colored wrap that held me tightly to the motherly back of a black nanny; or squatting on the back porch, eating *mieliepap* (corn porridge) with her, scooping handfuls from a black iron pot and moulding it in my small fist before tucking it away. I remember visiting my maternal grandmother in Bedford in the Eastern Cape, and the solemn family excursion every Sunday afternoon to the churchyard where, beside my grandfather's tombstone, my grandmother's own grave had already been dug, waiting to receive her body when she died. Other summer holidays were spent in the Western Province with its mediterranean climate; often on the fruit farm of my Oom Jannie at Tulbagh, where he was known as one of the country's expert vintners (having studied in France, something almost unheard of in his time), until my pious aunt, persuaded of the sinfulness of drinking, instructed him to eradicate every single vine on the property. I remember spending weekends or holidays on farms where all the boys would roam the veld together and make clay oxen, or cavort in the dam, or tend the sheep or milk the cows, without thinking about black or white: only later, by the time we turned twelve or thirteen and the farmers' sons began to attend boarding school in town, did the white boys settle into their roles as masters and the black ones become their servants.

In our sitting-room, for a long time, "Mum's election hole" used to be pointed out to visitors — a living reminder of the famous 1948 elections when my mother was so elated at the news of the then Prime Minister, General Smuts, losing his seat and the Nationalists coming to power that she jumped right through the floor. I remember how transfixed I was by the words of our "own" Prime Minister, Dr. Daniel Francois Malan, who intoned, at the inauguration of the Voortrekker Monument outside Pretoria in 1949: "Believe in God, believe in your people, believe in yourself." I was in my first year at university when Malan, after his re-election in 1953, travelled to Pretoria by train, stopping at every station to address the crowds: and we all bunked our history lecture to see the man of God in person. I remember, besides the motor cars, the horse and donkey carts abandoned haphazardly outside the station, and the gnarled bearded men and formidable women in Voortrekker *kappies* (bonnets), some of whom had travelled for twelve hours or more by cart in order to bring homage to their leader; and how, after the train had gone, one white-bearded old man exclaimed, while tears streamed down his face, "Lord, now lettest thou thy servant depart in peace, according to thy word, for mine eyes have seen thy salvation."

Such was the context of my Afrikaner consciousness in my youth: it was a natural part of one's life; there was no need to question or examine it.

Stereotypes persist; and a caricature of the Afrikaner has been perpetuated in the mind of the world by writers like James Michener: the rough-edged frontiersman, gun in one hand and Bible in the other, inspired by the conviction of his covenant with God, his divine mission to tame the wilderness and subject the black heathen; his life determined by an obsession with racial purity and an atavistic brand of Calvinism based on an Old Testament view of the world; suspicious of sophistication and most things modern; and ever ready, when confronted by dangers real or imaginary, to retreat into the laager, that ring of ox-wagons habitually drawn in nineteenth-century clashes with black enemies.

Up to a point stereotypes may of course be both useful and powerful. "The standard Afrikaner is a caricature — but an authentic one," argues Frederick van Zyl Slabbert, erstwhile leader of the white opposition in parliament, before he quit in order to broaden the base of his attempts to explore democratic alternatives for the country. "Otherwise Eugène Terreblanche would not be in business." (He is referring to the vociferous leader of the Afrikaner Weerstandsbeweging or Afrikaner Resistance Movement, an extreme-right organization modelled on Hitler's Nazi party.) "He has a preoccupation with his collective identity which reflects a latent sense of inferiority and lack of self-confidence. And there is fear too, about his continued life here and the manner in which he would like to live it. He knows it is not possible — because 'the world' is against him — but he is going to try and get away with it as long as he can. And so he tends to be socially uncomfortable, often appearing crude and insensitive. This disguises a natural warmth and simple generosity. Those who wander into his midden usually experience an awesome and debilitating hospitality. There is no doubt about it, as a white, he is uniquely and specially African. He has missed most of what Europe has gone through culturally, philosophically and economically over the last century — and it shows."

Still, if indeed there used to be a stereotype of "the

Afrikaner" it has changed drastically. Says the angry young poet Antjie Krog who lives in the small Orange Free State town of Kroonstad, "Sometimes I envy our parents. They knew exactly what it meant to be an Afrikaner. My generation no longer does."

The name "Afrikaner" was first recorded in 1707 during the struggle of Dutch and French Huguenot colonists against the nepotism of Governor Willem Adriaen van der Stel and his get-rich-quick officials, when the unruly young Hendrik Bibault resisted arrest: "I won't go," he said, "I am an Afrikaner, and even if the landdrost [magistrate] beats me to death or puts me in jail I shall not be silent." At that time the name simply referred to someone born on African soil, as opposed to officials of the Dutch East India Company who, from 1652, were sent from Europe to run the small victualling station at the Cape. For almost two centuries afterwards it designated mainly persons of mixed blood, just as the language that became known as Afrikaans was largely shaped by slaves and others who could not speak proper Dutch. Only in the last quarter of the nineteenth century, when the survival of the small Boer Republics established in Transvaal and the Orange Free State after the Great Trek was threatened by British annexation, did a sense of national consciousness arise among South Africans of (largely) Dutch descent; from then onwards "Afrikaner" acquired a more explicit political and religious connotation and Afrikaans was deliberately propagated as a "white" language. Even today the term "Afrikaner" remains loaded. Many whites insist that it embraces Afrikaans speakers from the white race only (some would go so far as to exclude even fellow whites who do not belong to the Dutch Reformed Church and the National Party); others distinguish between "white" and "brown" Afrikaners. Then again, some "colored" speakers of the language (many of them also members of the Dutch Reformed Church) accept being called Afrikaners, while others, affronted by the ideological content of the term, object vehemently. Which makes it necessary to explain that this essay deals specifically with what has become known as "the white tribe of Africa."

During the century following the clash with Governor van der Stel at least three different groups of Afrikaners — vastly different in social and economic terms and in terms of attitude — evolved during that crucial century.

In the environs of Cape Town, within reach of the harbor and the markets, a class of more or less well-to-do farmers was established; some, like the Cloetes, whose wine, produced on the estate of Constantia, became famous throughout the world. Others, inhibited by the strict controls and monopolies imposed on the market by the Dutch East India Company, survived closer to a level of mere subsistence, but because they remained in closer contact with Europe, a sense of stability, culture and even urbanity gradually began to characterize them. Many of the differences in attitude between present day Afrikaners from the Cape and those from the Transvaal or Orange Free State, can be traced back to the evolution of a humble version of "landed gentry" in the Cape region. Most of these attitudes were connected with labor, and with race. Initially, especially after the early importation of slaves which made the entire white community dependent on the labor of others, these relations were determined not so much by race as by class. Manual labor was associated, from the earliest years of the existence of the Cape as a Dutch trading post, with servitude, with social inferiority. Moreover, early colonists looked down on their slaves as they did on their indigenous Khoikhoi ("Hottentot") workers, not because they were non-white but because they were not Christian. (At the same time, slaves were seldom converted to Christianity, as it was difficult to advance moral reasons for keeping Christians enslaved.) There certainly were few inhibitions about miscegenation, and as early as 1675 three-quarters of all children born in the colony were halfbreeds. One of the results is that today's Afrikaners are still estimated to have an average of 71% of "non-white" blood in their veins.

A second group consisted of Afrikaners in the employ of the Dutch East India Company and, after the British Occupation of 1795 (which became permanent in 1806), in the service of the British. Unlike officials sent from Europe, these Afrikaners fully identified with their African habitat; but they acquired the sophistication of their European employers. Especially after 1806 they were largely responsible for the increasing process of anglicisation most Afrikaners underwent, usually without even being aware of it. In contrast with Afrikaners in the outlying districts and along the borders of the Colony, these officials developed a keen sense of law and order and of social structures. Among them were people like Egbertus Bergh (1758–1827), a member of the Cape Council of Policy, who, in 1802, lashed out at the way in which his compatriots subjected indigenous peoples to "the most inconceivable maltreatment," while describing the Khoikhoi as "freeborn and rightful possessors of the land in which they are now made subservient." Another was Andries Stockenström (1792–1864), landdrost of the remote district of Graaff-Reinet and son of a Swede who had lost his life in a skirmish with Xhosas on the Eastern frontier: confronting a group of angry frontiersmen protesting their hardship because they were not allowed to take the law in their own hands in dealing with "vagrants" (Khoikhoi) and "marauders" (blacks), he proclaimed: "From the principles to which I have always clung, I shall not deviate one hair's-breadth . . . In one word, equal rights to all classes, without distinction." But at the same time he defended Afrikaners against British: Boers, he said, never attempted to deny that they oppressed the indigenous peoples; but the notion that they were "irreclaimable savages, fit only to be exterminated," derived from the British; "the Cape Dutch at least did wrong with less hypocrisy, for I never once heard our aggressions attempted to be excused or justified by the pretence of spreading the Bible or Civilisation." A third example would comprise legal men like J. A. Truter or W. S. van Ryneveld, who represented different degrees of sophistication in trying to make the Cape of the early nineteenth century a better place to live in for all its inhabitants, black or white. Compare Truter's reference to the Khoikhoi: "They are, and remain, people, and free people at that"; and van Ryneveld's much less liberal, more pragmatic view of slavery: "That it would have been desirable that the Colony should have begun without slavery — on this point I am in full agreement with all the philosophers and all reasonable people. But that is something different . . . One must accept things as they are, and not as they ought to be."

The third group, the Trekboers or nomadic stock farmers, made a decisive contribution to the stereotype image of the Afrikaner. Lured by ancient tales about Monomotapa, the fabled kingdom of gold in the heart of Africa (associated nowadays with the early Mapungubwe in the northern Transvaal, or the later Zimbabwe), and pressed by the dual need to escape as far as possible from governmental control (so devastatingly demonstrated by the clash with van der Stel), and to find grazing for their herds, the trekboers crossed one mountain range or twisting river after the other, entering an historical period one may well term their hundred years of solitude. These were people — most of them desperately poor — who lacked the means to compete on the monopolistic markets of the Company, while their pride forbade them to enter into the service of others. Deep in the interior they spread across vast tracts of land and whenever officials of the Company turned up to exact taxes or impose justice, they simply loaded their wagons and moved on, further out of reach. Their only cash came from the sale — perhaps once a year at an outpost market, after weeks or months of travelling — of ostrich feathers, ivory, hides, horns, whips, and fat; for the rest they survived on subsistence farming, living either in their wagons or in small wattle-and-daub cottages or huts. The basic social unit in trekboer society was what the historian Martin Legassick terms "the patriarchal family: a master, his wife, his children, and his dependants," a set-up which evolved into a kind of petty chiefdom. Few of those poverty-stricken farmers could afford slaves: for labor, they depended on

Khoikhoi or San help, whose children were often simply "booked" into the service of a master who had captured them in the veld or on a raid. Judging from contemporary accounts by foreign travellers in the interior, even the poorest of these farmers would never dream of doing their own work. They preferred to live as far apart as possible: the mere sight of a neighbor's smoke on the horizon was reason for suspicion, as a neighbor might stake off a claim on the nearest waterhole, or get to game before one knew of it, or entice one's Khoikhoi servants away from one's own employ, or even poach one's sheep or cattle. And so a race of ferocious individuals emerged who regarded any stranger with suspicion or animosity; and yet, at the same time, an unexpected traveller would be treated with amazing hospitality — for strangers brought that rare thing, news, and some kind of contact with the remote outside world.

To these Trekboers survival depended on one's ability to tune in to Africa: to adjust to the rhythms of the seasons, to drought and flood, to read the veld and the skies, to find remedies and medicines in bushes and roots and shrubs. Freedom, to them, was no abstraction, but tangible reality: *this* piece of earth where one was free to take all the decisions on which one's life and those of one's clan depend. This life-style meant an escape from poverty and indignity: here even the poorest man was absolute master of his household and the servants he could coax or cajole or coerce into his employ. At the same time, some kind of *modus vivendi* had to be devised to co-exist with others: inferiors (like the Khoikhoi) could be subjected; enemies (mainly poachers, like the San; or, increasingly, blacks, ever since, by 1778, the trek into the interior had reached Xhosa territory in the Eastern Cape) could be killed; but equals and potential allies had to be befriended. Which means that race attitudes were, to say the least, paradoxical and — to the outsider — confusing. For example, if the commando system, requiring all the farmers in a given area to be called up for compulsory military service against Khoisan or — later — black tribes, tended to foster group consciousness and racial hostility, it is known that farmers often sent their servants in their place, which meant that black and white served together in the same commando. And if some frontiersmen in the early nineteenth century left the Colony because they resented the official recognition, in 1828, of the Khoikhoi as their equals, others from among these same "racists" readily submitted to the authority of black chiefs and married black wives; and on several occasions these early Afrikaners would ally themselves with black tribes *against other whites* (notably against the British, whom both blacks and Afrikaners regarded as foreign invaders of "their" territory).

The main concern of these frontiersmen seemed to have been the urge to be independent, to make their own decisions, not to be accountable to anybody. This pioneering attitude, and the paternalism that went with it, defined their notion of "freedom." It is revealing to read the notes made by Landdrost Andries Stockenström, that early prototype of modern "liberal" Afrikaners, of the objections farmers in his district made against the abolition of slavery: "Yes, emancipate the children as soon as you like. I will even volunteer to give up those already born, under a certain age, but do not deprive me of my paternal authority, under which both my children and slaves are happy, and which is necessary for their and my peace." This is echoed by a speech made by one Christoffel Brand in Cape Town in 1832: "Some people accuse us Afrikaners of being vicious oafs, but, my friends, the charge is false. Our children are beaten and punished when they deserve it. Yes, we chastise our own blood, and are the slaves better than that? . . . Why may we not punish our subordinates when they misbehave?" And a few years later, in 1841, the acting commandant-general of the Voortrekkers in Natal, Andries Pretorius, furiously berated a neighbor, one Zietsman, for capturing and punishing some blacks on Pretorius's farm: "Do you think Sir, that it could be possible for me, who professes the Christian belief, to have my subordinate creatures innocently punished and chastised without the least semblance of a trial, and not to defend their rights? No. Suppose now that some or other person, who abhors your illegal conduct regarding my kaffirs, should make an exact account of the matter and send it to the editor of the *South African Commercial Advertiser.* How would our Afrikaans character not be stigmatised anew as that of barbarous tyrants?'" How revealing, the references to "my subordinate creatures" and "my kaffirs"! Shocking as they may be to modern sensibilities, they also suggest a certain sense of responsibility and paternalism which explains a lot of subsequent attitudes.

Brief examples like these illuminate the precarious situation that arose during the first decades of the nineteenth century, when pioneers suddenly found the outside world catching up with them as the previously "open frontier" (the term used by historian Hermann Giliomee) slowly began to close around them, especially after the arrival of the British who took colonialism much more seriously than the Dutch ever had: insisting on extending their Pax Britannica to the most remote frontiers. For the Afrikaners in the frontier region this meant subordination, increasing impoverishment, a threat to their whole way of life and their sense of dignity.

This was the main reason why, especially during the years 1836–8, some fourteen thousand of them embarked on what became known as the Great Trek. Once again, it had very little to do with "national consciousness," or with an urge to found their own independent republics in the interior. True, there had been an interesting but brief upsurge of republicanism in the frontier districts of Graaff-Reinet and Swellendam in 1795 when, inspired by rumors of the distant French Revolution, small groups of zealous "patriots" tried to declare their own independence: but these minor insurgencies had been quelled without much use of force, and had had very little to do with any real sense of nationalism. They had mainly been emotional and impetuous responses to the threat their government in Cape Town and its masters in distant Europe posed to their fierce sense of independence, fostered by a century of almost total isolation. So the Great Trek, too, was a massive demonstration by a number of threatened individuals who wanted to be left alone to "do their own thing."

Internecine strife soon became a characteristic of the Great Trek as members of different groups rallied round their own leaders and viciously fought against others, whom — in the spirit of their previous frontier existence — they regarded as strangers and potential threats to their individualism and independence. Which accounts for another paradox: the urge to be left alone, and at the same time the sense of ferocious loyalty to a leader. These attitudes were carried over into the series of small Boer republics founded by the Trekkers in the interior: first Natal, ended by British annexation in 1843; then (after the Trekker women had threatened to cross the Drakensberg mountain range barefoot rather than accept British rule) the Orange Free State and Transvaal, the latter consisting of at least three separate groupings that sometimes insisted on their independence from each other.

"The civilized life of each nation consists precisely of their own activity," says a declaration from the Executive of the diminutive Republic of Lydenburg in 1860, which then goes on to make this significant statement: "We believe that the same God of the Old Testament still rules . . . Our belief in these matters (the occupation of the four continents) is, therefore, that the Almighty in His wisdom, having decided to spread His word and His law over the whole earth, is using the European peoples for this and has therefore given them the intelligence and power not only to discover these countries but also to occupy and possess them."

This introduces the element of religion into early Afrikaner attitudes. But this does not mean that Calvinism was decisive in shaping the Afrikaner mind during his hundred years of solitude. True, the Bible was invariably the only book in a frontier household, but there is little evidence that Trekboers or even Voortrekkers consciously modelled their view of life on the Old Testament story of Israel or on notions of predestination. It was only after the Great Trek, and usually in circumstances where Afrikaners in the interior found their independence and survival as a group threatened from outside, that the Biblical model — and a sense of history — was introduced into the argument. Historian Floors van Jaarsveld has argued persuasively, in *The Awakening of Afrikaner Nationalism,* that, having withstood the threat of Matabele and Zulu tribes during the Great Trek, the Afrikaners in the interior only became conscious of their freedom and of themselves as a group when threatened by the expanding British Empire. Until that moment, van Jaarsveld points out, freedom to them meant no more than "concrete proof of being free from British control, and the right to live unhindered on their farms with as little interference from the authorities as possible." But when diamonds were discovered and Britain, using the flimsiest of pretexts, promptly annexed the fields, a real sense of nationalism flared up. One Boer wrote to a newspaper in 1868: "Just see how we poor small group of Afrikaners are persecuted from without and within! Fellow Burghers! You feel now what the English do to us!"

And when Portuguese from neighbouring territories referred to Transvalers as "Hollanders," Pretorius was quick to insist that "we are not called Hollanders but Afrikaners." (At the same time, it is interesting to note, Cape Afrikaners, using the newspaper *De Zuid-Afrikaan* as their mouthpiece, were urging conciliation between Afrikaners and English speakers, and regarded English as the yardstick of education and civilisation.)

In 1877 Great Britain annexed the Transvaal. Through that one act, thirty thousand Afrikaners, who had experienced almost no national consciousness previously, who had regarded their own government as a body without binding power, and who had not felt any direct threat to their security from outside or from within, suddenly began to gear all their energies toward one goal, "to restore what had been lost." Supported by assurances from the Free State that "we are one with you in Language, Religion and Outlook," Transvaal went to war and achieved its independence from Britain in 1881. However, the discovery of gold and the influx of thousands of *uitlanders* (foreigners) made independence a short-lived experience. Constantly under threat, Transvalers turned more and more to their history, rewriting and remodelling it to discover Divine Providence in their past, consciously creating an entire mythology to foster the newly discovered national consciousness. The small Frontier uprising of Slagtersnek in 1815 (where a handful of farmers took up arms against Britain after one of them, summoned to court for maltreating a Khoikhoi servant, had been shot by a colored soldier) was transformed into a major symbol of Afrikaner resistance against imperialism; a vow made by the Voortrekkers before their battle against the Zulus at Blood River in 1838, and soon forgotten afterwards, was resurrected as a key event in the history of a Covenant between God and His chosen people; and the wanderings and sufferings of Trekkers in the wilderness were viewed, more and more explicitly, in Biblical terms. (Van Jaarsveld: "When people appeal to history, it means that questions about themselves are answered, i.e. that they are thinking about their nationality.")

Under these circumstances the Anglo–Boer War of 1899–1902 broke out, in which two small republics, with the moral support of most of the Western world, pitted their strength against the full power of the British Empire. For Afrikaners, an unforgettable aspect of the war was the way in which the British resorted to the use of concentration camps, in which some 27000 women and children died, compared to the 7000 Boers killed on the battlefield. This war, followed by a systematic campaign to eradicate Afrikaner nationalism and the Afrikaans language, so embittered the nation that even today it can be regarded as a touchstone of Afrikaner sentiments: in many ways, and on many levels, that war is still being waged in the minds of modern white South Africans.

Even before the Anglo–Boer War a new surge of national awareness had also manifested itself among Cape Afrikaners. Consciously adopting the designation *ware Afrikaners* ("real Afrikaners"), and claiming as their exclusive "white man's language" the vernacular which, at the Cape, had long been spoken mainly by "coloreds," the fight for official recognition of the language became primarily a political struggle, waged by cul tural and religious leaders based in the prosperous Western Province town of Paarl. The Anglo–Boer War gave impetus to the language struggle, and from the early years of the twentieth century Afrikaner poets and writers were in the forefront of a movement of Afrikaner conscientisation. Broken militarily, economically and politically, Afrikaners resorted to culture — specifically to the promotion of their language — as a means of rekindling national pride.

Two main streams of thought characterized Afrikanerdom through the decades following the Anglo–Boer War, both of them championed by popular generals from that war: there were those, led by Louis Botha and especially by Jan Smuts, who saw the only hope for survival in a movement of conciliation with the English; while others, led by General Hertzog, regarding Afrikaner nationalism as the solution, appealed to group anxieties (defined by the historian Newell M. Stulz as fears for the loss of class, status and power) to promote the cause of the National Party which, by 1929, was supported by 80% of all Afrikaners.

Socio-economics largely dictated the course of events. The war had driven thousands of Afrikaners from their farms, which had been the only way of life they had known for generations. Soon after the four provinces of South Africa formed a Union within the British Commonwealth in 1910, the First World War exacerbated the socio-economic situation, and an entire class of Afrikaner poor-whites came into existence in the cities, notably in Johannesburg. What war couldn't do was very nearly achieved by poverty — and a terrible drought in the early thirties, linked with a world-wide Depression, came close to destroying the Afrikaner people. They were saved by the efforts of a few Afrikaners in positions of political leadership, but mainly by social welfare organisations and sustained cultural efforts. Among these was the Afrikaner Broederbond or "League of

Brothers," a secret organization formed in 1918 or 1919 with the specific aim of promoting Afrikaners and Afrikaans culture in strategic positions and areas in order to save the volk from extinction. Members were predominantly civil servants, teachers, clergymen, and politicians. Once again the issue of divine providence became prominent: according to I. M. Lombard, secretary of the Broederbond in the mid-forties, the organization "was born out of the deep conviction that the Afrikaner nation was planted in this country by the hand of God and is destined to continue to exist as a nation with its own character and calling." As it happened, several of the most important cultural and political leaders — Geoff Cronjé, Piet Meyer and others — pursued their postgraduate studies in Germany during the twenties and early thirties, and returned deeply impressed by the way in which the vanquished German nation had reclaimed its pride and strength during the Third Reich: and these ideas were summarily transplanted among Afrikaners. In this way the existing anti-British sentiments were soon linked with strong pro-German attitudes. The situation was dramatised in spectacular fashion during the centenary of the Great Trek, when in 1938 a symbolic ox-wagon trek was organized throughout the country. It was as if, suddenly, an entire nation was reborn from the ashes, its ebullient new sense of nationhood based on a rewriting of history, a realignment of heroes, a political awareness ablaze with religious conviction.

This was the situation at the outbreak of the Second World War, when General (soon afterwards Field-Marshal) Smuts forced a vote in parliament and elected to take South Africa into the War on the side of Great Britain. This ended a brief spell of co-operation between the conciliatory and nationalist factions in Afrikanerdom and resulted in fierce blood-feuds which continue to divide some families and communities. The remarkable upsurge of nationalist awareness brought to a frenzy by the ox-wagon trek, seemed dampened by the trauma of the War; instead of uniting in their opposition, Afrikanerdom splintered into numerous small factions (repeating the scenario of the

Great Trek and anticipating the divisions of the eighties). But behind the scenes small groups of zealots were hard at work, with the Broederbond particularly active. With the elections of 1948 looming, the policy of apartheid was fashioned; the fact that D. F. Malan, leader of the National Party, was also a minister of the Dutch Reformed Church, ensured that it had the important support of organized Afrikaner religion (and soon, in fact, the very policy of apartheid was to be justified on Biblical grounds). The word became a battle-cry expressing all the anxieties and animosities in Afrikanerdom: fear of being swamped by a black majority; the long-smouldering resentment against Britain and everybody seen to be collaborating with her; the desperate belief in being God's chosen race; the deep-seated fear of being deprived of what they regarded, in their persistent exclusivist thinking, as the land they had bought with their own blood. "The history of the Afrikaner," proclaimed Malan, "reveals a determination and a definiteness of purpose which make one feel that Afrikanerdom is not the work of man but a creation of God. We have a Divine Right to be Afrikaners. Our history is the highest work of art of the Architect of the centuries." As a corollary, J. G. Strijdom (later to succeed Malan as Prime Minister) attacked the Smuts government's education policy for Africans, as it meant that blacks "would very soon cease to be barbarians."

Malan's National Party won the election. During the twenties General Hertzog had been elected in a coalition with the Labor Party; in the thirties he had collaborated with Smuts in a government that included several English ministers, and many members of other persuasions. But in 1948, for the first time in history, Afrikaners on their own had acceded to full political power in South Africa. They were resolved not to let go of it again. It is now forty years later, and it is time to assess what has become of Afrikaners in the meantime.

The most obvious discovery is that a large proportion of Afrikaners have become slick and sophisticated city-dwellers.

Rags-to-riches success stories characterize the lives of a growing number: some of them Yuppies, others already matured and established in positions of affluence and authority. One of the first Afrikaners to reach the top in the world of industry — until comparatively recently the near-monopoly of English or Jewish businessmen — was Albert Wessels, who progressed from barefoot farm boy in the Western Free State to managing director of Toyota South Africa with assets of more than $500 million. The white-haired, urbane Wessels, now eighty, recalls how, after the Anglo–Boer War his parents returned to their farm to find the homestead burnt down, the orchards and garden parched, the fields barren after three years, and with no stock or seed to start again. Yet somehow they managed to make a new beginning, and he remembers how his mother, strangely unscathed by bitterness, insisted on a sound education for her children: "If ever the Boers want to regain their independence, they must first earn equality in education and wealth." After embarking on a degree in theology (with teaching, the traditional professions for "clever" young Afrikaners), he soon found that he was too critical and independent of spirit to submit without question to the teachings of the church, and turned to politics and economics instead. "It became a matter of conscience to succeed in the economic sphere in order to prove to my Afrikaans compatriots that we could become the equals of the English," he says; and so he started the first Afrikaans clothing factory, Veka, progressing eventually to one of the top positions in South African industry. Significantly, the promotion of the Afrikaans language and culture has always remained an obsession with Wessels: big business has never become an end in itself, but has remained a spectacular means of furthering the "Afrikaner cause" and the image of the Afrikaner as a worthy citizen of the modern world. In this respect, his achievement is typical of that of the first generation of Afrikaner industrialists.

Among the younger achievers in the cities there seems to be less concern about consciously promoting Afrikaner values or about "demonstrating" something: achievement becomes its own justification. A case in point is Kobus Cloete who, at fifty-three, has reached the top in the mining profession in a position previously regarded as almost inaccessible to Afrikaners. "It's not a matter of what group you belong to," he says, almost vexed by the idea, "but of your personal abilities. You see, I grew up mainly in South West Africa where my father was a mining captain, so I never felt burdened by the conventional attitudes of Afrikaners as a group. 'Afrikaners' to us were miners, or refugees from the Union of South Africa, or railwaymen, or fishermen; or farmers who couldn't make it in Angola and drifted south, hat in hand, to beg for work, living in wretched little shanties among the blacks. 'Civilized' people were either Germans or English. And by the time I was sent to the Western Cape to go to school, it was a dual-medium, Afrikaans-English institution in Paarl, which confirmed the kind of openness with which I'd grown up. So it really was only when I went to the Calvinist university of Potchefstroom to study law that the traditional feud between Boers and Brits was driven home to me . . ." Subsequently he joined the diplomatic service where he scrupulously followed the dictum, "I serve each successive government with equal fidelity and equal contempt."

And yet . . . Taking me outside his home high on a *koppie* in the much sought-after Johannesburg suburb of Melville he shows me the gently undulating stretch of land far below where his grandfather's farm had been: he knew intuitively that he had to buy this house and complete a circle. It meant a return to his roots — not just geographically, but in a philosophic and psychological sense. His maternal grandfather had been a great peacemaker (after his death, for days on end, complete strangers — blacks, Indians, Afrikaners, English — would turn up at the house to spend some time sitting on the *stoep,* meditating in homage to the dead man); and it comes as no surprise to learn that in recent disputes between miners and management Kobus was one of the key negotiators.

Johann Jansen has a stronger sense of belonging to a specific group: "I'm an Afrikaner and I'm proud of it," he says. "To me a sense of identity is immensely important. Unless you know who you are, you can't set out doing anything." But as Chief Director of a powerful state-subsidised cultural organization (a position he reached before he was forty) his concern is not the promotion of group culture, but with bringing theater, opera, music and ballet to as many South Africans as possible. "We look at the arts as being totally anti-apartheid, being non-racial, and we're here for the benefit of everybody in this country." He is the image of the New Afrikaner: utterly at home at a theater performance, wheeling and dealing over copyright in London or New York, pulling in the fishing lines from a ski-boat off the East Cape coast, or having a beer or a whisky-and-coke while testing the succulence of the lamb chops for a *braaivleis* (barbecue) in his shady backyard.

On the farms, and in the little dusty villages of the interior, a new breed of Afrikaner has also made his appearance. Some seem to have amassed wealth, but no more; I remember one terrifying old man on the Cape West Coast who pays almost a million pounds per year in income tax (after he's lied down his income to rock-bottom), yet lives in a wretched little cottage devoid of the most ordinary creature comforts (the beautiful old homestead of past generations has been turned into a shed), and whose only diversion, apart from devising new ways of cheating his neighbours and the government, is inviting over a group of friends to join himself and his six sons, to be entertained by a cornucopia of prostitutes his black chauffeur has been sent to round up in the city, two hundred kilometers away, in his huge Mercedes.

But others have kept up with the times without neglecting a larger spectrum of values. There is Pieter Scholtz, working on a doctorate in agriculture while spending what seems to be fifty hours per day to build up an impressive, scientifically run holiday farm in the Eastern Transvaal. With his vivacious and enterprising wife Marianne, a qualified teacher, he keeps abreast with events in the outside world: last year he visited Taiwan; she attended a congress in the USA. They are knowledgeable about the arts, she is an outspoken feminist, he is a keen economist. If in some respects they have turned their backs on traditional Afrikaner values — neither of them cares much for religion (although, for the sake of the grandparents, they did have their baby son christened in church) — in others, they are extending the definitions of Afrikanerdom.

Another colorful couple is the wealthy lawyer Johnny Venter and his live-wire wife Esther, in a small town at the edge of the Kalahari desert: coming from conventional, religious backgrounds and having submitted to the Calvinist indoctrination of the university of Potchefstroom, they are now firm believers in the good life. After years of struggling Johnny, through his astuteness as a businessman and his charming manner, finally pocketed enough to build the most beautiful house in town (a mansion which would not be out of place in Beverly Hills), and built up a staggering collection of firearms: every year he and Esther set off to some remote region of the world — Central Africa, British Columbia, Alaska, the Pyrenees, or wherever — on hunting trips. The trophies from these expeditions fill a vast two-storied hall around which the rest of their home has been devised. Mayor of the town for nineteen years, his main worry is the Afrikaners' political swing to the right in recent years: "There seem to be more and more of them who cannot even think of a black man as a human being," says Johnny, "while our motto is to live and let live." Reading, art collecting, and organising concerts and cultural events enhance the quality of their life.

And then there is Oloff Hennig, lord and master of several farms on a small fertile plateau in the mountains above Piquetberg, a man larger than life in every sense of the word — well over six feet tall, with the physique of a buffalo and a voice like a peal of thunder. No wonder that, years ago, he should have been prop forward, first for Northern Transvaal, subsequently for Western Province, the two top rugby teams in the country. Like many succesful men of his generation, Oloff comes from humble origins: his father ran a mine in Namaqualand. It is rumored that, in their heyday, both his father and his grandfather had killed adversaries in fights. Asked about it, Oloff merely mumbles: "It isn't all that difficult to kill a man, you know." After a stint at university, studying dentistry, Oloff had to give it up. The father of the (English) girl he planned to marry needed him as a foreman; it was many years before Oloff owned his own land. Once he did, he became one of the first farmers in the area to buy a computer; using the most up-to-date scientific methods, he has turned his vineyards and his pear and plum and orange orchards into a multi-million rand concern. He is one of the major producers of *rooibostee* (bush tea) in the country; and he is the acknowledged *buchu* king of South Africa (*buchu* is a medicinal herb gaining popularity in many countries, causing Oloff to spend more and more time travelling). In addition, he has a stake in crayfish concerns along the West Coast, and he is a breeder of race horses.

The latest addition to the large thatched homestead on his farm is an enormous bar, its walls bedecked with the horns of kudu and buffalo and even an elk. Elephant and zebra and lion skins adorn the sofas and chairs (including two huge dentist's chairs he'd shipped from America). When his friends gather for a drink, each man is given his own bottle of whisky, or brandy, or whatever. His birthday celebrations often run to several days and nights. Once, shortly after the bar had been built, a friend complained that, well-equipped as it was, it didn't convey the impression of being on a farm. "Hang on," said Oloff, and disappeared. Soon he returned, leading a horse and a sheep, which he tied to the counter on either side of the friend. "*Now* does it feel like a farm?" he asked triumphantly.

Once a year Oloff goes hunting, using an enormous truck especially fitted out for this purpose: the rear has been converted into a comfortable room, with a full Chesterfield suite and a bed bolted to the carpeted floor; along the walls are deep-freezes crammed with fish and crayfish. The trip covers hundreds of kilometers, up to Namaqualand, through the Northwestern Cape and the Orange Free State and via the

Eastern Cape, stopping over wherever there is game to be hunted, exchanging fish for venison until the crates of wine and whisky are empty and the deep-freezes filled to capacity with the carcasses of springbok, blesbok, hartebeest, kudu. Even a trip to Cape Town, for a race meeting or shopping or business, can last many days, depending on which friends Oloff encounters where; and he has a "colored" chauffeur waiting on the farm, to be summoned at any time of the day or night when Oloff has emptied his last bottle or broken his last guitar and feels like coming home.

He rules over his domain like a feudal squire of medieval times; at the same time he has ensured that all his laborers are comfortably housed, with TV laid on and an extensive recreation center provided. "Don't talk to me about apartheid," he says, waving a colossal hand. "I can't stand all this meddling by the government. Look at the schools: white schools standing half-empty, colored schools overflowing. Why can't they be shared? They should leave it to us to make our own arrangements."

Clearly not a man to be toyed with. But he has a heart as vast as the Karoo: if there's a signal of distress from a friend, be it in Perth or Dallas or London, Oloff will be there next day to lend a hand. "Look, I want to *live* every day of my life," is his philosophy. "If there's something to be done, I want to do it right now, on the spot — I don't want any regrets afterwards." It is obvious that Oloff is not the kind of man you'll readily find in church. Yet, when the dominee (the Dutch Reformed pastor) turns up, this boisterous, outsized man is like a little boy, trying to hide his embarrassment about not being able to find his Bible, and blaming the children for mislaying it.

Not all present-day Afrikaners are well-to-do, of course. Someone like Don Riekert, who lives in a village of the barren Northwest Cape, regards wealth as the greatest curse of the Afrikaner. "Father Kestell was right, you know," he says, referring to a venerated church leader of half a century ago: "He prayed God to protect the Afrikaner from wealth. The day our people got rich, it lost its soul. I often think that the worst sin the Afrikaner has learned to commit is to want to hold on to everything: he's lost the capacity to *give.*" Riekert derives his own generosity from his intense communion with nature. "I still live among the symbols of my youth," he says, "oryx, Jonas stone, and camel-thorn." In his village he is known as the desert prophet; as the self-appointed historian of the region he feels himself closer to the San ("Bushman") culture of twenty thousand years ago than to modern civilisation. A poor man by city standards, Don was unable to attend university, but he worked in a café for years to support his studies by correspondence, and nowadays he runs a small photographic business recording weddings, civic events and the portraits of townsfolk while producing his amazing brand of folk poetry which he generally types and xeroxes himself and then sells by riding his bicycle through the dusty roads of his town. Here is a sample (even if it loses much in translation):

In the silent darkness
of the veld
the small plover cries out
in fear, and
God's full moon
unfurls
like a host of flowers

His father, one of five children and born when Don's grandfather was already seventy-five, grew up in dire poverty on a drought-stricken farm, feeding mostly on blackthorn honey, prickly pears and locusts; at the age of sixteen, claiming he was eighteen, he joined the army in the First World War to fight the Germans, then stayed on for several years to return as a lifelong convert to the German way of life, with Bismarck, Radetsky, Von Moltke and Hindenburg as his heroes. His children were taught these same ideals from early youth, and Don himself orders his life in a military manner. (He'd intended to call his own first-born "Maximilian Maria Joseph Reichsführer von und zu Weichs an der Glon," but unfortunately — or fortunately! — the baby turned out to be a girl.) Neither this child nor any of his two others has been christened. ("One of these days they'll begin to suffer for it," warns a neighbor. "God doesn't sleep.") Don is not a churchgoing man, although he has deep religious feelings and a mystical awareness of God in all things. Every meal begins with the saying of grace and Don wouldn't dream of setting out on a journey without asking God's blessing on it.

Ambiguous attitudes toward religion have become characteristic of many Afrikaners. Traditionally, the church has played a key role in the structuring and cohesion of Afrikanerdom — even though, characteristically, there are three different Dutch Reformed churches. The initial schism occurred after the Voortrekkers had left the Cape Colony, when the Transvalers founded their own versions of the mother church. All three have "exactly the same confessions of faith, the same language and the same people, in the same country," explains Dr. Frans O'Brien Geldenhuys, a leading figure in the Nederduits Gereformeerde Kerk, which has almost two million members, as opposed to the quarter million of the Nederduitsch Hervormde Kerk and about 130,000 of the Gereformeerde Kerk. (During 1987 the extreme right-wing in Afrikaner politics, rebelling against a recent decision of the NGK to open its doors to all races, formed yet a fourth branch, the Afrikaner Protestant Church.) In addition, of course, there are separate Dutch Reformed churches for "coloreds" and blacks; and the situation is compounded by the fact that more and more Afrikaners, especially of the younger generation, feeling ill at ease among the political tensions of the white church, become members of these latter branches. One of the first to do so was the renowned Dr. Beyers Naudé, member of a staunch Afrikaner family (his father, in fact, was the first pastor or dominee to use Afrikaans in a sermon in Graaff-Reinet) and an important figure within the Broederbond, as well as an acknowledged leader within the Dutch Reformed Church. In 1963, unable to agree any longer with the clandestine, Mafia-like methods of the Broederbond, he was instrumental in having the organization's secrets exposed in the press; soon afterwards, when he refused to give up his position as editor of the Christian publication *Pro veritate,* he was forced to resign from the church. In 1977 when, as head of the Christian Institute, his continued outspoken criticism of government racial policies became too much for the authorities, he was placed under banning orders. During those years of forced isolation, he joined the (black) Dutch Reformed Church in Africa, an act consistent with the profound conviction he recently explained to me: "When people become entrenched in their positions as enemies, the danger is that they can no longer think of any other form of existence. It has happened in Northern Ireland. It is also happening to Afrikaners in their attitudes toward blacks. We have lost our faculty of compassion."

The Mamelodi congregation of the church which Naudé joined, is served by another white dominee, Nico Smit, who has given up his comfortable home in a white suburb to live among the members of his flock in a black township. A recent member of the same congregation is the young Adrian Blom, also a qualified dominee, barred from preaching in the white church because of his liberal views: "In the township I am now accepted as an equal, as a Christian among Christians, no longer as the big white boss," he says.

Once the Dutch Reformed Church was a powerful factor in defining Afrikanerdom; the importation of Scottish Calvinist preachers by the British régime in the nineteenth century — ironically, to promote the anglicisation of Afrikaners! — actually strengthened the role of the church and promoted the vision of a people chosen by God. Toward the turn of the century, when the congregation in the small town of Reddersburg in the Free State was alarmed by a young teacher who taught his pupils that the earth revolved around the sun instead of the other way round, the church council solemnly decided, and recorded its decision in its minutes, that "From this day onward the earth shall turn no longer."

But this near-absolute power has been seriously eroded. The majority of Afrikaners still belong to the Dutch Reformed Church, but many have begun to feel uneasy about it, or simply shrug it off. "For the last six months I haven't been to church," confesses Hennie Lourens, a young teacher in Cape Town. "I am seriously considering joining another church. But I don't want to upset my father. He would see it as an affront to his authority." And Lenie Jansen, who lectures at a drama school in Pretoria, wistfully complements his remark: "In the case of most of our friends, the men have stopped going to church: they spend their Sunday mornings reading the papers. It's the women who feel it their duty to take the children to church. I used to do the same, until one morning, when I stopped at a traffic light on my way to Sunday school, my youngest son jumped out of the car and ran back home. Then I realised there was no point in it any more." In Cape Town, Hannie, married to the Afrikaans author Abraham de Vries, concurs: "It seems to be the traditional role of women in our society to keep the system going. And the church, realising it is losing the men, has begun to open certain positions — like that of deacon — to women. They simply don't have enough men to do the job any more. Anyway, the women have always been the organizers, haven't they? Still, it's hard to see the church allowing women as elders, let alone as dominees."

Martha Olckers, one of fewer than a dozen white women in politics in South Africa (she is a Nationalist member of the President's Council) insists that the church remains of primary importance in the lives of Afrikaners — "except it needn't be the Dutch Reformed Church only. It may just as well be the Anglican, or the Methodist, or whatever." Jeanette Ferreira, a writer and university lecturer in Natal, is more passionate in her reaction: "If you really want to know, the kind of Afrikaner woman I detest wholeheartedly, is the one whose whole life revolves round the Bible, but in such a way it's obvious that she's exploiting it only to camouflage her own inadequacies by resorting to the simplest of all formulas: Thou shalt, or thou shalt not . . . It makes me angry, because I'm a practising Christian myself."

And here is a final word from the young Afrikaner of my opening paragraph, whose relationship with a "colored" girl caused him to be disowned by his devout father: "The church played a central role in my youth. From as far back as I can remember I was dragged along, at least once — and often twice — every Sunday. That's without counting Sunday school, prayer meetings, and endless Christian societies. So I was brought up in true Christian and National fashion. The 'garden boy' was given his food outside, using his own utensils, old broken stuff kept in the garage. When I asked my parents about it, I was told that God had made people differently, and that 'non-whites' first had to develop to our standard of living before we could associate with them. My father gave large amounts of money to 'our' church, but when a black preacher once came to the door to ask for a contribution he was told very patronisingly to approach his 'own' people. So can you blame me for turning away from all that?"

For centuries, in some remote inland villages until well into the forties, the church fulfilled more than just a religious function in Afrikaner society: it offered almost the only occasion for social gathering. *Nagmaal* or holy communion, once every three months, brought farmers from outlying districts to town to attend the church services, but also to sell their produce, mingle with their fellow men, and enjoy, with great abandon, the great variety of events comprised by *Boeresport* — pillow fights, three-legged races, catching a greased pig, tug-o'war, and innumerable others. At New Year's Day this would invariably be rounded off with an all-night ball in a barn or on a farmyard, accompanied by drinking on a great scale — *witblits* ("white lightning," home-distilled spirits), *mampoer* (peach brandy), or more innocuous ginger beer or lemon syrup. With the dawn of a more secular and urbanised age, these social events have almost died out, although they are still in evidence on festive occasions like Heroes" Day or New Year's Day or agricultural shows. Along the Cape West Coast there are harvest home festivals which can last for several days and nights (and if Oloff Hennig is there, you are unlikely ever to forget it). For the rest, social recreation nowadays is mainly associated with robust sports like rugby, which is something of a secular religion, and whose champions acquire the status of pop stars in the rest of the world.

In small communities eating is still a popular pastime which brings people together, and one can listen for hours when the ladies of Namaqualand discuss their regional dishes: tripe, "puffadder" (springbok rectum stuffed with pluck), wild cabbage *bredie* (stew), kidneys roasted in caul, you name it. Even in the cities very few Afrikaner households do not indulge in *braaivleis* or *potjiekos* (stews prepared in iron pots over the open fire) during the weekend. A dying art is that of the storyteller; but in the Marico region of the Transvaal, in Namaqualand or in South-West Africa there are still old men who can hold an audience captive for many hours, telling their colorful anecdotes and hyperbolic tales of the feats or foolishness of country heroes. In recent years, it has been revived to a certain extent by the tremendous popularity of some storytellers who have brought the art to television. In other respects, sadly, television (introduced in South Africa as late as the mid-seventies) has brought an end to many traditional forms of entertainment.

The extent to which television has mesmerised people and broken down communication is illustrated by a recent event in Pietersburg in the Northern Transvaal, where the body of an elderly woman was discovered in front of her television set after she had been dead for three days: her husband hadn't even realised that she was dead. An equally amazing, but less morbid, incident is narrated with great relish by the author Abraham de Vries who recently saw his neighbor's farmyard at Ladysmith in the Little Karoo ablaze with light and went to investigate. It turned out that the neighbor, Oom Poens, had bought a television set, only to discover, when he arrived home with it, that it wouldn't work on kerosene (the farm had no electricity). So Oom Poens went back to town to buy a generator. Unfortunately, the only one he could find was so big that the salesman in the farmers' co-op warned him to make sure as much power as possible was drawn from it whenever it was in use, otherwise the machine might break away from its concrete block and destroy the shed. So Oom Poens rigged up about as many lights in the trees surrounding his house as a fair-sized town would use for its Christmas decorations. In the front room where the TV was installed, six 200-watt bulbs were blazing when Abraham arrived. As a result, nothing at all could be seen on the screen — even though Oom Poens and his wife were both wearing dark glasses, and sun hats to shield their eyes from the glare.

One of the greatest evils of TV, Oom Poens would no doubt emphasise, is that it cuts one's ties with nature, with the outdoors, the veld, the earth — those deep rhythms of Africa the trekboers had learned to adapt to. Now there is no denying that many of the younger, urbanised generation of Afrikaners would agree with Bessie Viljoen, a young television director in Johannesburg: "I'm a city girl. I can't survive outside this place." Yet a phenomenon which has never ceased to amaze me is the way in which even the smoothest city slicker among Afrikaners seems to cherish, somewhere deep down inside, a nostalgia for the bush, a desire to own a small piece of Africa. Johann Jansen regularly escapes to a bushveld farm in which he has a part share. "I feel out of touch with myself if I'm cut off from nature for too long. Simply to wander about the veld with a gun on my shoulder and a cartridge in the barrel — that makes one feel alive. Even if there's no game for miles around and not the slightest hope of bagging anything. It's just the *feeling.*" One is reminded of a classic story by the early Afrikaans writer Jan van Melle, "Oom Karel Neem Sy Geweer Saam" ("Uncle Karel Takes Along His Gun"), in which an old Boer on his death-bed comforts himself with the belief that he will be allowed to take his gun to heaven: His life has been filled with hunting and war. He has helped to clear the land; he's been in most of the frontier wars; he was in every battle against the English. How would he feel in heaven without a gun? Surely there must be something to hunt over there? The devil isn't dead yet. Somewhere beyond our known world there must still be places to be cleared; places where one would still find dangerous animals and kinds of savages and kinds of English to fight against?

Some Afrikaners devote their whole life to nature. Louis Hofmeyer, game ranger in the Kruger National Park, points out that out of twenty-two rangers in the park only five are English-speaking; he himself has been there for twenty years. He even met his wife there, years ago when she visited Satara camp with her parents. Love at first sight it was: he simply went up to her and said: "Come along, let me show you my zebras" — and off they went into the bush. No matter how modernised the park becomes, he assures me, a mere two hundred yards from the road you're back in the Africa of centuries ago. "I thank God every day of my life that computers can't take over everything: sometimes I'm even happy about things like veld fires or poachers, because they force one to intervene physically, not from a distance." It's the immediate sense of adventure, the urgencies of the natural world which make life worth living, he believes. "If I had to get up in the morning knowing the most exciting thing which could happen to me today might be to see an impala, life would be rather dreary."

City dwellers, too, have retained the dream of the veld, even if some are more pragmatic, or even cynical about it than others: "If I buy a bushveld farm," says Kobus Cloete, "it is to indulge the European in me, not the African. It's not a matter of 'the wide open spaces,' but having a retreat with a proper fence and a guard at the gate. And in any case, a farm should be a profitable concern, not just an emotional investment." In him, the old dream of the wilderness has expressed itself in a lasting concern with ecological and conservation programs. Others are more unabashedly romantic about it. Author John Miles (an Afrikaner in spite of the English name) lectures at Witwatersrand University in Johannesburg and has in many ways completely dissociated himself from the Afrikaner establishment. But one of the main joys in his life is his bushveld farm: "In most respects I'm hesitant about calling myself an Afrikaner: it's such a loaded term," he confesses. "But if my passion for the bush makes me one, then, all right, in that one respect I'm happy to be regarded as an Afrikaner."

It is an urge which often expresses itself in even more humble and private terms: my own father, a magistrate, couldn't wait to get home from his office in the afternoons to don his oldest, dirtiest clothes and get into his vegetable garden. On at least one occasion a stranger arrived in search of the magistrate and, taking him for a black gardener, enquired from him where *die baas* ("the master") was: it gave him great pleasure to tell the visitor that the master wasn't home, and continue with his digging and watering and weeding: that was his natural habitat.

Marianne Scholtz's parents, both of them teachers, have always held on to a small farm in the remote Northern Transvaal; some years ago they settled there permanently, driving in to school every day. In that part of the country, fears of "terrorists" from across the borders have drastically changed the patterns of life: safety wires, security systems, armed commandos, radio watch patrols characterize everyday existence; but it seems nothing will drive those Afrikaners from the land.

There is something painful about the tenacious way in which they persist, behind barbed wire, to pursue a kind of life associated with freedom and open spaces (in the small town of Kuruman Peet Vorster, a builder, told me with great conviction: "Ever since they started making wire, the world has become a fenced-in place: it's no longer ours"): but even in a shrinking and threatened world, it seems, one's life can remain determined by ancient urges — like a lion in captivity. In the Eastern Transvaal an energetic young doctor, Esmé van Rooyen, lives with her husband in a massive farmhouse. When I commented on the walls, which seemed at least a metre thick, and on the way in which the outer section of the house forms a laager round the inner core, Esmé replied offhand: "Well, you see, in these parts one has to provide for terrorists, mosquitoes and the heat."

In another form, something of the Afrikaner past seems to persist in a constant wanderlust: for if a traditional Afrikaner symbol has been the laager one should never forget that a laager was made of wheels, which symbolize the urge to explore, to trek into the unknown in search of uninhabited open spaces or of the mythical kingdom of Monomotapa — or the New Jerusalem, for increasingly, since the middle of the nineteenth century, the physical trek to the north was linked with a mystical search for the City of God. There even was a Transvaal trek, in the 1850s, the members of which called themselves the *Jerusalemgangers* or Jerusalem-goers.

One curious aspect of these historical evasions is singled out by Ronnie Melck of Stellenbosch, himself an eighth-generation member of a renowned vintner family which has never left the Boland. "On three occasions did Afrikaners trek right out of their country, mainly after the Anglo-Boer War, when they couldn't resign themselves to submit to British rule again. One group went to the Argentine, the second to Angola, the third to Rhodesia. And where did they end up? In the desert of Patagonia, or in the most barren and bleak region of Angola, or in the arid Enkeldoorn area of Rhodesia. It's because of the Calvinist streak in us: it makes us feel good when we suffer. We're a nation of moaners, always in sackcloth and ashes. Yet, at the same time, these experiences have strengthened us and made us more durable."

Present-day travellers are a different breed: they are either in search of fun or culture (often prompted by the need to keep up with the neighbours), otherwise they go abroad on business — and people like the well-known industrialist Anton Rupert may spend six months out of every year in other countries, or on planes.

But there is that other brand of traveller: the Afrikaners with itchy feet, whose restlessness can only be explained in terms of their nomadic past. Talitha Laubscher comes from a staunch family of political right-wingers. Her grandmother was one of the founders of the *volkspele* (folk-dancing) movement which formed part of the revival of Afrikaner national consciousness in the thirties. Her father was terse, her mother in tears, when Talitha joined a group of Afrikaners who travelled to Senegal in mid-1987 to meet leaders of the banned African National Congress. Her grandfather spent a lifetime translating the Bible from Latin into Afrikaans, as an act of contrition after a marital indiscretion. By any yardstick, it is a family bound by convention and tradition. But instead of settling down as expected of a model Afrikaner girl, Talitha is a compulsive explorer. Early in 1987 she journeyed to Barbados, there hitched a ride on a boat to the mouth of the Amazon, and set off into the interior, accompanied only by a companion she'd picked up in the West Indies. Somewhere in the jungle they lost their way, Talitha fell ill, and they were rescued by a tribe of Indians who nursed her back to health. On another occasion she ventured into the Okavango Swamps where, at night, one could see a crescent of lions' eyes glowing in the dark a few metres beyond the camp fire.

Of course, an excursion always leads to return, and it is important to know what one returns to, and what one brings back. This experience is epitomised by the author Jan Rabie, who now leads a Mediterranean existence in Onrust, a small coastal village near Cape Town, after spending many years in Europe, especially in Greece, where he went in search of the roots of Western civilisation. Well into his sixties, Rabie still has the physique of a young man, and his tanned, sinewy, weather-beaten appearance defines the outdoor man and the wanderer he's been all his life. Asked about his life-style, Rabie does not hesitate for a moment. "Europe taught me that the more my mind is opened to the whole world, the more I become responsible for a tiny portion of it, by being an Afrikaner in a small village, in a small language."

Perhaps this "small language" is the crux of the matter. There used to be a time when an Afrikaner could be defined as a white, Afrikaans-speaking South African who belonged to a Dutch Reformed Church and voted for the Nationalist Party. It should by now have become clear that most of this has changed, or is in the process of changing. But the language remains a touchstone, even if many Afrikaners are embarrassed by the presence of the phallic Afrikaans Language Monument erected on a granite outcrop outside the Boland town of Paarl, where the Society of Real Afrikaners was formed in 1875 to promote the language as a vehicle for white political aspirations. (Surely this must be the only nation on earth to erect a monument to its own language?) Any fully-fledged nation, argued two champions of the Afrikaans language, the brothers Nienaber in 1941, requires its own language and its own country; but since Afrikaners do not have a land of their own, *everything* is focussed on the language — with the supreme irony, as indicated earlier, that in the late nineteenth century, when Afrikaans was spoken mainly by "colored" people, the language was consciously wrested from that community and consciously transformed into a "white man's language."

For many years the language was intimately associated with the "Afrikaner cause"; since the thirties it was used increasingly as a vehicle of individual expression; since the sixties, in the hands of a new generation of fiction writers among whom Jan Rabie was a key figure, it became, more and more consciously, a language of dissent, breaking down the stereotyping of the ruling Afrikaner establishment. Says Chris Barnard, one of these *Sestigers* ("Writers of the Sixties") and currently president of the Afrikaans Writers" Guild: "The Afrikaans language is our only real achievement, the only thing which keeps us together. There is nothing else: neither politics nor religion nor anything else." And Jan Rabie: "The non-racist liberation of language is our only defence against the encroaching tyranny of skin color." To which he adds grimly: "Afrikaans is not the property of a political party which, in fact, has often acted with hostility against the vital interests of the language." (He may have in mind the curious fact that no Afrikaans writer of note was invited to the inauguration of the Language Monument.)

What is significant is the influence Afrikaans literature has had on the emergence of the new generation of Afrikaners. "In my first year at the University of Pretoria [a bastion of Afrikaner thought in the Transvaal]," confesses the young author Jeanette Ferreira, "I joined a mass demonstration of Afrikaans students against a handful of students from the University of the Witwatersrand who'd presented a petition against the arrest of the poet Breyten Breytenbach to the Minister of Justice. I sat there while tomatoes, songs and slogans filled the air, thinking we were doing something great. Now, fifteen years later, I have just completed a PhD on that same poet. I've come to know — and to be — a different kind of Afrikaner, mainly through journalists, writers, academics. They have taught me something different from the conventional Afrikaner values: humanity, which comes before heredity; compassion, which is larger than chauvinism." And the young student of my opening scene adds: "My resistance against the values of my parents grew in direct proportion with my interest in literature: the works of the *Sestigers,* especially Breytenbach . . . Today I dearly wish one could remove the stigma of politics from the concept of 'the Afrikaner.' If that were possible, I'd have no difficulty in calling myself an Afrikaner. For however much I reject the establishment, this deep emotional bond with the language, and all that goes with it, remains."

When it becomes difficult to define something in its own terms, it can be useful to describe it in opposition to something else. Historically, whenever there was some movement toward a national consciousness among Afrikaners (even in the rudimentary form demonstrated by young Hendrik Bibault), this awareness could be explained in terms of an enemy or a threat. Increasingly, since 1795, this threat to the survival of Afrikaners as a group, was posed by Great Britain. And it is amazing to discover, even today, and even in liberated, sophisticated and urbanised Afrikaners, a deep-seated mistrust (if not actual hatred) of the English. At the very least, there is an active sense of always having to compete with the English, having to "show" them — exacerbated by a persistent tendency among South African English to despise Afrikaners as uncouth or crude or uneducated, referring to them as "rockspiders," "hairybacks" or whatever.

When Marianne Scholtz had her baby son, she was still teaching in a Cape school where most of her colleagues were "liberal" Englishwomen. Upon her return from maternity leave, Marianne was drawn into a discussion of politics (all conversations in South Africa seem to drift into this domain sooner or later). "Your poor little baby," commiserated one of the ladies. "To think he may marry a black girl one day." Marianne's reaction came from the guts: "I'd rather have him marry a black girl than an English girl," she said.

Johann Jansen's father was a teacher of English at school, and he was very fluent in the language: but outside of the classroom he refused to speak it. My own father, a deeply religious man and an enthusiastic lover of rugby, turns off the television set or leaves the room if a church service or a rugby match is broadcast in English: both of these, to him, are sacrilegious actions. In Johannesburg I was bemused by a suave businessman who had long ago rejected all emotional links with the volk: when asked how he feels about being called an Afrikaner, he shook his head: "No, I'd rather be called a South African." Adding, after a moment: "Except, some people may then think I'm English."

In a more positive way, a sense of competing with the English has motivated many Afrikaners. From her early childhood in the Eastern Cape towns of Cradock and Somerset East, Martha Olckers was pained by the image of Afrikaners in English eyes: "Whatever went wrong in the country, was blamed on the 'retarded' Afrikaner," she says. "They didn't seem to know that there were élite Afrikaners too; they couldn't bring themselves to accept that we're their equals in culture, civilized manners, philosophy and so on. So I was determined to show them." After school she went to Grahamstown to study at an English teachers" training college. There, more than ever before, she had the impression of English-speakers looking down on her. "Fortunately, I'm the extrovert type," she says. "I decided to radiate the kind of warmth they couldn't resist. So they had no choice but to take notice of me."

In a small village in the desolate region of the Hantam which suddenly bursts into flower after the first spring rains, there is a store which has been run by the Hugo family for a hundred years. Both the owners, Sybrand and Hetta, attended the English speaking University of Cape Town, sent there by their parents "to learn English." Especially if you want to enter the business world, Sybrand points out, you're at a disadvantage unless you're fluent in English. But it was hell at first! After writing one of the first tests in Commerce, says Hetta, she left the lecture hall and noticed this forlorn young man looking through his paper. When she asked him, in English, how he'd fared, he replied in the same language — "but it sounded like a goose chewing cabbage leaves, so I immediately knew he was Afrikaans. We fell in love right on the spot." The store is small but flourishing (it sells everything from bicycles and hardware and foodstuffs and clothing to coffins), and they are looking forward to the day when their son, who also studied in Cape Town, can join the business.

Members of old Cape families seem less suspicious about English. Having co-existed with the English for so many generations, these Afrikaners are much more easy-going about the language. Ronnie Melck is a case in point: when he married his wife Annatjie, she couldn't speak a word of English. Now the two languages are mixed and matched at home; their two sons were sent to an Afrikaans primary school, but when it was time for secondary school they had to respect an old family tradition and go to the English-medium Rondebosch High in Cape Town. For the first three months the younger son didn't utter a single word, too intimidated by the Anglo-Saxon surroundings: but today the youngsters converse exclusively in English.

There is another "enemy" in terms of whom Afrikaners have traditionally defined themselves: blacks. At the outset, as we have seen, these relations were determined more by the labor situation than by race. "The despotic and barbaric treatment" to which free-born Khoikhoi laborers were often subjected was "neither a matter of accidental excesses nor attributable to the moral failings of the farmers, but inherent in the nature of the forced labor system," explain the respected historians and political scientists Hermann Giliomee and André du Toit. The situation was compounded by the practice of slavery, as well as, at the other end of the scale, the often peaceful and equally often violent co-existence of inland Afrikaners and independent black tribes. Today the social life patterns are so inextricably linked that attitudes are exceedingly complex to interpret.

Many of the younger generation have been raised expecting a volcanic eruption of black violence. "In the Northern Transvaal where I grew up," says Marianne Scholtz, "we were conditioned from our earliest childhood to expect a racial catastrophe. In the wake of Rhodesian independence we just knew that one day blacks were going to take over. So I was actually relieved when the first landmines began to explode near the border: we'd been waiting for it for so long."

This explains much of the extremes of rage and fear that characterize traditional attitudes. When the Afrikaner mission to the ANC in Senegal returned to South Africa, they were awaited by a hostile crowd of AWB members at Jan Smuts airport. A British Airways flight attendant carrying a small black baby was confronted by the demonstrators: "Put down that child," they shouted: "The Bible tells us not to consort with the animals of the veld." In the Transvaal village of Standerton a young shop assistant, Marietjie Petzer, expresses her unequivocal support for the Conservative Party: "They are the only ones who will make sure the blacks don't take over this country."

And the leader of the AWB, Eugène Terreblanche (a particularly apt name) proudly proclaims: "I am precisely what the Fatherland expects of me. I am a realist, a product of this earth as a place where the farmers must struggle and survive. I understand survival well. I am a pure Afrikaner nationalist. I am jealous of the rights of this people, the only white nation indigenous to Africa." Even further to the right of Terreblanche is the BBB or Blanke Bevrydingsbeweging ("White Liberation Movement") headed by a retired Biochemistry professor of the Rand Afrikaans University, Johan Schabort, who declares that "The black races pose a threat to all whites. Science has already demonstrated them to be an enemy to white survival, because they destroy the economy and morally subvert Western civilisation." As an illustration of the direst consequences of this attitude, Bessie Viljoen tells about an encounter with a farmer in a Free State village who has trained seven or eight blacks as his "dogs": wherever he goes, they are taken along on the back of his small truck, where they are expected to sit waiting for as long as it pleases him, often throughout a frosty winter's night; and should anyone offend the master they are sent in to attack the person and beat him to a pulp. They themselves are subject to barbaric beatings at unexpected times in order to keep them "sharp."

At the other extreme are people like the dominee Nico Smit who have forsaken white comforts to live among blacks (a practice not open to many, because the Group Areas Act severely restricts one's choice in residential matters). Or the young son of a leading Afrikaner industrialist in Johannesburg, who took great pleasure from being a member of a crack army unit that specialised in dangerous missions: studying at the University of the Witwatersrand changed his outlook and when he was called up for army duty in a black township he refused, left the country and is now associated with the ANC. Pieter Lourens, a Johannesburg personnel consultant whose daughter was recently released from prison where she served a term for High Treason (for "furthering the aims of the ANC") is quite blunt about it: "Whites don't seem to belong in Africa. Not even their skins can stand the sun." (Although he does add wistfully: "The blockheaded Afrikaner, white skin and all, has much to offer Africa. But he also has the potential of damaging his continent in a terrible way.")

In the middle ground between these positions one finds an attitude based on mutual respect. Kobus Cloete recalls how his grandfather had forbidden his children to go near the houses of his Chinese laborers to spy on those strange people: their privacy had to be respected. But the children's curiosity could not be inhibited, and one day the boy Karools crept to the Chinese quarters to find out what was going on there. One of the laborers discovered the boy and tried to catch him; in his panic to escape Karools jumped over a barrel and cut his foot on a broken bottle. When he arrived home, bleeding profusely, his father demanded the reason behind the injury: and when he heard that the boy had insulted the Chinese, he first gave Karools the thrashing of his life before attending to the bleeding foot. That was one way of ensuring that respect for the life-styles of others was inculcated in his children.

Another approach, but based on the same conviction, is demonstrated by a farmer like Jan "Boland" Coetzee (a legendary rugby player; nowadays a leading vintner in Stellenbosch) who devotes much of his time to the improvement of labor relations on the farms, in an attempt to draw young "colored" people back to the land. "For many years we farmers thought of nothing but capital and land. Now we're beginning to think of people again, and the result is a change in mentality difficult to explain — one has to experience it . . . I have enough faith in my countrymen, black, white and colored, to believe we can find a solution together." This relationship often fits within a paternalistic mold. In The North-western Cape, Don Riekert, having grown up with Tswanas as his "second fathers and mothers" wants his children to have the same experience (even though his attitude is colored by a hefty dose of paternalism). Wherever he goes he is accompanied by an old black man, Prys, "inherited" from his father, and acting as mentor to Don's children and as *agterryer* or "batman" to Don himself. And when, on one of his journeys through that Old Testament world in which he feels so much at home, Don stops for refreshments with friends or relatives, old Prys is sent round to the kitchen with his tin mug for his own draught of coffee.

Almost all Afrikaner children are brought up by black nannies who, more often than not, become "one of the family." And the nanny's children are encouraged to play with those of the "madam." Dr. Esmé van Rooyen freely admits that she couldn't possibly run her medical practice, pursue her studies, and manage her farm without the four black women who take charge of the house and children. "It can be embarrassing," she says, revealing a complexity of emotions and attitudes. "Once we were having a meal when my small son brought his black friend Andries with him to the table. Thank God we're out on a farm here, for can you imagine what our friends would have said if they'd unexpectedly come in to find a black boy at table with us?" And Martha Olckers readily admits that her public career would have been unthinkable without "old Violet" who runs the home. "It's just not my temperament to be bothered with cooking, washing up, keeping a routine going."

This is precisely what infuriates the poet Antjie Krog: "The average Afrikaner woman is a privileged species, unique on earth. She enjoys the limitless freedom of time granted her by cheap, intelligent, black domestic help. So she can select the tidbits and specialise in entertaining, or designing clothes, or studying, or gardening, becoming a connoisseur in roses and silver, and making her own pots for Christmas. She's a Bible boffin too."

In many cases, of course, a very special personal relationship may develop between "madam" and "maid." Marianne Scholtz, like many other farmers' wives, readily drives her servants in to town for shopping, or to see the doctor; often the newly married Afrikaner wife regards her elderly domestic servant as a mother figure who can teach her how to run a home and family. "But there's a real problem," says Karin de Bruyn, a postgraduate student of literature. "No matter how personal the relationship, it is confined to the kitchen. The moment the black woman closes the door behind her, she becomes one of the black masses, who live beyond the periphery of white experience and are therefore seen as a menace. Her life 'out there' remains an unknown quantity to the 'madam.' And, in fact, she *chooses* not to know more about it. So the distance, and the suspicion, and the misunderstanding, and the fear remain."

Still, there are some who approach the situation positively. Sarie Malan, who teaches at a "colored" college in Cape Town, hopes her work and her friendships with non-white people will enable her to enrol her child at a non-racial day-school or kindergarten when he gets older. "In that way things may be easier for him than for us, who still bear the burden we have inherited from our parents."

The Afrikaner woman occupies a difficult and ambiguous position in her modern environment. In a very strongly male-dominated society, her role has traditionally been that of wife-and-mother, subservient to her husband. And even today it is common to encounter the attitude expressed by Magda Delport of Standerton, a town where, according to one journalist, "the main streets are named after Voortrekker leaders, where a dentist's surgery still sports a sign indicating a 'non-white waiting room' and where taxi ranks are still clearly marked 'whites only.' " Asked about how she would be voting in the next by-election, she said, "Conservative — because my husband votes for the Conservative Party." Any woman wanting to enter public life or embark on a career of her own, is faced with an entire tradition of female submissiveness. "Hers is a cruel world," says Jeanette Ferreira. "She remains torn between a professional life which poses enormous demands because the forefathers decreed that 'a woman's business is to serve.' She's regarded as a newcomer who constantly has to prove herself. She suffers from guilt if her household or her home life doesn't come first. In the ten years or so of my life as an academic not one single person has encouraged me to devote more time to my research or my career. Instead, whenever I was exhausted, I would be told, 'Chin up, girl, remember your home comes first.' It's a kind of special permission you're granted to have a career: how you make out is your own problem; and any sign of success is greeted not with: 'Congratulations,' but with: 'You're an ambitious lady, aren't you?'"

Hannie de Vries, who used to be a teacher and managed a children's program on radio before settling into family life (although she still does some freelance work for the radio) counters firmly: "A woman knows she's got to make a choice between running a home or having a career. Inevitably, you give up something. But it's worth while. And by devoting her energy to the home she creates the possibilities her husband needs to do his thing outside."

Antjie Krog puts it in a broader historical perspective: "The Afrikaner woman survived the Great Trek and the concentration camps and the Rebellion of 1914: she's brimming with guts and talent, yet her life is wasted on trivialities. I blame the men for it. Because they know they can rely on black servants, they have remained totally unliberated, living the way their ancestors did. Because they're obsessed with 'fighting against the black peril,' they have no time to give a hand making up the beds or washing dishes or bathing the kids. They're constantly rushing from one meeting to another, bitching about the government, hunting on distant farms in the Southern Free State, or telling cruel racist jokes in clouds of *braaivleis* smoke." The result, says Marianne Scholtz, is that the emancipation of women in South Africa is inhibited by the political situation: "Women are conditioned to believe that the race problem has priority. And in order not to interfere with that, women hold back on their own issues. We know there's so much repression elsewhere to be solved first, that we meekly resign ourselves to being bottom on the list."

"Why," I ask her, "is it such a common thing in this country to come across witty, energetic, talented young women at university, who seem to live life to the hilt — yet when you meet them again after five or ten years, they've lost all their sparkle and ambition as they settle into a dreary pattern of running a home and breeding obtuse, tousle-haired children?"

"It's because all that promise you saw in them at university was part of the illusion," she replies. "Don't you see? It's a game, a long-established pattern. Her parents and her society *allow* her to live with such abandon, precisely because it's accepted that afterwards she's going to get settled. She can *afford* to be free when she's young: after all, it isn't real freedom at all, as there is no responsibility attached to it. Her responsibilities only start when she becomes a wife and a mother: that determines the model and the measure of the only success or achievement she's allowed to experience."

What happens to the woman who revolts? In a moving passage in *The Story of an African Farm* that clairvoyant author Olive Schreiner wrote in 1883: "Before us there were three courses possible — to go mad, to die, to sleep." In many respects it would seem that the options have hardly multiplied since. One stark reminder is to be found in the fantastic "Owl House" in the archetypal Afrikaans hamlet of New Bethesda near Graaff-Reinet in the Eastern Cape (a story made famous through Athol Fugard's haunting play *The Road to Mecca*). Although Helen Elizabeth Martin was only half Afrikaans (her mother was a van der Merwe) her life reveals some of the torments of the woman crucified to a preordained role. Helen tried to escape from her confinement in a puritanical rural backwater by marrying a man named Pienaar, but the marriage lasted only four months; subsequently she was married again, to a man with the revealing name of Niemand (which literally means

"Nobody"). Again the relationship seemed to offer no redemption; and after the death of her parents Helen returned to New Bethesda and withdrew, like a hermit, into the unprepossessing little house of her birth. Here she began to give expression to her weird fantasies, shaping from cement a menagerie of phantasmagoric creatures with strange religious and sensual undertones (camels and owls, distorted animal and vegetal shapes, tortured bodies, naked girls, the Magi . . .), and covering the walls and ceilings with ground glass of many colors that shimmers in unearthly hues in the light of her innumerable lamps and candles. But obviously there was too much life, and too much imagination, in that frail body caught up in an uncomprehending society which survived only in terms of its own rigid codes. And at the age of seventy-eight, on a Friday afternoon, she swallowed caustic soda and died on the Sunday.

The situation is less dramatic today, but still fraught with difficulties. When it comes to politics, the majority of Afrikaner women prefer to stay out of it. Because Martha Olckers's father was deeply involved with politics her own interest in this field was encouraged from an early age, but only as a hobby. And when her husband Jaap entered politics she had to content herself with "always remaining one step behind," although their relationship blossomed as a result of the many things they could do together. It was only after he'd lost his seat in parliament and fell ill that she felt free to become a public figure in her own right — both in local affairs, where she became deputy mayor of Grahamstown, and on the national scene, where she is one of only five women in the President's Council. "It isn't easy," she confesses. "As a woman you've got to be twice as good as your male counterparts. But once you've made it you have the subtlety of a woman on your side. I know my family went through difficult times, especially when my two daughters were growing up — most meals degenerated into pitched battles — but I think they've been strengthened by the experience."

But there is another side to being an Afrikaner woman. If she generally retreats into her home, she also turns it into a bastion. Behind the patterns of male chauvinist society one often discerns the outline of matriarchal structures. On the initially secret trip to Senegal to meet the ANC, I was struck by the unanimous reaction of most of the Afrikaner men in private conversations about the likely reaction of family and friends at home when the news broke. "What's my mother going to say?" they all asked in trepidation — all of them well-established and successful men in their fields.

"I think the Afrikaner woman is very much like a Jewish mother-figure," explains Rachel Breytenbach. "Always in the kitchen, always organising everybody's life, always in the very center of everything." Rachel's family is a remarkable illustration of this viewpoint. Her four brothers represent the full political spectrum among whites in the country: from Jan, the eldest, an army officer whose exploits during the first South African incursion into Angola in 1975 made him a hero in the military establishment, to the poet Breyten, who spent seven years in a South African jail as a convicted "terrorist" for allegedly plotting against the state, before returning to Paris where he lives in exile. "As you can imagine, the tensions in our family were almost unbearable at times," says Rachel. "The only one who kept us all together was my mother. Whenever quarrels broke out, she would retreat to the kitchen and come back with everybody's favorite food. That was her way of expressing her love and of patching up hostilities. And it worked." Since the mother's death Rachel, as the only remaining woman in the family, has done her best to take over the role. "But I'm not always successful," she admits. "Remember, I'm the youngest. I lack the authority which goes with a mother's role."

Annari van der Merwe, an editor with a publishing firm in Cape Town, has the same experience, if on a less spectacular scale. "Whenever something was wrong, my mother would never ask me about it outright," she says. "But just from the dishes she prepared, I could see that she knew there was a problem and was encouraging me to talk about it. Food was the code in which she expressed herself."

Because of her position in the family the Afrikaner wife-and-mother has been able to exert a strong influence on her children and, in fact, on the patterns of society and social intercourse. Which is why Marina Jansen can affirm: "Women, more than anybody else, have been the custodians of 'the system' in South Africa. By taking her children to church and keeping old customs alive, she has maintained both the good and the evil inherent to our society." Antjie Krog agrees implicitly: "I interpolated the Voortrekker past and the Boer War with the fairytales and the myths and the other stories I told my children, to try and counter the victim syndrome from which all Afrikaners seem to be suffering." From here it is but one more step to the positive perspective offered by Jeanette Ferreira: "I can see a whole younger generation of mothers like myself emerging, who are lovingly but resolutely beginning to liberate their children from all the preconceived roles."

In almost every sphere of life one comes across evidence of an old Afrikaner order breaking down, introducing a period of transition toward new patterns and relationships yet to be established. One of the final walls to crumble in the ancient edifice was the concept of patriarchal authority and unquestioned leadership. The so-called "Information Scandal" of 1977–8, which brought about the fall of the father figure, Prime Minister (and eventually President) John Vorster and revealed corruption and shady deals in most of the high places of government, came as a particular shock to Afrikaners whose Calvinist creed had inculcated in them a respect for authority as something ordained by God. Having discovered in devastating fashion that even their own national idols had feet of clay, a sense of bewilderment took hold of the Afrikaner people. The processes of urbanization and secularisation which had been going on for so long, were now accelerated and opened up by a new brand of cynicism, facilitating the splintering of the granite monolith of Afrikanerdom which, since 1948, had seemed so intractable.

Grossly simplified, two main trends were highlighted: on the one hand, to the right of the socio-political spectrum, a more aggressive insistence on "traditional values" and patriarchal systems; on the other, an increasing openness and fluidity in attitudes.

Sociologists have lately been grappling with the disturbing escalation of family murders among Afrikaners; statistically, says the Rev. Jan van Arkel, more Afrikaner men wipe out their families than men in any other society in the world. And it has been suggested that the excessive notion of patriarchal power (aggravated by the awareness that it is increasingly threatened by a changing world) may have contributed to the phenomenon. It would seem that when the father finds himself in trouble, financial or otherwise, he cannot conceive of his family continuing without him as he has been the sun round which all their planets have revolved, and so he takes them all with him. Within the family context, this is the attitude of those Afrikaners who, rather than adapt to changing conditions, prefer to see the whole tribe annihilated and their land destroyed. But even less extreme forms of this syndrome characterize what is disapprovingly termed "the super Afrikaners." At one stage the term referred almost exclusively to members of the Broederbond, but today it is applied loosely to all Afrikaners whose lives are ruled by ideology and convention rather than by significant values.

"Super Afrikaners are a pain in the neck," says Ronnie Melck, descendant of the German colonist Martin Melck who in the middle of the eighteenth century was a leading light in the cultural life at the Cape and a personal friend of the much-admired Governor Rijk Tulbagh. "Then I'd rather just be known as an Afrikaans-speaking South African, for I resent the use of politics or religion as a yardstick to determine one's quality."

Talitha Laubscher had experience of the super Afrikaners even beyond the reaches of her own family: when she came back from Dakar she was summoned by the principal of her school, who forced her to resign from her post, as discussions with the ANC — "the representatives of the Antichrist" — were against the constitution of the Education Department; "and to make it worse," he stormed, "you chew gum." And Hendrik Verwoerd, son of the assassinated Dutch-born architect of apartheid, Dr. H. F. Verwoerd, confident that "Afrikaners are a clearly defined people in Southern Africa," demands territorial segregation to create a separate state for his people. As secretary of the Vereniging van Oranjewerkers (Orange Workers Association), he tries to sound reasonable: "Those Afrikaners for whom I speak do not wish to dominate others, as we will not let others dominate us." It is, clearly, the last trek of the *Jerusalemgangers,* the final stand of an outdated form of nationalism.

"I'm scared by the notion of nationalism," responds the Cape artist Hardy Botha, who divides his time between painting and tending a marvellously chaotic old farm in the process of being restored. "It is shaped by the same instinct which causes gangs and mobs, and my worst nightmares are about mobs. What repels me in Afrikaner nationalism, as in any other, is the way in which it immediately defines an 'us' opposite a 'them' — and then it becomes so easy to blame 'them' for everything."

The publisher Daantjie Saayman agrees: "What matters is not the group you belong to but the person you are. I know wonderful Afrikaners, but the moment you start talking about 'the Afrikaners' it becomes a pain in the neck. I can't stand people who can only define themselves in terms of an ideology: it's not dogma that makes an individual but the values he believes in. I mean, where are you going to fit *me* in?" Where indeed? He is the proud descendant of the first recorded marriage between a Dutch colonist and a Khoikhoi woman in the mid-seventeeth century. His grandfather once owned a wheat farm in the Riversdale district. When feathers became the vogue he changed to ostriches and in due course lost everything. As a result Daantjie's father had to find work on the railways, and Daantjie was born in Witbank in the Transvaal, the youngest of five sons. When he was xonly a few months old his father died and his mother returned to the Cape, where she struggled to make ends meet. By the time he was fourteen or so there was no more money to continue with school and Daantjie became a clerk in the traffic department; but as soon as he turned eighteen and could legally obtain a motor-cycle licence he became a traffic cop. What made him unusual was his passion for books; most of his spare time was filled with reading. At twenty-one the old Afrikaner urge to explore Africa got the better of him and with a friend he set out on a walking tour through the entire length of Africa, up to Cairo, spending some time with a Bedouin tribe in the Sahara. After a year he returned home and became a truck driver for a large publishing firm. This was an excellent opportunity to catch up with his reading again, and in due course he became branch manager of the firm. After rising through the ranks in publishing he finally acquired his own small business. In the early seventies, when all the established Afrikaans publishing firms were intimidated by the looming threat of censorship, he published my novel *Kennis van die Aand* (*Looking on Darkness*) and took the rap when the book was banned. The imprint of Saayman & Weber still proudly survives. At home, Daantjie and his petite ballet-dancer wife Nici have a splendid collection of paintings; books are to be found in every room of the house, while his garage makes do as a cellar for his formidable wine collection. Through books — and wine — he has made friends all over the world; and a vast number of foreigners carry his name in their address book as a "contact" when they first set foot in Africa. There probably is no better guide for any prospective mountaineer in the Cedarberg range; and whether his guests are professors, economists, architects, journalists or adventurers, they all find in this permanently tanned man with the mephistophelian goatee a companion not easily forgotten. If he demonstrates, sometimes on a scale larger than life, many of the most notable characteristics of the Afrikaner, he is — like his great friend, Oloff Hennig — in other respects a breed unto himself. Indeed, it is a matter not of ideology (he has no time for politics or the church) but of values: generosity, humor, compassion, enthusiasm, a respect for knowledge but none for pretence, and an abiding love of nature and life in the raw.

In the end it comes down to a question of definition. And Breyten Breytenbach eloquently makes the point: "I am an Afrikaans-speaking South African, bound to Africa, and living in Europe for the time being. But one cannot escape from what one *is.* According to the narrower definitions I don't qualify as an Afrikaner — yet I was born an Afrikaner and I cannot renounce it. What is required, it seems to me, is constantly to transcend one's Afrikanerhood into a larger whole, without ever having to deny who you are." Late autumn sun beats on his tanned face on the terrace of the Paris café where we sit talking; passers-by glance at us, intrigued by a language most of them have never heard; then the world streams on again. "To be an Afrikaner is a schizophrenic experience," says Breyten. "We belong to Africa, yet we cannot escape the Europe in us. With everything we do, both halves of our personality are involved. Our very survival depends on trying to find peace within ourselves. That's why politics in South Africa is such a deadly serious business." He smiles gently, and proceeds to tell me of an encounter with an English-speaking South African student some time ago. "He asked my advice: he'd decided to be an activist for a few years. 'And afterwards?' I asked him. 'What then?' 'Oh, then I must take over my father's business,' he said." There is both amusement and bemusement in Breyten's eyes. "You see, that's the difference. We Afrikaners do not have the scope to experiment with political attitutes, playing games while we wait to take over Dad's business. We are what we do. With everything we do our whole future is at stake."

Africa and Europe: always it comes back to this. The Africa discovered by early Trekboers who survived because they had learned from indigenous peoples to tune in to the heartbeat of a wild continent, but which they betrayed when apartheid was devised to justify white supremacy. The Europe with its human values and culture shaped through centuries of trial and error, which we betrayed when only a minute and distorted portion of its legacy was imposed on Africa. These are the poles between which the white tribe of Africa finds itself oscillating.

"The enduring tragedy of the Afrikaner," says van Zyl Slabbert, "is that he is a white African who refuses to come to terms with his own continent and its people. Most of them still wish to be here but apart, and after more than three centuries the sadness of 'the Afrikaner' is that he still has not come home."

JANUARY 1990

Mandela Free

i am the man you will never defeat
i will be your shadow, to be with you always
and one day
when the sun rises
the shadow will move

— Mongane Wally Serote, "No Baby Must Weep"

And now the shadow has moved, is moving. For over a quarter of a century, and more and more insistently over the years, the cry *Free Mandela!* has reverberated across the world. Now he is free, and the myth is about to change into a man. In that resides both the exultation and the anguish of the moment.

Although even the unlamented P. W. Botha during the last years of his dark imperial rule had hinted at the possibility of liberating Mandela (subject, of course, to the condition that he unilaterally forswear violence while violent oppression by the State continued), the present step should be seen against the background of what is usually referred to as the de Klerk "reform initiative."

This is a context which should be approached with great caution. To what extent is it really a matter of "reform," to what extent an "initiative"?

Article written in anticipation of the announcement that Mandela was to be liberated from prison; published in the *Independent on Sunday*, January 1990.

No one can deny that there have been changes, some dramatic, in South Africa in recent months. But it is easy to lose sight of the wood through becoming too impressed by the spectacular fall of a few rotten trees. It did not require much insight or imagination to realise, after the traumatic September elections, that South Africa might go up in flames — or down the drain, depending on one's choice of metaphor — unless a few bold steps were taken without delay. So peaceful demonstrations and public protest, still officially banned under the Emergency Regulations, were allowed: not necessarily because of greater tolerance and realism in the new régime, but because pressure at grass-roots level had become so enormous that an explosion was imminent, which de Klerk could quite simply not afford (especially after the possibility of a widespread revolt among "colored" police had surfaced). Beaches were desegregated (although the Separate Amenities Act is still untouched), not because apartheid is on the way out, but because in the light of increasing foreign pressure and local resistance the régime could not afford a repeat of the recent spectacle of tanks, helicopters and machine-guns driving small black children from the beaches. The security surveillance system in local communities was dismantled (although less obtrusive but highly effective forms of surveillance continue and may even be increased), not because it was discovered to be odious or repressive, but because it represented a power-base of the discredited Botha régime that had to be dismantled. High-profile political prisoners were released because the government needed Thatcher's support at the Commonwealth Conference to ward off more stringent sanctions and renegotiate its international bank loans. And now Mandela's release has been ordered, not necessarily because the new government is more enlightened than its predecessors but because that is the price demanded by the international community and by a groundswell of pressure among the vast majority of South Africans for postponing a final turn of the screw.

The South African government is prepared to face a free

Mandela, as it has demonstrated itself prepared to abolish certain glaring trappings of apartheid, because it believes this is the only way in which it can be allowed the respite it needs to reorganize its structures and reinforce its hold on power. For as I read the government's mind (and I did spend five years with de Klerk at university, if that counts as a qualification) *this* is its ultimate concern: not the abolition of apartheid but the retention of power. As long as the concept of (ethnic) groups — entrenched in the Group Areas Act, the Population Registration Act, the Land Acts, etc. — determines the thinking and the actions of the de Klerk régime, apartheid remains alive and well and more sophisticated than ever.

i came from the isle of Makana
the beacon of liberty
that enfolds the spring of struggle
petal by petal
listen to the fire in the timbre of my voice
for i am the subdued multitude
— Dikobe wa Mogale,
"Bantwini Ngcipe's Testament"

Now the myth is to be set free; soon the man will be among us. And whatever the reasons or intentions or calculations behind it, the event in itself is momentous, his presence is now a fact which cannot but influence the whole situation. If his imprisonment cast a shadow on the possibilities of profound change in South Africa, his liberation may shed unbearable light on the inadequacies of what has so far passed for reform.

His liberation is not yet enough to ensure the next move toward those "negotiations" all the parties involved talk about without necessarily having the same process in mind. But it is a starting point: *without* it the stalemate would have been permanent. Other preconditions will have to be met: the unbanning of the ANC and the lifting of the State of Emergency, the liberation of young Mass Democratic Movement leaders, and at the very least a statement of intent to abolish the infrastructure of apartheid legislation. But the Wall has been breached, in Pretoria as in Berlin. And since South Africa has learned so much from the Germany of the thirties, perhaps it might yet decide to take note of the Germany of the nineties as well.

It would be logical to expect repercussions from Mandela's liberation in at least four areas:

1. The Extreme Right in white (mainly, but by no means exclusively, Afrikaner) politics. Even since the September elections there have been indications of further growth at this end of the spectrum. It should be taken seriously, as it involves more than just a lunatic fringe. But precisely because it also involves more sensible and sincere minds (prejudiced as they may be), Afrikaner history itself suggests that many of these Rightists, perhaps the majority, may exchange their present do-or-die mentality for more resilience, even generosity, once they are faced with a *fait accompli*. This has happened in Namibia; the experience may well be repeated. Afrikaners have survived in Africa not *merely* because they were better than anyone else at subjugating others, but — much more positively — also because they have learned to tune in to the rhythms of the continent. They share with black Africans the collective memory of a tribal, peasant, nomadic past, a fierce sense of freedom, a desire for justice, above all an allegiance to Africa which is far beyond romanticism. Much of this has become obscured, especially since 1948, by the negations and the destructive exclusivity of apartheid. But deep down this awareness and this allegiance smoulder on; and the historical processes set in motion by Mandela's release may in due course allow them to resurface.

2. Other black organisations, notably Buthelezi's notorious Inkatha. It is often alleged, usually by Buthelezi himself, that he represents some seven million people. The truth is, of course, that a minuscule minority of the Zulu people was responsible for his accession to power through an adroit manipulation of the structures of apartheid. After the inevitable initial posturing by others, it is more than likely that the ANC will soon be recognized for what it has been for so long — not merely the

major organization of liberation, but the true representative of the overwhelming majority of South Africans.

And such divisions as do exist — and which should exist in any more or less normal democratic society — have been minimized by the long and tragic experience of apartheid which has ensured a development toward solidarity unparallelled in Africa.

3. Factions within the ANC itself. The South African government has for a long time been spending its taxpayers' money in local and international campaigns to promote the image of an ANC internally riddled with factions and leadership struggles; one of the motivations behind Mandela's release may in fact be the expectation that, especially with Tambo ailing, rifts may develop between "internal" and "external" groupings, between older and younger generations, between communist hawks and nationalist doves. Very recently Foreign Minister Pik Botha returned from Hungary with the gloating message to the ANC that in view of the latest developments in Eastern Europe the policies of the ANC are hopelessly outdated. The point is, of course, that in terms of the Freedom Charter which lies at the base of ANC policy, and last year's Harare declaration about a future constitution, the kind of democratic dispensation the ANC foresees for South Africa is exactly what the mass movements in Hungary, Czechoslovakia, East Germany and Romania have begun to introduce in their countries (whose ousted régimes, communist as they may have been, so strikingly resembled the apartheid system perfected by Verwoerd, Vorster and Botha).

The democratic and non-racial nature of the ANC, proven by a proud record of more than three-quarters of a century, guarantees an accommodation with the released Mandela to ensure a smooth, efficient and resolute movement toward the future.

4. The international community. Mandela's physical absence and symbolic presence through a quarter of a century have kindled expectations which no ordinary human being could hope to fulfil. It is one thing to be a living myth in prison, the sym-

bol of freedom for the world at large. It is something else to become the one person millions look up to — after decades of deprivation — for solutions to problems created by centuries of misunderstanding, hatred, exploitation, oppression and violence. What will be demanded of him now will not be the inspiration and wisdom emanating from a jailed martyr, but the practical answers and maneuvrings and compromises of a human being among other human beings. Sometimes, inevitably, he must become despondent, annoyed, angry; sometimes he must make mistakes. The world at large, even his own organization, may then feel that he has failed them. History can be notoriously unjust and cruel in its treatment of myths turned men.

Yet I have faith in Mandela. Precisely because, from the testimonies of many who have been in prison with him, it is known that however great his mythical status may have grown, he has never given up being a man; and however isolated and deprived he may have lived in incarceration, he has never lost touch with the world:

> *Supposing all this,*
> *do you think they'd assume*
> *this shadow play was real?*
> *That these prisoners could forget*
> *the struggles of their brothers and sisters*
> *there outside where these sounds*
> *bathed in the daylight, may*
> *someday, grow into words?*
> — Jeremy Cronin, "Plato's Cave"

It might have been different in another kind of society. But Mandela's release does not mark a simple progress from imprisonment to freedom. Robben Island, Pollsmoor Prison, the Cape Town clinic, Victor Verster Prison, Soweto, South Africa as a whole — all of these are but different confines, wards and dungeons. From the many reports that have filtered through, Mandela's experience of his island prison has fully prepared him for the exigencies of whatever new task is now required of him.

How many times over the years have I listened to his ex-colleagues newly released from jail entertaining others with stories about Mandela: his natural leadership, his dignity which could not flinch even under the worst humiliation, his respect of others, his ability to listen to all possible opinions before cutting straight through to the heart of the matter and giving his own, his perseverance, his respect of education (even while breaking stones and crushing granite his teams were organized into groups involved in seminars on politics, history, sociology, law, languages, whatever), his generosity, his compassion, his concern for others, his laughter. (No leader of a future South Africa can hope to succeed without a sense of humor.)

I shall single out only three respects in which I believe this man could reassure all his would-be critics or opponents and persuade them to accept his integrity and leadership:

— His relations with prison warders. To the most outrageous assaults, viciousness or stupidity he would respond, his comrades invariably testified, with restraint and dignity. In fact, in due course he succeeded in winning the respect of his own warders, whom he helped with their legal and domestic problems, and whose children he coached for their school examinations, even in Afrikaans.

— His sympathy with Afrikaners and their language. "One of the first things Mandela would ask a newly arrived convict on the island," more than one ex-prisoner has told me, "was whether he could speak and read Afrikaans. If not, he was told to do so without delay. Mandela believed that the only way to get to know Afrikaners was to read their literature."

— His attitude toward black organisations outside the ANC. Whatever strife there may have been among members of different organisations on the mainland, once they landed on the island Mandela involved them in discussions and inculcated in them all a profound mutual understanding and respect, based on the passionate belief that they were all involved in the same struggle, for the same goals, within the same land.

Transferring these attitudes, this wisdom, to the larger prison in which he now finds himself should not be difficult for Mandela, even though the demands and expectations will be more daunting, more urgent, perhaps more dangerous. The entire situation is precarious, if not explosive. But Nelson Mandela, I believe, has the charisma, the humility, the authority, and the experience — always seen within the context of the ANC as a whole — to break out of the present circle of violence scarring the country. Certainly, the prize is worth the effort and the sacrifice:

And the wounds that are deep as the dongas
the wounds shall begin to heal,
And the scars that are grim as the ghettoes;
the scars shall begin to heal,
And the grass on the hills of freedom;
the grass shall be green again,
And the grapes on the vine of freedom;
the grapes shall be sweet again,
And the dogs in the days of darkness;
the dogs shall cower in the sand
And peace shall come to Azania;
when love is lord of the land.
— Chris Mann, "And Peace Shall Come to Azania"

1990

Reflections on Literature and History

Official historiography in South Africa has traditionally dealt with the dark era of slavery (introduced by the Dutch soon after the original settlement of the Cape of Good Hope in 1652; abolished by the British in 1834) by making two main assertions: one, that slaves at the Cape were in general better and more humanely treated than in most other parts of the world at the time; and two, that the master/slave relationship had no marked influence on the future of race relations in that country. (The pattern of race relations, it used to be stated, was determined by the meeting between white settlers — largely Dutch, with a significant proportion of French Huguenots added in 1688 and 1689 — and free, independent indigenous peoples: the Khoisan — derogatorily known as "Bushmen" and "Hottentots" — and, at a later stage, the Bantu-speaking black races.)

These "truths" had been uttered over such a long period, and by so many reputable historians, that they became accepted as historical fact, along with a number of other assertions about the South African past.

I became involved in this particular problem, not as an histo-

Essay published by *De Balie*, Amsterdam, as part of a symposium on "Collective Memory," 1990.

rian but as a writer, when in the novel *An Instant in the Wind* I first began to explore the ways in which early Cape society (in the mid-eighteenth century) conditioned people into carefully circumscribed roles as slaves and masters, and extended those models to all black/white relations. But that was only a beginning, and although the background material was factual, based on a close examination of contemporary documents, notably the accounts of foreign visitors, the story itself was fictitious in the ordinary sense of the word.

Writing this novel had opened my eyes to a number of startling correspondences between early Cape society and the modern apartheid state; I knew that what I really needed to explore was a slave revolt. But unlike the wealth of comparable material from other Dutch, Portuguese, British or French colonies of the time, there seemed to be no instance of an extensive and organized slave revolt in Cape history. And it took a considerable time of research before one of the most astute historians of a younger generation, Hermann Giliomee, unearthed the kind of episode I had been looking for: an organized revolt by a score or so of slaves on several farms in the "Bokkeveld" in the deep interior of the country, which resulted in several deaths. The revolt was quelled before it could attain its aim of spreading across the whole colony and liberating the entire slave population.

What fascinated me most at the time was the episode that unleashed the revolt: although, over the years, the leader, Galant, had been subjected to the most horrendous treatment by the man who had been his closest companion in youth (floggings, deprivation, the murder of his one-year-old child . . .), he had willingly endured it all, accepting that his *baas* had the right of life and death over him. But the one thing he could not stomach, and which triggered the revolt, was a promise (even if it was only a rumor) of liberation — which was not kept. It seemed to me to echo, most alarmingly, what was happening in South Africa in the Botha era, when all kinds of reforms were promised, but never realized.

If this was the starting point of the novel *A Chain of Voices,* the most unsettling and unforgettable aspect of the experience of researching and writing it was the confrontation with some 2000 pages of handwritten documents in the Cape Archives, in which the entire trial was recorded. Behind the ponderous nineteenth-century Dutch one could hear the vernacular, the fear and anger and outrage, the authentic suffering, of those — masters and slaves alike — who had all become the victims of what even then was recognisable as an evil system of exploitation and oppression.

I shall never forget those voices addressing me, across a divide of 150 years: the men and women expressing, perhaps for the first time in their lives, the full horror of what it meant to be alive as a slave.

This experience brought into doubt most of the official versions of slave history in South Africa. (The very way in which such a significant episode had become "lost" in official history, speaks volumes.)

On the one hand, the single, authoritative voice of "history": on the other, the innumerable, often contradictory, often inarticulate, inchoate voices of the people enmeshed in it. It was a dismaying demonstration of that passage from a letter from Engels to Marx which I subsequently used as a motto to the book:

> *History makes itself in such a way that the final result always arises from conflicts between many individual wills, of which each again has been made what it is by a host of particular conditions of life . . . What each individual wills is obstructed by everyone else, and what emerges is something that no one willed . . . Yet each contributes to the result and is to that degree involved in it.*

Perhaps the best illustration of this is the well-known children's game in which someone whispers, very quickly, in his neighbor's ear, some abstruse message; which is then repeated down the line until the child at the end of the line is required to say out loud what he has heard. Then, invariably, everyone collapses with laughter. Because the final message sounds so totally "wrong," has, perhaps, nothing at all in common with the original sentence. Is that not the way in which official history, too, comes into being? A chain of voices — resulting in the babble of Babel. And yet, if it is repeated often enough, and with enough emphasis, it is accepted as a canon of received wisdom. And whole societies base their way of life on these "messages" transmitted by official history.

This is the stage where literature may step in.

During the last decade or two, and most particularly since the State of Emergency was declared in South Africa in 1986, until its repeal in 1990, the relationship between literature and (official) history was highlighted in a most spectacular manner. In this case it concerned not the canonised history of a more or less distant past, but the living history of the present in the process of unfolding.

What happened was that the media were excluded from all events pertaining to what was euphemistically termed "unrest." No newspaper, no radio or television station, could report what was happening — even if journalists were there to witness it — unless the report had first been cleared by the security forces. And since these forces were invariably implicated in the events (and often the instigators of them), it was evident that hardly anything of what was occurring in the country was reported openly. Most of the "unrest" inevitably occurred in black townships. Not only have these traditionally become more and more remote (in every sense of the word) from the white experience, but, as the "unrest" escalated, they were cordoned off by police and the army, so that outsiders had no way of finding out what was happening inside. A blanket of silence descended on the country. Most black people knew what was happening: they were there, in the midst of it. The vast majority of whites did not know, were discouraged from trying to find out, and so were largely left in ignorance.

Only writers of fiction — playwrights, poets, short-story

writers — were, curiously and paradoxically, allowed greater freedom. If the government feared and hated journalists, they adopted the attitude that other writers were writing "only" fiction, and so need not be taken seriously.

One inevitable result was a volcanic explosion of creativity in the country. Painters, sculptors, photographers, poets, dramatists, fiction writers, singers, dancers, all of them were drawn into a massive cultural movement that mobilized the masses into resistance by writing the history of their time in the form of fiction.

And, as in the case of the slave rebels, they were speaking in their own voices. Even if officialdom, or aesthetic tradition or whatever, tried to anesthetize or distort their communication, the real timbre of their voices broke through. And when, one day, the official history of this period is written, it cannot but draw heavily on the testimonies of those who spoke through the silence imposed on them.

My only regret is that, abroad, so few people seem to be interested in these voices narrating their own story. So few of the great number of magnificent black writers and poets are known beyond the borders of South Africa: if some white voices have been heard increasingly, the more is the pity that the world should be ignorant of the voices of Miriam Tlali, or Wally Serote, or Njabulo Ndebele, or Mtutuzeli Matshoba, or Sipho Sepamla, or Ellen Kuzwayo, or so many others. Through them the authentic history of our time is expressed in words like jets of blood.

History: story. Fact: fiction. How strange that these pairs should still be experienced as opposites, as dichotomies. It is time to explore, once again, their intricate relationship.

In the infancy of literature, when all is magic, all is invention, and all is real, such distinctions do not exist. Myth encompasses both the "real" and the "imagined." Neither Homer nor his successors, Apollonius of Rhodes or Xenophon of Ephesus, were bothered by what they would have regarded as casuistry;

Herodotus and Thucydides would not be reproached for inserting invention into their history, neither would Chariton for mixing history into the flights of fancy in *Chaereas and Callirhoë.*

In heralding the modern novel, Cervantes had no problem in introducing, into the imaginary life of his brainchild Don Quixote, a myriad of social and historical details: this had little to do with the anxiety about "verisimilitude" that so haunted some of his successors. It was part of a world vision. But perhaps Cervantes, as a Spaniard, was spared the inquisitions of a more rectilinear mind: after all, he could draw on an ancient Spanish narrative tradition according to which all stories began with the ritualistic phrase: *Once upon a time, there was and there was not . . .* In the same sentence, the same story, the same book, in the same view of the world, *was* cohabited with *was not.*

The watershed was the eighteenth century.

It became a characteristic of the novel of that remarkable age, both in England and in France, that novels should be offered to the public, not as products of the imagination, but as "true histories": whether the author was Aphra Behn, or Madame de Lafayette, or Defoe, Richardson, Fielding, or Prévost, Marivaux, Rousseau or Laclos, he or she was at pains to disguise and deny fictitiousness, presenting a novel as anything *but* a novel: memoirs, diaries, letters, documents, surveys — but not a novel. This was, of course, a result of the bad reputation novels acquired so soon after their inception (most especially in an Age of Reason!), when the *novella* (the "little new thing") was severely frowned on as escapism, as frivolity, as nonsense; while what was regarded as "fact," as direct access to the living and lived world, was held in esteem.

The interesting consequence was, of course, that offering invention in the guise of fact (the memoirs of Robinson Crusoe or of Des Grieux, the letters of Marianne or of Clarissa), readers entered into a contract with authors/narrators: no one "really" believed that those were "true histories." They were read *as fiction,* that is as invention (*fingere* = to fabricate), but they became acceptable because they so closely resembled the *kind of world* readers encountered in their daily lives. The result was, as a commentator said with reference to García Márquez, that "fiction acquires an amplitude that information lacks." It is this "amplitude," this magnificent weight (the bearable weight of being) that became the prime *raison d'être* of the novel, of fiction.

But why should this be so?

In a remarkable recent study of the eighteenth-century novel, *Story and History,* William Ray suggests that the reason lies in the fusion between "narrative authority" and "social identity"; more specifically, "between personal story and public account, between the social act of relating one's perceptions or events to some listener and the collective narrative or history that framed such acts." In that century, Ray indicates, "fiction suddenly emerges in the critical discourse as the primary vehicle for representing contemporary social reality, and even shaping that reality."

The core of Ray's argument is that, "Freed from the limitations of factual fidelity, assured of representing the biases of the culture it depicts by virtue of its own enclosure within that culture, the novel can formulate, analyse, and illustrate general paradigms of social interaction explicitly through its plot structure, at the same time that it exemplifies in its gesture of narration the conventions of communication and representation underlying such interactions."

We are moving closer to a new perception of the relationship between history and story, fact and fiction. That relationship can be one of opposition only if one accepts, rather naïvely, that in "history" we have direct, unmediated access to the factual world of events (that is, if we believe that, in history, language becomes a transparent window through which one looks directly into "reality," whatever that might be), while in "fiction," in literature, the world is mediated, and reinvented, through the imagination, through language that draws attention to itself.

But this is simply not true, of course. There may indeed be a difference between "history," defined as a representation of a situation which is accessible, and can to a certain extent be corroborated, through *other* sources (both Churchill and de Gaulle, among innumerable others, wrote the "history" of the Second World War; and in spite of vast differences — one is, after all, British, the other French! — a reader can painstakingly wade through those accounts and deduce from them "what really happened," even if that may in itself be an illusion), whereas a fiction is unique, has no support outside its text, exists wholly within that text.

However, it is not the degree of subjectivity or objectivity, nor the degree of factuality or fictionality, that concerns us, but the way in which human experience — which includes whatever we may wish to term "reality" or "imagination," "exteriority" or "interiority" — is embodied in language. Literally, as Wittgenstein said in that famous aphorism from the *Tractatus,* "the limits of my language are the limits of my world."

We are back at the image of a row of children playing their language game.

The question is: if language cannot be "trusted" (especially not since Saussure, Wittgenstein and Heidegger), why should we set any store by literature? Or even by history, for that matter? Although it might yet be argued by some, in spite of what I have said above, that history at least *attempts* to interpret facts that can, in one way or another, be corroborated, whereas fiction appears like a private indulgement.

The answer, again, lies in the nature of language, and in its role in our lives.

Postmodernism, especially, has in recent years opened our eyes to the way in which our entire empirical world is "storified." One recalls a seminal passage from Bakhtin:

> In real life, people talk most of all about what others talk about — they transmit, recall, weigh, and pass judgement on other people's words, opinions, assertions, information . . . At every step one meets a "quotation" or a "reference" to something that a particular person said, a reference to "people say" or "everyone says," to the words of the person one is talking

with, or to one's own previous words, to a newspaper, an official decree, a document, a book and so forth.

The Dialogic Imagination

But even outside that part of our lives that exists, as "primary experience," in the form of language, we turn everything into language: at the end of each day, as we review it, we transform the events of that day into story; each of us is perpetually involved in making a story out of our own experiences: it is the only way in which we can *interpret* the world to ourselves.

This is the point where story and history meet and mingle, where the private experience (expressed in language) intersects the public or the social or the political (also expressed in language).

And it is from *this* vantage point, rather than from the dubious and misleading distinction between "fact" and "fiction" that one should review the contemporary situation.

The major problem of the present tension is, undoubtedly, the way in which "history" has become associated with the official, hegemonic interpretation of the world: even after the withdrawal of the colonial powers, the written history of their domination — written, more often than not, in the language of the oppressor — extends the cultural, sociological, and especially economic domination over the allegedly "liberated" territories and peoples. And the only way to counter this insidious form of exploitation is to counter it *from inside.* Obviously political, economic and social action is required: but unless a change is effected on the level of culture — which is, in any society, the level on which the *production of meaning* occurs most overtly — other changes will remain only temporary, and superficial.

In some societies (Kenya, for example), indigenous authors who achieved success and recognition through writing in the language of the erstwhile opppressor (Ngugi wa Thiong'o) have now begun to write their stories in the indigenous languages in order to interpellate the individual and collective consciousness and conscience of their still-oppressed compatriots.

In many instances the ordinary channels of literary expression have been blocked by totalitarian régimes: in such cases the most incredibly ingenious ways of storytelling have been found. To me, the most moving instance is that of the illiterate washerwomen of Chile who, unable to write about what had happened to them (because written accounts were forbidden; and also because they could not write anyway), began to make embroideries and tapestries to narrate the "stories" of the "disappeared" or the "forgotten." This form of visual literature was their way of countering silence: ultimately, of countering death.

Which is the primordial function of literature.

Confronted with the mass of archival material at my disposal for the writing of *A Chain of Voices,* I experienced very lucidly the essential problem of the writer within the context of the relationship between literature and history: the literary text can never be a mere transcription of the historical document, but a reinvention of it. To me, the problem was that of *imagining the real.* What "had already happened" (on a cluster of farms in the Bokkeveld, in 1825) had to happen again, anew, in the language of fiction; within the voices that addressed me from the court documents, I had to come to grips with the full weight of biographies, lives, existences underlying their utterances. The fiction writer always, on every page, reinvents the wheel. Without it, our minds cannot move. This means that, far from opposing literature and history, one discovers, more and more, their interrelationship, their essential symbiosis. *Within* the historical documents I had to discover — rediscover — the stories of the lives behind them; and on the other hand, the lived experience of the individual, history, assumes meaning only in the act of turning it into language and story. Neither can exist without the other.

★

In recent decades a revolution has begun to effect a radical change in historiography: even in "official historiography." For centuries, history has become the encoding of the values and actions of the ruler class: the feats and exploits of kings and generals and "leaders of men" (both terms are illuminating, both "leaders" and "men": because this canonised form of history was also the canonisation of phallocracy). It endorsed, and maintained, the hegemony of the few, of the élite, of the powerful, over the many, the "nameless."

But through studies like Leroy Ladurie's *Montaillou,* or in a slightly different vein, Schama's *Embarrassment of Riches* and *Citizens* within the field of historiography; and the work of Truman Capote, Norman Mailer and others in the field that traditionally belonged to literature, the boundaries have become more and more ineffectual, more and more effaced. Historiography itself is turning increasingly to the private accounts of "ordinary" citizens, of "small" people, to rewrite itself. In more and more courses in history, anthropology, politics, etc. at universities all over the world, novels are being introduced as key texts. Whereas within the domain of literature itself, the work of feminists is rewriting literary history too, bringing to light "forgotten" texts that change our entire perception of cultural history and of ourselves.

At last, we are writing ourselves into history. South African history of the future will not look exclusively at the misbegotten actions of a Verwoerd or a P. W. Botha, or even at the innovations of F. W. de Klerk, nor even, exclusively, at the Mandelas or the Tutus: but at the innumerable small poems and plays and stories, the often almost illiterate expressions of those who previously had been regarded, not as the makers but as the victims of history.

JULY 1992

Reimagining the Real: English South African Fiction Now

A LITERATURE IN CRISIS

The award of the Nobel Prize for 1991 to Nadine Gordimer has confirmed a world-wide interest in South African literature which has existed for a long time. It would be no exaggeration to suggest that, ever since the publication of *Cry the Beloved Country* in the fateful year of 1948, much of the international preoccupation with apartheid has in fact been stimulated and directed by South African fiction. But this interest has been largely political, extending occasionally to the domain of the ethical or the moral; now (inasmuch as it is feasible or even possible to distinguish between "literature" and "politics") the Nobel Prize has simultaneously broadened and sharpened the international interest into a consideration of the aesthetic. After many years of both writing and reading South African literature as an "essential gesture" (cf. Gordimer 1988) in a stern world of blood and tears, fiction in our part of the world can at last be approached *as* fiction (whatever that may mean).[1]

But this international attention comes at a peculiar moment

Paper read at the Winter School of the Grahamstown Festival of the Arts, July 1992.

of our transition from one state of consciousness to another, which goes beyond an awareness of our "here and now" as the not-so-still point where past and future meet: it is, in fact, a moment of crisis. This crisis, which contains, as crises do, both negative and positive elements, concerns *all* literature, and all literatures, in the country, but for reasons of time and space the focus will be restricted to fiction written in English, specifically to the *novel,*[2] and even more specifically to novels produced by writers resident in the country, not by exiles.

DIVISIONS

Read negatively, the crisis reveals English South African fiction as a deeply divided literature, involving, among others — ever since a whole generation of *Drum* writers was driven abroad — a tragic division between writers "outside" and others "inside," whether living or dead: on the one hand, the Heads and the La Gumas, the Nkosis and the Hopes and the Mosses; on the other the Rives and Copes, the Gordimers and Coetzees, the Ndebeles and Sepamlas. There is even a group of writers straddling the divide, those who were exiled and have returned, bearing in their writing the scars of both experiences: the Matteras and Wicombs and Serotes.

Another division, imposed by more than forty years of apart heid, is that of racial or ethnic "streams": on the one hand one finds what Rive termed "writing black" (1981), on the other what Coetzee terms "white writing" (1988). And however much one would wish, or try, to discuss in one rubric, or as one whole, all writing in English by authors from different sides of the racial divide, to ignore the divisions imposed by apartheid — divisions in terms of style and focus and narrative approach; often of genre and theme and aesthetic system; invariably, sadly, of audience — would be to distort the image. Even if there has been an increasing dedication among South African writers to the exploration of a "common South African identity," the *fact* of different traditions, audiences, and existential experience imposed by apartheid cannot be wished away. And the movement toward a "South African identity" in literature may well be increasingly interrogated, if not subverted, by the inevitable development of *language* divisions (like those already separating Afrikaans and English literatures) among writers who, for political and cultural reasons, have in the past turned largely to English in order to foster a necessary solidarity that supersedes ethnic divisions: more and more, as a still largely mythical "new South Africa" unfolds, black writers, like their predecessors in Nigeria, Ghana, Kenya and elsewhere, may turn to their indigenous languages as the arena of cultural struggle shifts more markedly toward the post-colonial. Ngugi's arguments about "decolonizing the mind" through language are well known: "We . . . cannot develop our cultures and literatures through borrowed tongues and imitations" (Ngugi 1981:65); and "by our continuing to write in foreign languages, are we not on the cultural level continuing that neo-colonial slavish and cringing spirit?" (Ngugi 1986:26).

DIVERSITY

But there is also a positive side to the present crisis in English South African fiction.

A particular feature of the prevailing situation is precisely the rich diversity of its sources: and in many respects the centrifugal forces in the situation are countered by a centripetal dynamic. This operates on both spatial and temporal levels.

In terms of space, English fiction in South Africa is fed from the entire spectrum of — for want of a better word — "ethnic" experience. The fact that both District Six and Sophiatown enriched an evolving tradition of local *English* fiction has helped to accelerate the breakdown of colonial traditions which, in so many parts of the world, have been paralyzed by the persistence of old distinctions between "center" and "margin," between "metropolis" and (erstwhile) "colony"; from native Zulu, Xhosa, Sotho or Tswana speakers, from "colored" and "Indian" writers, a constant, and expanding, input has enhanced the diversity of cultural expression contained within the local "English" tradition. What British fiction has been experiencing in recent years, when winners of the Booker Prize have included writers originating from New Zealand (Kerry Hulme), Australia (Bruce Chatwin, Peter Carey), India (Salman Rushdie), South Africa (J. M. Coetzee), Japan (Kazuo Ishiguro) et cetera, is replicated, in a much more dazzling demonstration of interrelationships, in South African fiction. And the local English tradition is being enriched even further through increasing translation of significant Afrikaans texts by Stockenström, Joubert, Schoeman, van Heerden, and soon also Miles, Goosen and others.

On the temporal plane there is another fascinating dimension to this experience. When the *Drum* generation was silenced in the early sixties a vital part, not only of English South African writing but of the South African *memory* was excised from the public consciousness. And without memory, Kundera more than any other modern writer has reminded us, a whole society, a whole culture becomes maimed, if not paralyzed. Now, as part of the reform processes introduced in 1990, most of those suppressed texts have been made available to South African readers once more. If, inevitably, some of them have a depressing air of datedness about them, much of vital significance has also been resuscitated. In a very real sense Alex la Guma, Can Themba, Bloke Modisane and many others have suddenly become our *contemporaries.* And this, too, adds to the splendid diversity of the present fiction scene.

But the problematic of division and diversity constitutes only an introduction to the crisis in South African English fiction.

THE MOMENT OF TRUTH

A crisis is a turning point, a moment of choice, a moment of truth: it is that moment when movement seems briefly arrested before it flows on in an unpredictable direction. Everything is possible. It is that instant when, as Barthes has it, "the garment gapes" (Barthes 1976:9) and one glimpses what is normally concealed, and who can tell if it is truth, or illusion, or mere possibility? It offers, as Barthes again suggests, "a discursive site" (Barthes 1979:3).

To guess the direction in which the movement may continue, if it continues, one has to know how it has arrived at *this* point "where past and future are gathered."

A young and intrepid Margaret Atwood once suggested (in trying to answer the question "Where is here?" in connection with Canadian literature) that "every country or culture has a single unifying and informing symbol at its core" (Atwood 1972:31). For America, she proposed, that symbol might be "The Frontier," for Britain "The Island," for Canada, "undoubtedly, Survival." It is much more than a game (unless in the seriously ludic sense in which Kundera uses the term) to try and find a corresponding symbol for (English) South African fiction. But perhaps, at least in the last few decades, one might be justified — with all the caution that inevitably accompanies generalisations — in finding that shibboleth in "The Struggle."

The term, I think, is large enough to embrace at least great tracts of South African literature, containing as it does the notion of "grounds of contest" which Malvern van Wyk Smith recently proposed (Smith 1990): it is large enough to accommodate not only Schreiner's *Story of an African Farm* but also Jordan's *The Wrath of the Ancestors* (which, in translation, has entered the tradition of local English fiction), the muted interior battlefield of Pauline Smith, the tussle between memory and forgetting in Gordimer's *The Conservationist.* In a very specific sense it has room for the political struggle of the last half-century. And perhaps that is part of the present crisis: that such a potentially expansive notion has become, in recent decades, so urgently restricted to only one *kind* of struggle, defined or explored in only one *set* of terms.

But even if "The Struggle" *has* been an acceptable symbol of South African fiction in the past, the very nature of the interregnum we have entered may force one to take another look at it. Part of the anguish that accompanies South Africa's present experience may well arise from the *silences* implicit in the old symbols, in what is *not* invoked by them; and, concomitantly, in the need to find new symbols, to revisit the familiar which has suddenly become disconcertingly strange, to rediscover the ordinary (as Ndebele puts it), to reimagine the real.

What used to be "adequate" no longer suffices.

But *what* "used to be" adequate in our literary, fictional experience of The Struggle?

LIBERATION

It is one thing to die for liberation: it is something entirely different to live with freedom. This is, of course, a platitude. Yet it seems to me it is part of a pervasive malaise that has swept across English South African fiction in recent years at the very least since Albie Sachs put his cat among the literary pigeons of establishment and ANC alike with the seminal essay "Preparing Ourselves for Freedom" in which he rejects the notion of art as "an instrument in the struggle." "In the case of a real instrument of struggle," he argued, "there is no room for ambiguity: a gun is a gun is a gun, and if it were full of contradictions it would fire in all sorts of directions and be useless for its purpose. But the power of art lies precisely in its capacity to expose contradictions and reveal hidden tensions." (in de Kock & Press, 1990:20.)

The problem cannot lie in the urge to freedom as such: the urge becomes problematic only when "freedom" becomes, entirely unwittingly, synonymous with "death": death as the ultimate utopia, the ultimate peace, the ultimate escape-from-it-all. And undoubtedly this death-wish has informed much of *white* South African fiction in recent years.

One of its manifestations has been a morbid proliferation of apocalyptic fiction. Traditionally, of course, apocalyptic texts have emerged within oppressed minorities attempting to counter history with eschatological fervor, through the prophetic revelation of an end to present misery and the advent of a divinely inspired new world order. In the hands of white South African authors curious distortions have been effected in the Biblical model, turning it into a secular, racially based *cri de coeur* of a privileged but embattled power group so overwhelmingly conscious of the imminent destruction of its power that the prospect of a new order is almost wholly obscured.[3] And although fascinating traces of the original cosmic dimensions of Armageddon remain, most of these narrators tend to turn the gaze inward, exploring the agonies of the private conscience *within* a context of a society falling apart.

From the very first page of a seminal apocalyptic text like Gordimer's *July's People* individual characters do indeed tend to function "on behalf of" the groups locked in final battle: while it focuses on a remote settlement in the margin of a country going up in flames, we are constantly reminded that July represents "his kind," the Smales family "their kind." Yet when a helicopter finally arrives, Maureen Smales runs out toward whatever it brings with it — whether "saviors" or "murderers" — and in this urgent birth of a new consciousness (the whole final scene is weighted heavily with images of sex, insemination and the agony and ecstasy of being reborn) the end of the Gramscian interregnum invoked in the epigraph is signalled — but it is a private ending and a personal choice, and what Maureen does here, in spite of very perceptive arguments by some critics,[4] is no longer done "on behalf" of anyone else but purely for the sake of her own future: "She runs: trusting herself with all the suppressed trust of a lifetime, alert, *like a solitary animal at the season when animals neither seek a mate nor take care of young, existing only for their sole survival*" (Gordimer 1981:160, my italics).

Possibly the most "typically" liberal-white apocalyptic text in recent white fiction is the startling, often moving, sometimes exasperating *The Arrowing of the Cane* by John Conyngham in which the violence of the ancestors is visited upon their present-day descendants. The first-person narrator, the sugar-cane farmer John Colville, is faced by relentlessly approaching cane-fields (reminiscent of Zulu impis armed with assegais) and by the nightly fires creeping ever closer to his homestead; yet his only response is to retreat into writing and to secrete his account of his own end and that of his tribe in a mossy fissure in his cellar (a sad substitute for the sex he is no longer capable of).

J. M. Coetzee is the most persistent — and the most impressive — prophet of apocalypse in most of his novels, notably in the allegorical nightmare *Waiting for the Barbarians* (1980), and the deceptively lucid *Life and Times of Michael K* (1983), the latter replacing traditional visions of utopia or distopia with one of what Barthes would call "atopia" (Barthes 1979:34–36). As an all too recognisable South Africa sinks into the total devastation of its ultimate war, Michael K retreats not only from history but even from language, as he finds salvation in a purely imaginary feminine order where "reality" is displaced by vision — the vision of the archetypal Voltairean gardener who lowers a bent teaspoon into a shaft in the earth: "and when he brought it up there would be water in the bowl of the spoon; and in that way, he would say, one can live" (Coetzee 1983:249).

Significantly, and in keeping with the increasing radicalisation of her ideological position, Gordimer attempts to bypass the white despair of apocalyptic fiction in *A Sport of Nature* (1987) by offering, instead, in a bold if controversial ending that reaches beyond the historical perspective of her contemporary reader, a deliberately optimistic view of the dawn of a new world *after* the Struggle.

In many novels not primarily determined by what Kermode termed the "sense of an ending" (Kermode 1977) another problematic — if highly understandable — aspect of South African English fiction is illuminated: that of reportage. It is necessary, of course, to bear in mind the extent to which South African journalists throughout the seventies and eighties, and most depressingly from 1984–1989, were prevented from reporting even the basic "facts" of events they witnessed. As state security took precedence, newspapers were browbeaten into complicity, or silence, or — at most — angry but muted opposition. In these circumstances it was not surprising that writers turned increasingly to reportage as an indispensable supplementary function of their fiction. Newspapers might be barred, for example, from reproducing publications of the Soweto Students Representative Council (among many others): but through a novel like *Burger's Daughter* (1979), arguably Gordimer's masterpiece, a writer of "fiction" could disseminate a pamphlet by this student body.[5] Gradually fiction became a repository of knowledge about the contemporary scene in South Africa. This was particularly true for black audiences. In those dark years following the uprising of Soweto and the murder of Biko and other activists of Black Consciousness, literature became sloganised as "a weapon for liberation" or "an instrument in the Struggle."[6]

At the same time this fiction became marked by the postcolonial urge throughout Africa (as in the rest of the Third World) to democratise culture, to draw it into programs for literacy, political solidarity and mass action. More and more numerous, and more and more vociferous critics and theoreticians began to demand new approaches of African literature as a peculiar form of cultural-political expression. And this was necessary, in a world conditioned for too long by the exclusivist readings of metropolitan (European) aesthetics. The problem, however, was that gradually, for many readers and writers alike, political commitment became the *only* criterion for the evaluation of African literature.

Brave attempts have been made by a number of South African fiction writers to introduce a personal, subjective dimension into reports of the "black experience." The first-hand, yet fictionalized accounts of black suffering and anger in the stories of Mtutuzeli Matshoba (*Call Me not a Man,* 1979) are indelibly inscribed on the South African mind. And it is significant that his harrowing fictionalized account of a labor farm in "A glimpse of slavery" (Matshoba 1979:77-64) marks the reader more unforgettably than its early factional model, the eyewitness report Henry Nxumalo wrote in the fifties for *Drum* on the horrors of a Bethal prison farm. Mongane Wally Serote, in many respects the natural heir to the *Drum* generation, brings to life, amid more "dateable" representations of oppression and resistance, the sharply focussed personal image of Tsietsi Molope, the narrator of *To Every Birth its Blood* (1981) in his attempts to master, not only "the name of the game . . . 'them and us'" (Serote 1981:96) but the subtle relationships with his wife, his brothers and sister and their families. Both victim and trickster, "somehow I kept pace with the fury of my town" (Serote 1991: 139) — and in the end he narrates, in an intensely personalised scene that appears to go against the grain of the preceding account of life under apartheid, the bloody but liberating birth of a baby.

In *And They Didn't Die* (1990) Lauretta Ngcobo inserts the struggle, not only of a "women's movement" but of a woman within that movement into the larger framework of racist and economic exploitation; if the novel often slides into sloganising and stereotypes, especially in the portrayal of the protagonist's abuse by a white man, it also offers poignant and sharply etched scenes representing her refusal "to wait [any] longer for other people to do things to make decisions about her life; she would make them herself" (Ngcobo 1990:10). Of particular interest is Jenzile's struggle on two fronts: it is directed as much against exploitation by whites and the apartheid system as against an oppressive black patriarchy which attempts to imprison her in custom and tradition.

The problem in much of this writing arises when aspects of the sociopolitical experience are *stated* rather than explored, *reported* rather than interpreted. It involves a terminology once used by Dorothy Sayers to distinguish between "poetry of statement" and "poetry of search." There may not be anything disturbing in the reader's encounter with any individual text: the uneasiness arises from the *accumulation* of texts that content themselves with the mere representation of exploitation, oppression, suffering, resistance and rage: Cope, du Plessis, Ebersohn,

Kuzwayo, Mathobe, Mattera, Mutloatse, Ngcobo, Nkosi, Rive, Ramgobin, Sepamla, Serote, Tlali . . . The sheer weight of such a fiction becomes depressing.

Not that its existence was and is not justified! One is reminded of a Neruda poem:

> And you will ask why doesn't his poetry speak of dreams and
> leaves and the great volcanoes of his native land?
> Come and see the blood in the street
> Come and see the blood in the street
> Come and see the blood in the street.

What was at stake was infinitely more than the reproach of fiddling while Rome burned: it was believed, and with reason, that at least part of the South African writer's "function" (all the more so if he or she wrote in English, which offered access to the whole world) was to *report,* to keep memory not only alive but ablaze, lest anyone be tempted afterwards to reiterate those dismal words of Nuremberg: "We didn't know." And the risk — often, for the black writer especially, the danger — of reporting the real lent an urgency to the interaction between writer and reader which, in itself, largely justified the enterprise.

But in the last few years, as we entered the interregnum between the darkness of apartheid and the as yet undefined future, there have been startling changes in the writer's position. With the press largely unmuzzled, the problem has become not the *lack* of information but the public's *bombardment* by it. Massacres at Khayelitsa or Pholla Park or Boipatong appear in their full horror on our television screens within hours, to be explored at length, and in gory depth, by newspapers in the days and weeks and months following the event.

In some respects the change in the novelist's position can be compared to that experienced by painters of the late nineteenth century when the emergence of photography dramatically displaced painting's immemorial monopoly on "representing the real," on capturing "true likenesses" of the visual world. Initially, photography was treated as an impostor and a rival and a threat; what happened in due course was the *liberation* of painting from the need of representation. Far from being a justification for painting, representation was now discovered to be an almost incidental aspect, at most a by-product, of visual art. And it seems to me that this is the challenge facing the South African writer at the moment. If we continue to be conditioned by what used to be a significant, but supplementary, function of the novel, namely reporting, fiction will lose its readers.

For Njabulo Ndebele, perhaps the most astute interpreter of South African black literature, the danger in much of that literature in the past lies in the fact that its "aesthetic validity . . . to its own readership lies precisely in the readers' recognition of the spectacular rendering of a familiar oppressive reality" (Ndebele 1991:45). This results in "an art of anticipated surfaces rather than one of process" (Ndebele 1991:27). And: "It establishes a vast sense of presence without offering intimate knowledge; it confirms without necessarily offering a challenge" (Ndebele 1991:46). Reporting here becomes equivalent to shocking, as each writer tries to outdo the other, partly out of fear that *not* to do so might be interpreted as avoiding the issue.

In conventional terminology, it seems to be a problem of the comparative weight of different "realities" or "authenticities": that of the inner life of the individual as against that of society; but also that of the word as against that of the lived experience — most particularly against that of *violence* as lived experience. As such it forms part of a much larger anxiety in the literature of our time. In his latest novel, *Mao II,* Don DeLillo expresses it as a twofold concern: about people, notably the world's young generation, becoming "immunized against the language of self" (DeLillo 1991:8); and about "the emergence of news as an apocalyptic force . . . The novel used to feed our search for meaning . . . But our desperation has led us toward something larger and darker. So we turn to the news, which provides an unremitting mood of catastrophe" (DeLillo 1991: 72). Or, rephrased: "What terrorists gain, novelists lose. The degree to which they influence mass consciousness is the extent of our decline as shapers of sensibility and thought. The danger they represent equals our own failure to be dangerous" (DeLillo 1991:157).

But the problem becomes more acute if DeLillo's notion of "danger," like Ndebele's notion of "spectacle," is linked to Baudrillard's concept of the "hyperreal": that blown-up, distorted and spectacular *image* of reality (created by the propaganda and the hype of the media, of advertising, of supermarkets) which, at least in the West, has almost completely supplanted the real. This is not the place to go into the Derridean notion of the non-existence of "the real" and the subversive supplementarity of language as the only "reality," there being no outside to the text; but the deconstruction of the real is inevitably a crucial part of the dilemma of the English South African writer, and much of the rest of this paper will be concerned with it.

THE CHANGING SCENE: TOWARD DEMOCRACY

Before we can look at responses by English South African writers to their changing world, the nature of at least some of the pertinent changes involved has to be clarified. Because these changes are so radical in their implications that the whole course of our indigenous literature may be affected. It may even go so far as to require a redefinition of the Atwoodian "symbol" of that literature.

As the country moves painfully, convulsively, from the structures and the mentality of authoritarianism toward — hopefully — greater openness and more freedom (however that is to be defined), the most obvious disappearance is that of an easy sloganised "target" or "enemy," an Other in terms of which the self is to be described.[7] It affects, in other words, the very notion of "self" and of "identity," which shifts and even subverts a basic preoccupation of indigenous literature since its inception.

The problem is compounded by the post-colonial authority's strategies of appropriation. Ndebele significantly points out, for instance, that in its manipulation of "the reform process," the

South African government has appropriated many of the ideals of the Struggle. "The potential result is that a moral and visionary desert is being cultivated precisely at a time when vision and morality are needed" (Ndebele 1991:8). This in itself provides us with at least two useful terms to test in our (re)definitions of an increasingly elusive South African "reality": *morality,* and *vision.* There is, more urgently than ever before, a need for images that transcend reportage, and for a morality that goes beyond expediency, pragmatism and "literary effect." This involves acknowledging that leaving the nightmare of the past need not mean, by the same token, the end of dreams.

As we approach democracy, the ideological map of our country needs to be redrawn. Writing has a place in it: and it is neither an easy nor an enviable place. Because for a long time "freedom" has been the slogan of indigenous literature. But in our changed circumstances the very nature of each version or possibility of freedom, as it presents itself, will have to be interrogated. In many respects "democracy" has become a keyword in our Newspeak, which in itself should alert the writer to new responsibilities.

NEW DIRECTIONS

As one way out of the impasse of the past Ndebele has suggested "the rediscovery of the ordinary" through stories which "remind us, necessarily, that the problems of the South African social formation are complex and all-embracing; that they cannot be reduced to a single, simple formula" (Ndebele 1991:55). Apart from illuminating Ndebele's own endeavor in *Fools* (1983), one of the landmarks of black writing in the last decade, this observation also highlights the redeeming features of those novels from the Struggle — by black and white authors alike — that went beyond "recognition" toward "transformation" (Ndebele 1991:27). But it does not seem to me to go far enough. It is the real itself — whatever we collectively or individually perceive as "real," especially when it threatens to become "hyperreal' —

which requires reinvention. Fiction, after all, does not (or: no longer) involve "representing" the real but *imagining.* As Musil suggested long ago, "Reality has in itself a nonsensical yearning for unreality" (Musil 1988:343).

And there are signs in English fiction presently produced by South African writers to suggest that this is already happening. A few forms in which it manifests itself:

The private vision. In its most obvious form it involves the interpretation of the world in terms of a heightened private awareness, a subjectivised vision. This is evident, for example, in Menan du Plessis's attempt in *State of Fear* (which is much more convincing than the patchy and overstated *Longlive!,* 1989) to break down "such simple polarities" (du Plessis 1985:175) as she explores the invasion of the private space of her narrator Anna Rossouw by the outside world represented by two fugitive colored children, an irruption which breaks down all her previous "myths" and questions language itself in "the breathless, wordless pause before an utterance that makes most spoken meanings possible" (du Plessis 1985:24).

A comparable invasion of the private by the public occurs in Coetzee's *Age of Iron,* in which, as in Solzhenitsyn's *Cancer Ward,* the terminal illness of the individual is symptomatic of a larger social misery. Here, too, a stranger, the enigmatic vagabond Vercueil, intrudes into a woman's private space and forces her first to see, then to acknowledge, and ultimately to imagine a violent world she — good harmless liberal that she is — would have preferred to exclude. And here, too, but more subtly and more urgently than in the du Plessis, it becomes an interrogation of language itself, as the narrator is forced to grope ever more dangerously, ever more exposed, for "my own words" (p. 91), those "other words" (p. 133), that "anagram" (p. 158) which may — or may not — solve the riddle of the real.

Gordimer's most recent novel adds a new dimension to her lifelong preoccupation with the interaction between the private and the public. The mystery of the Other is approached through the title: whereas the text represents a son's story of his father (significantly called "Sonny") the title designates it as *My Son's Story,* which is both elucidated and complicated by the Shakespearean epigraph, "You had a Father, let your son say so." This suggests that the "real" subject is constantly displaced: identity becomes too private ever to be grasped (as the father hides within the story of the son manipulated by the father as imagined by the son . . .); at the same time it becomes too public to retain "originality" (as the most private actions of the father become part of his public involvement in the Struggle).

Another demonstration of a private world emerging from, determined by, yet also in opposition to, a public space is Damon Galgut's skilfully crafted *The Beautiful Screaming of Pigs* (1991), constructed around the independence of Namibia and the assassination of Lubowski while focusing on the precariously balanced relationship between a Hamlet son (the narrator), his Gertrude mother and her lover. The conventional opposition inside/outside is itself shattered when, in response to the mother's lover's remark, "You'll live here in exile till your country's free," the narrator answers, "There are other kinds of exile" (Galgut 1991:114).

Two more texts deserve to be mentioned here. The first is Zoë Wicomb's *You Can't Get Lost in Cape Town* (1987) in which the successive chapters (which may also be read as separate stories) trace through a series of personal crises the life of a young "colored" girl as she migrates from the West Coast to the University of Cape Town to London and back. Passages of curiously stilted writing alternate with an almost Mansfield-like understatement to end in a startling revaluation of "reality": back from abroad, the narrator visits her aged mother, whom the reader, in earlier stories/chapters, has been led to presume dead, and who reproaches the daughter for the "lies" she has told in her writing. It reminds one of the second book of the *Don Quixote* where the hidalgo and Sancho Panza encounter readers of their previous exploits. In its best moments (cf. the title story) *You Can't Get Lost in Cape Town* must rate with the best English fiction recently produced in South Africa. At the same time it opens new possibilities for postmodernism (as defined and redefined most persistently in the work of Coetzee, extending it to one limit in *Foe,* 1986).

And then there is Joël Matlou's *Life at Home and other stories* (1991), arguably the most remarkable fiction by a black South African writer in years. Like Wicomb's text it can be read either as a series of short stories or as a (very short) novel. The most "ordinary" reality — life on a farm near Magaliesberg, working in a mine, courting a girl — is informed by a deceptively low-key imagination which unexpectedly erupts into "madness" (in the Erasmian or Quixotian sense of the word), especially in the final chapters, "Carelessman was a madman" and "My ugly face." The warning that "people thought he was mad, but he was really facing up to his future" (Matlou 1991:80) retroactively changes the reader's perception of all the previous events in the narrative. Coupled with a line from "Man against himself," "The life of a man is very heavy in his bones and his future is a deep unknown grave" (Matlou 1991:53), this vision illuminates quite disconcertingly events like the escape from the farm or the descent into the hell of the mine ("Suffering takes a man from known places to unknown places" — Matlou 1991:72).

History as story. The most striking feature of both the Wicomb and the Matlou text is the way in which personal history is transformed into *story.* The significance of this is perhaps highlighted in a revealing remark by Ellen Kuzwayo in her introduction to *Sit Down and Listen* (1990:i); referring to narrative tradition in the black communities of South Africa, she says, "We have owned our stories while owning so little else."

As the reimagination of the past has featured strongly in much of my own work, I have a particular interest in it as an alternative to representations of the "real." Turning *history,* whether "objective" or "subjective," into *story* involves more than drawing it into the private space of the observer and subjecting it, consciously or unconsciously, to the play of language. Above all, it involves the prestidigitations of the *image,* of "vision" (which, of course, cannot operate in literature except through language). That is: the obvious links with the determining influence of tradition are suspended; an imaginary opening is created which makes it possible for events that originally appear fixed in time and space, canonised by convention, sanctioned by authority, to be *re*imagined. Coetzee, as early as 1974, was perhaps the first to attempt this in what remains one of his most disturbing texts, "The narrative of Jacobus Coetzee." Revisiting a past already "officially established" in travel journals and public records, he uses history to redraw the map of the future—just as it may be said that, from a vantage point in the present he "prophesies" the past. "Looking back," says Kuzwayo (1990:15), "we can all find a new land in the past."

The possibilities of revisiting the past are endless. A more recent past is revisited, this time in a completely different mood and mode, with strident satire, in Rive's *Buckingham Palace District Six* (1986). Stephen Gray's *War Child* (1992), on the other hand, is a delicate and almost dreamlike evocation of the war years revisited through the sensibility and the imagination of a small boy. But as far as the transformation of history into story is concerned, the most exciting new English fiction writer on the South African scene is Mike Nicol. His latest novel, *This Day and Age* (1992) is much less convincing than his first and the debt it owes to Llosa's *War of the End of the World* (among others) becomes a burden it never completely succeeds in shaking off; but there is powerful potential in his compression of different historical massacres—the Killing of the Cattle, the Bondelswart rebellion, and particularly Bulhoek—into the conflict between the motley rebel band of Enoch Mistas and the armies of the South African President. Elias Canetti once wrote that, "I am not interested in grasping precisely a man I know. I am interested only in exaggerating him precisely." It is in the precision of his exaggeration that Nicol falters; but there are haunting cameos in the narrative, and the portrayal of the President who, phoenix-like, continually recreates himself, is particularly impressive — even if he lacks the impact of Luisa Valenzuela's grotesque and fantastic ruler in *The Lizard's Tail.*

"Magic realism." In a situation where "life itself is too fantastic to be outstripped by the creative imagination" (Moyana 1976:95) Mike Nicol also signals another possibility of reimagination as a means of escaping the tyranny of the real and the impasses of the past: it lies in taking a cue from the great South Americans of our time. (Where it borders on allegory there are indigenous forerunners too, notably in Coetzee's *Waiting for the Barbarians.*) The very danger of emulation may make such a strategy suspect. But in Nicol's first novel, *The Powers That Be* (1989), unmistakably postmodernist in its procedures, he offers the kind of explosive image of South African "realities" that makes the novel, in spite of its more labored moments, something of a *tour de force.*

The setting is a small nameless fishing village populated by a collection of perambulating stories rather than individuals and terrorized by the archetypal ruler Capain Nunes ("policeman, upholder of law and order, defender of Christian ways and God's word aaargh": p. 167) who is convinced that the place harbors a dark criminal secret; this delightfully eccentric microcosm offers a multiple eye-of-the-fly image of the South Africa of past, present and future. The captain's search for an elusive reality leads only to a proliferation of possibilities ("We've told him so many stories he doesn't know fact from fantasy," says Lady Sarah on page 51); the novel as a whole becomes "a flood of history with its visions of apocalypse" (p. 127).

It is a pity that a sense of fantasy occasionally lapses into the merely funny or idiosyncratic. Nicol is by no means a Marquez or an Allende, a Llosa, a Donoso or an Amado; but young South African writers and readers in search of "something different" and perhaps of "a way out," may well find in this novel, as in some others I have referred to, flickerings of hope for the future.

CONCLUSION

English South African fiction has undoubtedly established its own indigenous traditions, drawing on a rich and varied heritage, both African and European. If in many respects it has tuned in to international developments in fiction (post-modernism, neo-realism, magic realism) it is also impressively self-assured about its involvement in the local scene. It is marked by the often painful processes of post-colonialism. It is scarred, in many respects, by the inhibitions and anger of the apartheid era — and as this legacy of oppression and injustice extends well into the foreseeable future, old battles may continue to be fought for a long time to come. But there are exciting signs of renewal and reimagination; and even if, in the process, it shifts its focus toward new defining symbols in Atwood's terminology (if indeed such symbols can still serve a purpose), struggle of one kind or another may continue to inform it, challenge it, and revitalise it.

APRIL 1993

The Dove in the Grave

At the funeral of the anti-apartheid activist and South African Communist Party leader Chris Hani one of the white doves released by members of the family fluttered, not up into the clear sky, but downward into the grave. Was this a rather crude symbol of the significance of the moment?

Certainly South Africa has staggered through terrible events in its most recent history (one need go no further back than the massacres of Boipatong and Bisho in 1992); but it would be hard to a find a moment more devastating in its impact on the country's tenuous hopes for a free and democratic future than the murder of Chris Hani. There have been many occasions since Sharpeville in 1960, and even more urgently since the Soweto uprising of 1976, the assassination of Steve Biko in 1977, and the successive states of emergency of the eighties, when it was hard to resist the temptation of despair.

What has helped me, personally, through many of these crises, has been something the Great Rabbi of Paris once told me when he found me despondent about the future of South Africa: "To despair," he said, "is an insult to the future." But this time it was hard to make the words work their magic. The murder of Hani seemed to go beyond the grasp of reason: a

First published in the *Guardian*, April 1993.

blackness perhaps anticipated by the Afrikaans poet Ernst van Heerden in his recent lines about a time "when even our dreams/ humiliate and betray humanity."

The reason why the impact is so particularly shattering may be that it happened at a moment when, emerging from a spiral of deepening violence, for the first time in many years South Africans across the political spectrum, from far right to extreme left, appeared at last to be moving toward negotiation, reconciliation and cautious hope. Unlike the unrealistic euphoria that swept the country in the wake of the white referendum which endorsed the peace process exactly a year ago, the new signs suggesting a triumph of reason over violence were based on realistic considerations.

What was destroyed in the Easter weekend, in that darkness between crucifixion and resurrection, was not merely an extraordinary man and a leader unique in terms of his charismatic appeal to a turbulent "lost generation" of black youth conditioned to such an extent by rage and violence that their attitude to most father figures, including even Mandela, was, if not overtly antagonistic, at the very least fraught with suspicion. What was negated was the voice of reason itself. In the soldier who carried the Collected Works of Shakespeare to the battlefield was symbolized the man of action inspired by the conviction that we shall not live by the sword alone but by the word. He managed to reconcile in himself — thereby affirming the possibility for others — these two urges normally regarded as incompatible. And through his assassination the forces of sword and word were dangerously returned to their initial positions of antagonism, mutual exclusion and otherness. Once again, only more fatefully than ever before, South Africa was returned to that situation in which Sartre once paired (in an otherwise dangerously misguided essay) "the dehumanisation of the oppressed" and "the alienation of the oppressor."

What seems like a dark wave has broken over South Africa; and all the space of experience available at the moment appears invaded by an incomprehensible clamor of rage, pain and fear.

Yet behind the sound and fury some of the terrible silences of history may be discerned.

Since President de Klerk's landmark speech of February 2, 1990 which announced the dawn of a "New South Africa" many observers (especially abroad) have perceived a gradual rapprochement between white and black; a climate for co-operation seemed to be taking shape; and the overwhelming white vote in favour of negotiations in 1992 appeared to confirm that the dismantling of the framework of laws that had held apartheid in place was actually being accompanied by a change in attitudes and in mindsets. This was reinforced by the ANC's own long history as an organization not only intent on negotiation but demonstrating, as much in its Freedom Charter as in its membership, that racial harmony and co-operation was both a lofty ideal and a practical possibility. These perceptions were severely shaken by the increasing violence in the country (the demonstrable result, at least in part, of covert operations and provocation by government agencies): yet below the violent surface there seemed to be a very real and unstoppable basic groundswell toward understanding and the resolution of conflict through peaceful means. Certainly, if in early 1990 there were people in South Africa — including some of the most lucid minds in the country — genuinely persuaded that violence was the only way out of the apartheid impasse, by early 1993 no one could argue convincingly that violence was still the only option. In fact, the increase of options available both to individuals and organisations was the surest marker of the real change happening in the country (however long and arduous the road to relative democracy and a measure of political freedom still remained).

Hani's murder has changed all that.

This is manifested in the hysteria surfacing in pronouncements of leaders from right and left, in the reactions of whites barricading themselves in their homes or brandishing guns in public or buying one-way plane tickets to Europe, Canada or

New Zealand; in the desperate destruction by young blacks burning shops and vehicles and people or turning against their own leaders.

"Mandela's time is past, it is time we take the law into our own hands," I am told by a young "colored" student in Cape Town; and a white taxi driver in Johannesburg counters, "I've been called up by the army for township duty, but I've told them they can stuff it: there's no way I'm going to set myself up as a target for black hooligans. I'd rather take up my gun and pull the trigger myself."

If such reactions are to be dismissed as the uncontrolled emotions of "ordinary people" who, somehow, "don't know better," the most revealing — and the most sickening — responses have come precisely from those who *are* supposed to know better, including President de Klerk himself. Confronted by the news of black rage following the murder, his gut reaction was to summon his State Security Council; after a day of massive dignified mourning marred by some outbreaks of violence (nothing compared to the destruction of Los Angeles following the acquittal of the Rodney King accused in 1992), all de Klerk could do was threaten strong action against "unruly elements." Nothing has exposed this man so mercilessly for the petty and vicious little securocrat he is at heart than the events that have shaken South Africa since April 10.

Like Chesterton's donkey, de Klerk has had his moment of glory, when it seemed he took charge of history: what he must have discovered by now is that history does not need him for its unfolding. He has, in fact, been largely bypassed by it, cut down to a very paltry size by recent events which revealed nothing so much as his utter inability to grasp what is really at stake. His thinking, and that of his wretched régime, is still based exclusively on "them-and-us"; and criminally oblivious of what was happening in the mind of the great majority of South Africans, he allowed the black week between assassination and funeral to run its course as if it concerned only blacks — those dangerous and inferior others who, in his besieged mind, continue to bite the hand that feeds and beats them and cannot rise above the level of uncontrollable emotion and brute violence.

How little was really required! To have announced, the moment the news broke, a state-supported Day of Mourning for the whole country (when even the least informed mind should have been able to tell that in *practical* terms the country would come to a standstill anyway), would have drawn the whole of South Africa into a communal act of contrition and concern; in the meanest political terms it would have earned de Klerk the goodwill of the large majority of blacks. But he has, of course, a talent for making the wrong choice. Hours after the Boipatong massacre, in which the police were perceived to be heavily implicated, he appeared in the streets of the stricken township like a curious tourist ogling the excesses of "angry natives" from behind bullet-proof windows, escorted by the very police the township believed to have been responsible for the outrage. This time, at Hani's funeral, the most massive in the history of the country, the government was not even represented. It had, explained de Klerk, already paid its condolences in an adequate manner. And so, as the country ground to a sad and massive halt, Parliament continued with business as usual, celebrating its own irrelevance in a society which had so fervently been hoping for democracy.

This moment, more than the many others preceding it since de Klerk took office, represented the final abdication of vision, of dignity, even of ordinary decency from the present régime. And de Klerk is not even conscious of it — just as he remains blithely oblivious of the need to show remorse for apartheid (it was not an evil, he continues to assert, only a policy that somehow "didn't work"). Because he has remained the prisoner of apartheid which he personally helped to keep in place for so long; a prisoner of his own whiteness; a prisoner of history in its narrowest and crudest sense. In his predecessor I had occasion to remark on the phenomenon of apocalyptic arrogance. In de

Klerk it is merely ignoble ignorance. Ignorance, above all, of his own — that is, his régime's — mortality.

This is the core of the historical silence lurking in the heart of the present clamor: the silence that divides white from black, the silence of unknowing and of unreason — of an *unwillingness* to know — which manifests itself as a series of lacks — lack of understanding, lack of compassion, denial of simple human dignity. This is the price of alienation, of a process of othering that has gone so far as to appear irreversible.

As a counterweight to the pettiness of the scale on which de Klerk operates, Mandela has assumed, in the wake of Hani's murder, a stature and a dignity that appeared to invite, as something not only inevitable but *normal,* his being introduced at the funeral service as "the President of South Africa"; and the way in which, on the night of Hani's murder, he took charge of the television broadcast to the country confirmed an authority he'd already had in all but name.

Yet Mandela's contemplation of the grave into which Hani's coffin was lowered could not but evoke in spectators the speculation that he was watching the premonition of his own death.

In the crowds attending the ceremony on Wednesday April, 14, where Mandela was a main speaker, were many youngsters who booed when he spoke of reconciliation. Never has the generation gap in the ANC been so devastatingly demonstrated. And, as a desperate gesture, perhaps, to recapture the imagination of the young, Mandela has announced a program of continuing "rolling mass action" to harness young energies in order to impose the announcement of a firm date for elections and a transitional authority — *on which agreement between the major partners in negotiations, the ANC and the minority government, has already been reached.*

In this announcement one may be justified to read that, if de Klerk knows too little, Mandela knows too much: and in its own way this knowledge is paralysing. This means that if Mandela, too, has come to represent an historical silence, he, too, is a prisoner of unfolding history — especially if history is seen, as Engels formulated it, as the interaction of numerous wills, the frustration of each separate intention, yet the involvement of all within its outcome.

But history is also, as Barthes has pointed out, a choice — and the limits of that choice. To at least some extent these limits are defined by de Klerk's belief that he is immortal; by Mandela's assumption of his mortality. In the gap between them falls the choice. It is impossible at this stage (I am writing a mere day after Hani's funeral) to say which way the country will go. But perhaps, rather than indulge in prophecy, it is more important to acknowledge this *as* a moment of choice, in which the only freedom is that of many wills interlocking in the tussle of history. What is necessary is the lucidity to evaluate the options available in that space where choice is happening.

And in defining those options it is, at the very least, helpful to know that South Africans have been amazingly resilient in past moments of crisis; and that even now, in the face of all odds, a deep current of goodwill continues to run between the banks of two apparently intransigent extremes. (And since their very intransigence stems from the same ferocious attachment to the territory, this in itself may paradoxically turn out to be a source of hope rather than of despair.)

Above all, Hani's own example demonstrates an option not to be ignored: the example of the soldier with Shakespeare in his pocket. The word, the mind, the nobler achievements of the human spirit, need not be ruled out in this moment of choice: on the contrary. We *are* a violent species; but humanity — and South Africa with it — has demonstrated that it can rise above mere mindless violence. If we have triumphed over Auschwitz, or the murder of Gandhi, or that of Martin Luther King, we can also emerge from the shadow of apartheid and the death of Chris Hani. It is by no means certain that reason, or compassion, or decency *will* triumph. But it *can.* We need not insult the future. And acknowledging this within our set of choices is already much.

Before Hani's coffin was lowered to its ultimate rest, a soldier of umKhonto we Sizwe, the armed wing of the ANC, clambered into the open grave to retrieve the bewildered white dove, to save it from being crushed, to set it free.

This, too, should be remembered.

MAY 1993

Literature and Control

As South Africa stumbles from its dark past toward an as yet undefined future, its literature inevitably reflects much of the soul-searching that accompanies the move. And already writers, still somewhat dazed by the transition, are beginning to wonder about the extent of freedom to be expected in the much-vaunted democratic future (which is not quite such a foregone conclusion as wishful thinking sometimes makes it seem).

But it is impossible to discuss any future scenario without reference to the present situation; and the present cannot be evaluated in isolation from the past.

That specific past, characterized for writers by apartheid and by censorship (the Publications Control Act of 1974 is still on the statute book), demarcated a peculiar space, a peculiar set of possibilities, for the enterprise of literature. If the writer pursued his or her functions "in the name of," or by virtue of long established aesthetic traditions, these functions also acquired an unmistakable *moral* dimension: writing, even for those writers who would have liked to define their operation as apolitical, implied — willy-nilly — the assumption of an ideological position. One was reminded only too often of Brecht's much-

Paper delivered at a symposium on "Literature and Control" organized by the Cape Provincial Library Services, May 1993.

abused warning: What times are these when to write about flowers means being silent about so many other things! The very silences of a text — the *nature* of those silences — became a system of signposts demarcating the writer's operational area. And the moral weight of a text lay, more often than not, in what it attacked rather than in what it supported. Camus's injunctions about freedom, justice and truth as the writer's great directives were expressed largely in terms of a struggle *against injustice*, *un*freedom and the lie. What was said had to be weighed largely against what one was not allowed to say. However impressive some of the individual products from this period may have been, the limitations of a literature directed primarily *against* certain targets, rather than *in favor of* others, are only too obvious.

That those were evil times is universally acknowledged. Working under such constraints marked all of us, in one way or another; even those of us who were prepared to do battle against the forces of apartheid and censorship still bear the scars of those battles, ranging from the deformities of anger and spiritual violence to the dangerous pride of victims. Even in the midst of those dark days I warned about a shift I could not but notice in the attitude of the young generation: more and more as censorship asserted itself, the first question posed by young writers who sent me their manuscripts for comment would be, not *Is it good enough?*, but *Will it pass the censors?* And whether this attitude resulted in exaggerated caution or in exaggerated defiance, the distortions of the creative mind were only too visible.

Censorship imposed itself not simply in the banning of books, but in the creation of a climate of fear, suspicion, and insecurity. Publishers who became overcautious (not all of them did); printers who refused risky assignments; bookshops that preferred to carry only "safe" titles — all of these contributed to the situation of continual risk in which the writer had to operate. Even more dangerous — in the first place for black writers, but in one way or another it affected also whites who dared to question the proscriptions and prohibitions of the System — were the attentions of the security police: nothing demonstrated quite so eloquently the fact that censorship was primarily a *political* strategy as the way in which "suspect" writers were intimidated and victimised by the Security Police. And the inhibitions imposed by the apartheid mentality must to a large extent be blamed for a certain lack of density and variety in South African literature over the last few decades. (That a number of quite remarkable texts were produced, is reason for celebration; but in spite of much vitality the spectacle of the literature *as a whole* — especially when compared to the contemporary output in Canada or Australia, let alone several of the South American countries — was disappointing.)

But there was another side to the censorship era: the very existence of censors created *challenges* to those writers who refused to be intimidated. There was a special exhilaration, a sense of adventure, in knowing that one never operated in a vacuum but entered, with every publication, every poetry recital, every performance of a play, into an urgent and dramatic interaction with one's whole society; and at the same time there was an enriching and encouraging experience of *solidarity* with all the other agents of culture and creativity in the country. One might be persecuted: but one was never alone. And no censorship could impose absolute silence on the community of writers. The most murderous action of censorship — banning a book — turned out to be wonderfully counterproductive: the very knowledge of a ban imposed, or to be imposed, created a feverish interest among readers and would-be readers, resulting in a hectic clandestine circulation of precisely those books the régime was most scared of. Never before in South African history had the word carried so much weight; never before had writers acquired such notoriety and such importance; never before had literature contributed so immediately and so forcefully to the social and political debate. With the increasing proscription of overt political contestation, literature became the battlefield where conscientisation and resistance and revolt could take shape. There was power in the act of imagination.

But danger lurked even in the dizzying experience of engaging in literature in a time of repression. The danger of potentially valuable texts reduced to vehicles of easily digestible "messages," of slogans for mass consumption. The danger of overestimating the role writers *could* play or the misjudgement of the nature of their "efficacy." The danger of "enlisting" writers for causes, however noble in themselves. The danger of the direct hit: an enemy so visible, so seemingly coherent, so defined, so monolithic, invited an increasingly univocal and unifocal approach. If apartheid was the enemy, it was all too easy to reduce it to even simpler symbols: the National Party, Vorster, Botha, the security police . . . And with the dismantling of apartheid and the dismissal of those targets, it might well seem — as it does to many members of the public, and even to some writers — that, suddenly, there is nothing left to write about.

Which brings us to the problematic present. Problematic, because in the first instance one has constantly to remind oneself that it is not yet a post-apartheid epoch. If the framework of laws supporting that destructive system is indeed in the process of being dismantled, the *mentalities* of apartheid continue to inform our actions and reactions, our writing, our thinking. This is evident in every utterance of F. W. de Klerk and his sad entourage of vicious and/or incompetent mediocrities; in their inability to discover and acknowledge that apartheid was not merely an unsuccessful policy but a crime against humanity; in their transparent attempts to predetermine the shapes of the future. But it is *also* evident in the opposition's continuing exploitation of the role of victim (which is as pernicious in its denial of human potential as the role of oppressor); and in the classic psychological syndrome of "identification with the aggressor," visible in the obscene pursuit of status symbols, the reliance on autocratic decisions or unilateral resolutions in the name of democratic expediency, the "softness" on violence in the young generation for fear of losing support, the increasing recourse to political expediency when statemanship is required, the prevarications and the avoidance of straight answers, the parades of male chauvinism . . .

In this situation of ambiguities and vacillation — some of the "morbid symptoms" of Gramsci's concept of an interregnum — the writer has to redefine radically the space available to him or to her. In many respects there is an appreciable improvement: since the liberalization of censorship after the banning of Etienne Leroux's *Magersfontein o Magersfontein,* Nadine Gordimer's *Burger's Daughter* and my *Dry White Season,* and even more especially since the beginning of the de Klerk reform process (however suspect its motivations), the situation has opened up so much that no writer, black or white, need lose any more sleep over fears of censorship; the police, themselves in disarray, have other priorities; there is almost nothing — whether political, moral, sexual or otherwise — that cannot be said, shown on film or the stage, or experimented with.

And yet there is a debit side to the experience as well: if censorship used to heighten public interest in literature and other cultural manifestations, that urgency has now dissipated. The Market Theatre in Johannesburg, once a center of cultural resistance, has lost most of its audience; far from being lionised or even seriously considered, writers, no longer able to rely on a situation which automatically dramatises or highlights their work, have to find other ways of captivating readers — at a time when economic recession has already turned books into a luxury item (and also at a time when more than ever before South Africa has to face the dangers of élitism in producing literature for a small literate public surrounded by masses of illiterates).

Writers can now exploit the new freedom by experimenting with the boundaries of the permissible: for some this involves processes of self-questioning and of interrogating the very medium in which they work. For some others, especially those minor talents who in more dangerous times lacked the guts to ply their craft, it is simply an opportunity to indulge themselves and perform the easiest and most obvious little tricks in order to draw attention, not to the quality of their writing but merely to the shock-value of the surface. ("Look at me! Look at me!" Or: "Mine is bigger than yours!") This, they proclaim, is their freedom. But freedom has little to do with it. Years ago, when a famous American author was invited to write an article for *Esquire,* he was told that he was free to write whatever he wished and use any language he wished, on the sole condition that he didn't use the word *fuck.* In these conditions, the author replied, his only freedom consisted precisely in saying *fuck.* What makes so many of today's literary performers in South Africa pathetic by comparison is their insistence on saying *fuck* at the very moment when everyone else is saying it, and everyone *knows* that it can be said. O brave new world.

A more serious problem to be confronted in the new situation is the disappearance of the obvious and blatant "enemy." No longer can he (the enemy is invariably male) be dealt with in the univocal and unifocal manner I have referred to earlier. On the one hand, even if apartheid and its mentalities are still with us, there is little point in targeting it as the enemy, because there is no sense of *discovery* in the statement: and without the adventure of discovery literature loses its power to enthral and to challenge.

Perhaps the key to this aspect of the problem is the acknowledgement that apartheid as such has *never* been the enemy. It has always been only a symptom and a sign, a footprint, of the enemy. For the true enemy to the human is *power,* in all its forms. The power of the lie; the power of the corrupt; of oppression; of injustice; of bondage. These things outlive apartheid: they exist, and have existed, in all human societies, at all times. This is precisely the key to what I shall have to say about literature in a future South Africa — when apartheid may be finally eradicated, but not injustice, not corruption, not lies, not intolerance: in other words, not power.

And this enemy is not so coherent or visible or obvious as apartheid: and it is not only a more complicated and subtle process to track it down, but it is also more difficult to persuade readers of its menace, sometimes even of its existence. Quite simply because this enemy, power, is never "something out there," but very much "in here," in ourselves, part even of our attempts to define and confront it. *This* is the difficulty inherent to the precarious freedom writers enjoy at the moment, and will have to deal with in the future.

For me as a writer there is freedom in the acknowledgement that *I do not need apartheid in order to write.* If it has informed everything I have ever written, it is because it has determined every aspect of my life as a South African: to write about flowers, or love, and pretend apartheid wasn't there, would have been a denial and a lie: and literature can only take root in one's attempts to face the truth — about one's world, about oneself. But if that world and that self are changing (even though, as I cannot insist too often, apartheid persists in many pernicious forms), the literature that springs from, and reacts to, them must also change. This means that the scope of experience available to the writer is in the process of expanding immeasurably. Above all, perhaps, writing returns to its basics. What concerns the writer is writing, is language: all literature (even the most "committed" line of Struggle poetry) springs from the relationship between an individual and the word — and *through* the word with the world, with the "real" (whatever anyone, at any given time, conceives of as "real").

This does not mean that the writer can only "write about writing": it does mean that he or she *writes writing.* It means, in the largest sense of Derrida's notorious phrase, that "there is no outside-text": the world itself is a *written* world. So instead of severing or isolating onself from the world through the word, writing becomes an act of connecting the two, of redefining both Self and Other.

This experience, which involves *re*discovery rather than discovery, also involves a constant revaluation of the stages we have passed through to arrive where we are now. Even as we try to clarify the Other in order to arrive at a deeper understanding of our*selves,* our vision is obscured: we are all maimed, in one way or another, as I have said, by the experience of apartheid. And as one's awareness of that wounding process deepens, it informs one's choices for and approaches to the future: to the literature which may evolve in it, and to the possible constraints placed on it and its evolution.

At the moment there appear to be largely two main mindsets about the way to go about it. They have been highlighted by the continuing debate between the ANC's Department of Arts and Culture (DAC) and the National Arts Initiative.

The DAC has as its main objective (formulated most explicitly at the Culture and Development Conference organized in April this year) "the cultural liberation of the disenfranchised people of South Africa." The *raison d'être* of its strategy is the acknowledgement that a long tradition of oppression has left the majority of South Africans culturally deprived and marginalised; simply "opening up" the whole field of culture cannot restore the balance, as it would continue to silence most of the voiceless. For one thing, as the majority of South Africans cannot read or write, a massive education program has to underlie all cultural activity in order to extend the very possibility of access to culture. And education involves government and power structures. Consequently, argues Mtutuzeli Matshoba of the ANC, "As it was the apartheid régime that stifled South Africa's cultural development, it will take a democratic government guided by the vision of the people to create circumstances conducive to fruitful cultural development, not only the cultural community" (*Weekly Mail,* May 28–June 3, 1993).

This is an important argument; and it takes cognisance of the fact that culture is not a concept or activity that can ever be "innocent": it is permeated by politics — which (depending on how it is defined) need not be a simplistic experience determined by the exercise of power but, instead, a process of enrichment dependent on relationships and interactions among individuals and groups of people. Also, if the concept of "government" is read, as the ANC consistently does, as the "will of the people," that is, as a true reflection of what people (or "the people") "really" wish, one cannot but endorse it. The problem is that "the people" has become a questionable slogan, often with little or no connection with reality. In the Cultural Desk that preceded the ANC's Department of Arts and Culture the machinations of power had already become all too sickeningly obvious: and even the DAC itself has spawned — among many more dedicated members — a number of commissars and petty dictators on the cultural scene who are there, in very basic terms, for what they can get out of it, not for what they can put into it. Even a liberal newspaper like the *Weekly Mail* was constrained to comment that the Culture and Development Conference organized by the DAC itself demonstrated alarming tendencies toward authoritarianism, for example in the constitution of a previously nominated board of trustees about which no discussion was allowed at the meeting and no attempt at election was made. In fact the *Weekly Mail* reported, in its edition of May 7–13, 1993, that only five of the fifteen new trustees had been present: most had not even attended the conference and were ignorant of the resolutions taken there.

In addition, much of the talk about "redressing the imbalances of apartheid" and "democratizing culture" or "returning culture to the people" never transcended the level of sloganeering. The very use of clichés — even (and perhaps especially) when used by artists of acknowledged sensitivity and integrity — is a sign of the inhibition of freedom, not only of speech but of thought. It is another of the scars of the apartheid era, revealing as it does an inability to liberate the mind from the constraints of a necessarily narrow political definition of the objectives of the Struggle, and an inability to adapt to changing circumstances. As such it bodes ill for future freedom of speech and for the very democratic principles and processes the ANC has defended for so long.

It is all the more dangerous in a multicultural situation, where — even in terms of traditional democracy — a majority group arriving in a position of power may dominate other groupings, not only politically, but culturally. Or, phrased differently, it would be political domination in the guise of culture.

The very need to rely on organisations and "bodies" is suspect. Any "body," most especially a body close to, and in fact established by, political power, poses the threat of appropriation, domination and censorship. Any attempt at "protection" initiated by political concerns contains the possibility of exclusivist practice, just as any program of Affirmative Action (however necessary, and with whatever noble intentions it has been established) runs the risk of promoting favoritism. Many of these risks — and this, too, is an important consideration — may be worth running. Compared to what we have lived through, some of them may pale by comparison. But what is important, for writers and reading public alike, is that the dangers be *recognized* and the advantages and disadvantages be very carefully weighed. It is a matter of rational, and informed, choice: and choice is always a marker of freedom.

The second school of thought about the "management of culture" is expressed in the formation of the National Arts Initiative (NAI). Led by the widely respected writer Njabulo Ndebele, this was launched at a National Arts Policy Plenary in December 1992 as an attempt to assert the independence of the arts from politics by insisting on the need for artists themselves, rather than politicians or bureaucrats, to formulate and control their policies and expressions. There is a certain naïveté in the Initiative's belief that such a divorce of interests is possible. Surely the harsh experience of the Struggle should have brought home the need to revise old exclusivist Western notions of the aesthetic and to acknowledge the incorporation of a broadly defined "relevance" into any description of the arts. While one can sympathise with the motivation behind the exclusion of the

ANC and other political organisations (but not of governmental subsidiaries!) from the Policy Plenary, this decision did expose the NAI to criticism of hypocritical "purism" and even elitism; here, too, was evidence of intolerance and incomprehension. And by focusing exclusively on the producers/creators of art, the grass roots were ignored — i.e. the reality of a massive public of individuals, without whom art would remain a suspect ivory tower. Surely we have shed by now the Romantic illusion of seeing artists as the unacknowledged legislators of the world.

In spite of these misgivings, one must confess to a sense of alarm at the reaction of some ANC spokesmen to the NAI. "Once artists and independent thinkers were labelled communists," wrote NAI spokesperson Mike van Graan in an open letter published in the *Weekly Mail* of May 7–13, 1993, "now they are reactionaries. Once they were enemies of the state, now they are enemies of 'the people' . . . With horror, we watch again as the arts are sacrificed on the altars of political expendience, held ransom by the egos of commissars, conscripted by party political agendas."

Yet it seems to me that the real danger lies in approaching these two formations, DAC and NAI, as mutually exclusive. Their real potential lies in recognising the positive qualities in both: as regards literature, the DAC approach foregrounds the freedom (in fact, the right) to *read,* the NAI the freedom to *write.* And these two concerns are interdependent. Censorship, which inhibits the production of literature, also strikes a blow at the reader's freedom of choice; on the other hand, there would be little point in allowing writers all the freedom they wish if there were not sufficient readers with whom to interact: readers not only from a small privileged enclave, which has largely been the situation in the past, but from the whole broad spectrum of people and cultures in South Africa.

But freedom, of course, also involves responsibility. And whatever choices we make, there will always be dangers threatening both the creativity of the individual and the cultural space of a society. In this lies both the anxiety and the adventure of the writer. What is needed is that precious and precarious equilibrium in which the inspiration of the individual is respected *because* it is individual, but also because it is steeped in, and informed by, a sense of what the individual shares with humanity in general and a specific society in particular. This requires, above all, tolerance. But it also demands a certain kind of *in*tolerance: intolerance of all attempts to harness or subjugate or use the free mind of the creative artist; intolerance of all attempts to exclude anyone from the artistic experience — whether through decree, through illiteracy, or lack of education, or through poverty, or any form of discrimination based on race, religion, gender, language or any other criterion imposed on society.

For the writer this requires the space to operate in as unencumbered and unprescribed a manner as possible. Of course, no artist, no individual, can ever be a "free agent" in the absolute sense. Whether we wish it or not, whether we are conscious of it or not, we are all implicated in one ideology or another. But this does not exclude the need ceaselessly to strive for more freedom than obtains in any given situation. This is why I cannot join any political party. I may be a passionate supporter of the ANC, but not a *blind* supporter. When the ANC was a banned organization without the opportunity to explain its own cause in opposition to the campaign of lies and distortions, I often pleaded its case, in my work and in other actions, to ensure that its voice would be heard: that was part of *my* freedom in a closed society; now that the ANC is available to offer its own explanations and pursue its own policies I have other functions to fulfil (without for a moment abandoning the pursuit of justice and freedom which the organization, throughout its long history, has demonstrated in the face of oppression and persecution).

One of those functions, now as in the dark days of apartheid, is to go beyond the immediacy of political events and organizations, and try to express — from my small corner of the world, and from my limited experience — not only my opposition to whatever threatens the reality of human beings in the world, but also my celebration of those qualities that safeguard and promote our common humanity.

If this function is threatened, in whatever manner and by whatever manifestation of power, the writer should oppose it, in the future as in the past. There is neither posturing nor heroism in this stance: it is a simple statement of fact — the fact of being a writer in a troubled country, scarred by the past, uneasy in the present, anxious yet resolute about the future.

JULY 1993

Literature as Cultural Opposition

Within the general framework of this seminar, *Literature as a Political Force,* I have been invited to focus more specifically on literature as a form of cultural opposition. In other words — and this is an important preliminary caution — politics remains the context, not only as the institution "against" which culture may find itself in opposition, but also as a driving force within culture itself. If this is not always evident in sophisticated Western democracies, the situation in what used to be the Third World and what is now more commonly referred to as the South, continues to foreground the way in which politics permeates and informs every choice and every action of civic and even of private life. A "political novel" in the US or in Europe is a very specific *kind* of novel (i.e. one which overtly interrogates — or promotes — a given ideological system or stance); in South Africa *all* novels, whether so intended by the author or not, are "political" — because in that country, even as it moves out of the dark night of apartheid toward something new, every action, and utterance, and thought, every book and play and poem and song, carries a political load. In the mid-eighties, prompted by a French journalist who had asked me almost flippantly whether it was possible for me to write "a simple love story" if I wished, I

Paper delivered at a seminar on "Literature as a Political Force," Salzburg, July 1993.

tried to put it to the test: and in *States of Emergency* I used as my narrator a man who in a situation of siege tried to write (and live) a love story untainted by politics. Both he and I discovered, inevitably, that a country like South Africa does not allow it. (The difference between us was that, disheartened by the intersection of the private and the public, the narrator of my story abandoned the attempt; *my* novel, on the other hand, was written.)

The experience illuminated the immemorial debate between the "aesthetic" approach ("*l'art pour l'art*") and that of *littérature engagée.* And I must confess that I more and more believe this dichotomy — like all dichotomies? — to be false. Rather than conceiving of "pure art" and "political art" as radical and mutually exclusive opposites, it seems to me, it would be more profitable to regard them as two extreme points on a sliding scale: and the kind of literature produced in any given situation, or by any given author, would be determined simply by the *point* on that scale where one happens to find oneself at that given moment and/or by the *manner* in which the tension between the two extremes on the connecting line is activated. (I am indebted to my wife for the image.)

In the kind of environment that obtains in South Africa, politics is not something which can be abstracted from "real life" as an ideology, a system, a theory, a philosophical "position," but is, instead, a presence in the most ordinary and the most private moves across the chessboard of daily life: the food you eat and where you buy it, your means of transport, the suburb or township in which you live, the work you do, the school your children attend, the person you love and marry, the friends you associate with, *everything* has a political implication. Even an option "out of" politics — in art as much as in life — is a political choice.

In such conditions culture also becomes charged in a different way. To avoid getting bogged down in endless preliminary definitions or redefinitions of politics and of culture, I wish to propose, as a rough working approach, a view of culture as, pre-eminently, that territory in the life of the *polis* where meaning is engendered and shaped — most specifically as a product (but also as a condition) of the interaction between individual and society. It involves society in the process not simply of "performing" or "undergoing" actions within the unfolding of history, but of *reflecting* on that process and that history, trying to *make sense* of it. In what we normally regard as a relatively stable society, these cultural processes surround and inform those of politics, i.e. those which most specifically concern the exercise of power in that society, in the attempt to play the game of the possible. But the moment the internal stability is disturbed, culture finds itself in a position of interrogating, opposing and contesting the workings and instruments of power. This becomes all the more precarious if one considers the basic drive within power politics toward co-option and appropriation: a régime under threat almost reflexively attempts to draw culture within the framework of its own operations.

South Africa provides a particularly dramatic illustration of this kind of historical process. Apartheid, from the very beginning, like Nazism and Stalinism before it, persuaded organized religion, education, even sports, to collaborate with it in its classical colonization of hearts and minds as an accompaniment to the extension of its more blatant political excesses. What made it particularly insidious is that the hegemony of Afrikanerdom itself had begun as a culture of opposition: opposition to the imperialism of Great Britain, but also to the religious and linguistic domination of Dutch which, toward the end of the nineteenth century, came to be perceived more and more as a foreign-based power threatening the evolution of a local culture. In this struggle for independence (within *white* South African society) there was something particularly attractive: and the flourishing of Afrikaans literature, especially after the Anglo-Boer War, made an appreciable contribution to indigenous white culture. Culture, in these circumstances, not only reinforced the struggle for political independence but to a large extent provided it with its moral *raison d'être.* During its long march toward political domination (finally confirmed in the fateful whites-only elections of 1948 that brought the National Party to power), it continually attempted to consolidate its base — by harnessing artists and writers to its cause. And while Afrikaners were in political opposition, i.e. while Afrikaner writers and artists could be persuaded to believe that they belonged to a culture threatened by awe-inspiring economic and political forces from abroad, as well as by a vast multitude of hostile "barbarians" in Africa, their literature remained firmly allied to the cause of what they passionately saw as their emancipation.

But soon after 1948 this began to change. As apartheid emerged as the great consolidating force within Afrikanerdom (and increasingly within the whole of the white community in South Africa), it also adopted more and more overtly the power strategies of the very imperialist establishment that had been dislodged. Instead of learning from their struggle against power the need to avoid the destructive and appropriative exercise of that power, Afrikaners showed themselves only too eager to do unto others what had been done to them. One of the results was that writers within this new establishment began to question the bases of the cause they had previously promoted: initially this was done very cautiously, hesitantly, tentatively — which was understandable, as what they did was regarded as backstabbing within a previously tightly knit family. But gradually they became bolder in their protests; and when as a result, in a move traumatic to both sides, they were ostracised by the new power establishment and ejected from the fortress of Afrikaner interests, they found outside that enclave a new culture of liberation among the black masses, directed against the very hegemony they had previously assisted in establishing. And so another culture of opposition was fostered by the abuses of power by the apartheid régime. Now we are witnessing the dismantling of that dispensation and the likelihood of another historical changeover.

It seems to be a moment that invites celebration. Yet as a writer, having witnessed what has happened before, I also approach it with caution, wondering whether, once again, a culture of opposition may in due course ossify into its own framework of repression. Certainly, one thing has already become clear: the enemy of the writer in South Africa has not been something as readily definable as apartheid, but a much larger and much more ominous force of which apartheid has been only one, localised, avatar. The real enemy is *power:* power which, whatever its form and shape and manifestation, always and ultimately means only one thing—and that is what Musil called "the power to kill." And as long as human society is characterized by the organization of power there will be a need for a culture of opposition to it. In fact, unless there is space for oppositionality and otherness in a culture it cannot really, ever, flourish.

At the same time a cautionary note is appropriate: in opposing power, literature is not innocent of power. The very fact that as writers we believe in "the power of the word" suggests that the enemy, power, lurks in the heart of our very oppositionality. The enemy is also part of ourselves. Even as we use the word to empower ourselves we should acknowledge that this same liberating power is dangerous and may turn against ourselves. This means that, once again, the old forms of binary thinking have to be treated as suspect and we have to move toward more "lateral," more "deconstructive," more "sliding-scale" modes of thinking and of definition.

The question remains whether the power of the word can ever successfully confront that of the state. Are the two not so intrinsically different as to rule out any possibility of contest? (There is the old question whether an elephant and a whale can do battle.) A democratic government is to be contested, and if need be replaced, at the ballot box; the removal of a totalitarian régime requires a total strategy of resistance. Surely violence demands counter-violence, does it not? And if so, then how can one hope to oppose a *political* régime — most pertinently one that abuses its power and represses its citizens — with *cultural* means?

Is it at all *possible* for culture to respond effectively to a political challenge? I know it cannot be quantified: but that does not mean that it cannot happen. It is eminently sensible not to *over*-estimate what literature can effect. Undoubtedly it would be ludicrous to ascribe the present political changes in South Africa (or recent changes in Czechoslovakia, or the USSR, or Chile, or wherever) exclusively to the pressures of culture and the power of literature. And yet it remains an open question, I think, whether those changes would have been thinkable *without* the cultural onslaught. I know from my own experience, from many letters from black and white readers alike, that a novel or a poem or a play *can* work a sea-change in the mind and the perceptions of individuals: helping them to keep faith when all the "facts" appear to shout against it; helping them to discover solidarity in the reassurance that one is never entirely alone; helping them to acknowledge that the Other is no different from oneself. And in these ways, in one mind at a time, a climate has been prepared in South Africa — not only by literature, but by literature among many, many other experiences — in which change has become possible. The *mere* change of political or economic systems amounts to very little unless it is accompanied by a deeper, and more personal, change in attitudes, susceptibilities, and perceptions. And this, as I have argued so many times over so many years, is precisely the domain — inter alia — of literature.

In the play *Sizwe Bansi Is Dead* Athol Fugard demonstrates, in terms both moving and exquisitely funny, how a black man without any means of physical survival in a big city can endure by adopting the identity of a dead man whose passbook (known with terrible irony as the "Book of Life") he has appropriated. What it means in ideological terms, is that he learns to "play the system," to work within it; what it means existentially is that he accedes to an existence without authentic being; what it means in psychological terms is that he survives at the cost of his real identity and his dignity. In all respects a dismal ending. And yet I have seen audiences weep and shout and laugh and cheer as they watched Sizwe Bansi outwit the system. This play has inspired a generation of oppressed people to resume or reinforce their defiance of oppression. From the simple demonstration that — whatever the cost — survival is possible, they have derived the courage to resist in their own lives. And two decades later the system that once held Sizwe Bansi prison has now released him, a free man to the world. There have been many Sizwe Bansis over the years; many deaths too. And from all of those a resurrection has come about. Even in the midst of this process of resurrection Fugard's play has not become irrelevant: in changed circumstances the play serves a new purpose by reminding its spectators never to forget. In its own way, in South Africa and in many other societies, it will continue to correct the insidious silences of history. Kundera has shown all of us how power exercises the faculties of forgetting; surely one of the enduring functions of literature as an oppositional force is to make it impossible for us to forget.

There is little need still to argue that as human beings we not only have physical needs, but *also* spiritual needs; that the mind needs food as much as the body does; that caring for those who require to be fed, or sheltered, or rested, does not preclude, or exclude, the profound need for meaning in our lives. If we need political organization to cope with social and economic demands, we *also* need culture to help us make sense of what is happening to us.

In *The Fixer* Malamud paraphrases Spinoza: "If the State acts in ways that are abhorrent to human nature it's the lesser evil to destroy it." But the question remains whether culture, per se, can offer an *adequate* response to political abuse or outrage *on the level where such a response can be practically effective.* What I am moving toward is the assertion that *if* culture in general or literature in particular is set up as a response to a political challenge, in at least one sense it may be seen to *displace* a different response, or a response on a different level. In other words: if we wish to avoid the use of force, i.e. violent confrontation, by resorting to literature, that text, in this situation, displaces more obvious forms of opposition. Most specifically, literature may then be seen to *take the place* of violence. What I'm arguing now is that *if* we do propose the "use" of literature (to the extent in which literature can ever be "used") in these circumstances, it means that we see in literature at least the possibility of *another kind of violence.* And this, I think, is what literature as cultural opposition comes down to. In *An Act of Terror* I have tried to suggest that violence resides not only in the protagonists' attempt to blow up the State President, or in the moves of the security forces to destroy them in return, but in something as small, yet as momentous, as a heron lowering its foot into a pool of dark water to set in motion ripples of water and light that assault the eye of the beholder.

This view of violence may not be so far-fetched after all. All that is required is to acknowledge that violence, like power, need not be only destructive but that it can be a creative force in its own right; that, in fact, violence determines our being in the world. Not only rape and assault and death are acts of violence: the act of love itself is violent; the division of cells that results from it is a violent process, as is birth, growth, interacting with an environment or with others. Violence resides in our testing of limits, in all the processes of transgression through which we confront and interrogate our world in order to extend its frontiers. Every question we pose, to ourselves or to the world, affirms a species of violence without which we shall remain forever imprisoned in a very narrow space preordained, from outside ourselves, by a system of power: by custom or tradition, by the law, by others and by otherness. What concerns me at the moment, in the context of the familiar Sartrean equation, is to validate literature as a form of human — specifically cultural — involvement which goes beyond the gesture of the actor on his stage: it is that kind of "*essential* gesture" Gordimer has spoken about, which acquires the weight of an act — an act of (creative) violence to counter the (destructive) violence which is the hallmark of power. What I am appealing to is that mind-set which inspired Wallace Stevens to describe the mind as "a violence from within that protects us from a violence without. It is the imagination pressing back against the pressure of reality."

In a relatively free and democratic society, as I have already intimated, this is not so obvious, as (state) power can be countered on a "purely" political level (in parliament, in public debate, in the press, in elections); but in a closed society like the one we are still in the process of dismantling in South Africa, overt political contestation may often be proscribed. The successive states of emergency proclaimed by the beleagured minority government of my country during the eighties imposed a distressing silence on community life: state-controlled radio and television broadcast only stunted, truncated, officially sanctioned versions of reality; most organisations in political opposition to the régime were banned and thousands of individuals jailed, exiled or silenced in other ways; newspapers, their functions controlled by over one hundred different laws, were not allowed to report freely on what was euphemistically called the "unrest" in the country — in fact, they were not even allowed to leave blanks which might alert the public to the machinations of censorship. In these circumstances culture was one of the only territories of public life left relatively free as a forum of opposition and contestation. Culture became, as Joyce says in Stoppard's *Travesties,* "the continuation of war by other means." This happened precisely because the government, composed largely of culturally ignorant individuals, either did not take culture seriously or lacked the manpower effectively to continue controlling the arts as it had done in the seventies, the attention of the security police being required more urgently elsewhere, to contain the growing black trade union movement, contestation within education and religion and the mounting pressure exerted by the United Democratic Front.

In the seventies censorship had been a real menace to creativity, almost succeeding in stifling, among other things, a generation of young writers in Afrikaans (after an explosion of new talent in the sixties only two novelists of some significance emerged in Afrikaans during the entire decade of the seventies). Censorship created a stifling climate of fear in which the security police had their hands full keeping writers under surveillance. I was personally subjected to interrogations, house searches, the confiscation of books, manuscripts, notes, even of typewriters; attempts were made to sabotage my car and to set my house on fire, and there were endless threats to kill members of my family or myself. Even so this, it should be emphasised, was nothing compared to the indignities, the persecution, and the dangers black writers were subjected to. Many of them literally placed not only their freedom but their very lives at stake by continuing to write, and to read their stories, recite their poems, perform their plays.

At a time when the media were denied the possibility of performing their most basic duty, that of reporting, writers, actors, dancers, musicians, painters, sculptors were forced to assume much of this function — in order to ensure, quite simply, that people were informed about what was happening in the silences surrounding them.

In the process, the limits of culture were constantly tested, and expanded. Even in writing that was often reduced to reporting and to sloganeering there was a vital experience of giving and taking, of being enriched by the processes of cultural communication. Critics, especially from the outside, tend to see this as a process only of impoverishment and of reduction. Recently one of them (Vincent Crapanzano) wrote in an American newspaper:

> Writers writing in South Africa are served, as one is served a summons, their subject matter: apartheid — its scandal; its moral and political consequences; the separation, the misunderstanding, the un-understanding it produces. Even when they have tried to refuse that summons they are caught by it,

for whatever they write is read in terms of racial politics. The rift produced by apartheid limits the imagination.

I shall return to this remark. But for the moment I wish to pursue my image of the other side of the coin, the dark side of this moon: the important positive qualities of this experience of cultural opposition to a deadly system. Far beyond the needs of reporting, the kind of writing that emerged during the dark years of apartheid fostered a spirit of sharing, and of solidarity in the face of a defined and definable enemy. Black society, menaced by divisions into a multiplicity of language and culture groups, was inspired by the affirmation of what all its members had in common.

And white writers too — at least those of us who found our writing informed more and more by our experience with and among a community of black friends — began to function not only as "reporters," but as "interpreters" of what we had been privileged to witness among those whose lives had been so effectively sealed off by apartheid from the eyes and the awareness of the white minority. Literature became indispensable to the many new processes of conscientising at work throughout the community. And we, too, as white writers, began to experience that solidarity, that heady intimation of a new South African identity beginning to announce and define itself behind the official definitions.

What apartheid effected, notably through the seventies and eighties, was an increasing interaction among writers from different cultural streams, a new sense of solidarity, a new perception — and a testing — of at least the *possibility* of an emerging common identity. Of course many differences still remain — and this need not be a negative perception at all, as the affirmation of cultural diversity may well be as important as that of solidarity — but the appreciation of such an interaction has already had significant consequences for an emergent culture.

This emergent culture is enriched by forms stimulated

through the context of the struggle for liberation when access to traditional and formal means of production and distribution was fraught with many difficulties and threats. Many of these forms reached back to a long tradition of African orature: poets who could not risk publishing their verse, playwrights denied access to regular theatres, resorted to the reading and reciting, or the haphazard performance of their work at impromptu gatherings arranged at short notice and ready to disperse at the first warning of police approaching. Fugard, Mda, Ngema and others brought new meaning to the Grotowskian experience of "Poor Theatre" by fusing it with African traditions of improvisation; great poetry recitals drew the kind of crowds one would normally expect at a soccer match. Even today, when Mandela addresses a crowd, there is invariably a poet on the stage to combine the functions of the traditional *mbongi* or praise poet and the revolutionary poet of fiery contestation. Much of it may be demagogic, much of it remains on the level of sloganeering: but the surprising thing is that so much of it (witness Serote, Gwala, Dikeni and many others) is good by any standards, opening whole new ranges of possibilities to old established traditions.

Another aspect of the functioning of literature as a form of cultural opposition has been highlighted by the South African experience of the seventies and eighties: that is the *dual* nature of the writer's position in society.

There is, first, her or his *text,* the work, the written product of private and interactive battles, agonies, explorations and celebrations. Because of the nature of the textual challenges they pose, some of these, like the poems of Breyten Breytenbach or the novels of J. M. Coetzee, may be accessible only to a relatively small group of highly sophisticated readers; others, like the work of Struggle poets who would be horrified if anyone found their verse "beautiful" (as beauty, in their perception, would stand in the way of the political conscientisation and galvanization that is their stated aim), have the widest imaginable appeal. If in the West poetry has become perhaps the most reclusive of the literary arts, among South African blacks it has the audience of a TV soap opera.

But apart from, and in addition to, the *texts* produced by a given writer, that writer, by virtue of her or his notoriety, is empowered as an *individual* within the wide community. Thousands of people who have never read a poem by Breytenbach — thousands who cannot read at all — are inspired by the writer who has demonstrated, through his life, his solidarity with their cause. And *because* he is a writer, yet irrespective of what he has written, Breytenbach occupies a position of influence which charges cultural opposition with political force.

None of this necessarily means, as Crapanzano (quoted above) so readily jumps to conclude, that apartheid has curtailed the imagination — in the sense that during that period of threat and deprivation South African writers should have felt "obliged" (whether by external circumstances or by an inner compulsion) to produce overtly political texts. To begin with, as my reference to Breytenbach and Coetzee should have made clear (and any number of other names may be added to theirs) not all South African writers *did* write "Struggle literature"; and not all "Struggle literature" was facile sloganeering. At the very least the texts produced under those circumstances can only be read contextually. But, more importantly, I know of no South African writer who wrote "political literature" simply because he or she believed that it was "expected" of her or him. In the best of the texts that emerged from apartheid one cannot but discover the remarkable coincidence of what a given writer *wanted* and *chose* to write — and what circumstances *expected* her or him to write. In this respect there was no "summons" served on any writer. If it is a truism that one can only write about one's most urgent personal experience then apartheid *was* that experience, determining every waking and sleeping instant of one's life.

Culture, it is true, presents a space in which the writer confronts the real (i.e. whatever passes for "real" in any given context). But this does not mean that, working within the conditions and constraints of a closed society, some kind of social realism is the only dreary option. Even when the writer is involved in the real, as has been dictated to such a large extent by the apartheid experience, the writer's vocation — if one dare presume, if one dare generalise — has always been, not to *report* the real but to *imagine* the real.

When I was working on *A Chain of Voices* I came to know almost by heart the archival documentation about the slave revolt the novel attempted to re-present: the depositions, in the trial court, of all the accused and all the witnesses involved in the case; I familiarized myself with whatever I could lay hands or eyes on that had anything to do with that time and that place; I visited the region of the Bokkeveld where the action had taken place; the house in which slave and master confronted each other in that ultimate turbulent silence; the oven in which the wounded woman tried to stow away from the insurgents; the loft where the slave Galant and the white woman Hester hid — in an intriguing enclave of silence undisturbed by all the documents — while the others went on the rampage downstairs. But *knowing* all this was to no avail. It was only when I attempted that dangerous fire-leap from self to other, that history could become what it had always yearned to be, namely *story:* and for this it was necessary to try to *imagine* what it is like to be a slave who has been promised his freedom and sees that hope frustrated; to imagine what it is like to be a woman who has to sacrifice her independence to the inarticulate domination of a husband; to imagine what it *means* to be fierce patriarch or uncomprehending child or dour matron or protective mother or wild adventurer — slaves, all of them, locked in an inescapable chain of voices, sprung from earth, cleansed in water, seared in fire, wanton with wind. Only in the leap from history to story, and from world to word, does literature as a form of cultural opposition find its true voice: opposition to the lie, opposition to injustice, opposition to the unfreedom which in one form or another holds us all.

★

This is the freedom of writing, demonstrated most urgently in writing in the state of siege South Africa experienced under apartheid. But there can be danger even in this experience—and South African writers, like others throughout the erstwhile Second and Third Worlds, are beginning to make this discovery as they emerge from their many forms of oppression and try to map the new world unfolding around them. The very openness of this new space can be frightening, because it is so indefinite, so undefined. There can be something very reassuring about knowing your enemy very well: he is *there* (the enemy is always a "he"); he is visible, circumscribed, present, known. How disturbingly intimate the relationship between the oppressed and his or her oppressor, the self and the other. And when that other falls away, or begins to disintegrate and become diffuse, opaque, amorphous, inchoate, one is threatened, suddenly, by the discovery of a loss of something that has become indispensable to one's definition of oneself. This is when the danger of power—in this case, apartheid—becomes so distressingly evident: in the discovery that one has come to rely on that very enemy, power, to sustain oneself. A literature of opposition now becomes a questioning of the *self.*

It is a difficult thing to face, and a precarious experience: but it is, above all, necessary. Only now can one begin to establish the implications of that "summons" issued by apartheid which Crapanzano has referred to. But the problem was not a "limiting of the imagination" as he so confidently asserts. The imagination has always been active within the cage of apartheid: decorating and masking the bars or painting them in such stark colors that the awareness of their presence was dramatised; intensifying the exploration of the cramped space inside; reaching out into the limitless Beyond. The problem was, instead, that the *functioning* of that imagination remained predicated on the presence of prison bars. This favored a reliance on easy oppositions and binarities, on manichean models, and on predefined otherness (*however understandable—and sometimes necessary—those reactions may have been at the time*).

What I mean is this: that a culture of resistance can become a habit like any other. A literature which becomes used to asserting itself only in the face of a menacing opposition may in the long run dissipate all its energies in expressing what it is *against* rather than what it is *for.* To learn to define oneself *only* with reference to the other (that is, as the *object* of the other rather than as its own *subject*) is to deny a whole dimension of existence. And even before the darkness has entirely withdrawn from South Africa it was becoming obvious that it no longer sufficed to portray apartheid as evil or to take up a stance against it: everybody more or less in her or his right mind knew that, and was that. Perhaps, as Gordimer once pointed out, part of the South African sickness was precisely that people began to term "courageous" or "heroic" that which was only normal and natural. Even that may not be so bad (especially not if it involves at least an attempt to define the sickness, to recognise it as such): the problem arises when a whole literature threatens (and I mean this literally) to become oppositional and *only* oppositional in the most elementary sense of the word.

In the late nineteenth century many painters were so discouraged by the rise of photography as the medium *par excellence* in which to capture the "true likeness" they had been laboring to reproduce that they abandoned painting; this, it seems to me, is the kind of artistic and moral crisis many writers in recently liberated societies are experiencing at the moment. But does this *malaise* not result from an altogether too restricted, even fallacious, concept both of "writing" or of "the real"? There were painters at the end of the nineteenth century who made the exhilarating discovery that, in fact, painting had never had anything to do with the production of "true likenesses": instead, it had everything to do with working in paint on canvas. And it seems to me that this is the true challenge of the newly evolving situation in writing: the (re)discovery of the fact that literature arises out of a peculiar relationship with *language,* and with that reality which can be made accessible only through language.

Part of the present problem faced by literature in South Africa is that it can no longer slip so easily into the silences previously imposed by the government and — literally — circumscribed by the media: in the present circumstances there is a frenzy of *over*commentary and *over*exposure. Rather than articulating against silence the new literature has to make itself heard against the clamor of the media, the babble of too many other voices. And it is the function of the media both to globalise and to trivialise. More than ever before — acknowledging that there is no point in trying to make oneself heard by shouting more loudly than anyone else — literature has to find space for the private vision, the personal imagination, the individual small, still voice. This does not mean a return to nineteenth-century heroic individualism or early twentieth-century Freudian egoism, or mid-twentieth-century existentialist solitude, but the articulation of a personal space *informed* by an experience of suffering and witnessing with others.

It is not just a matter of freeing the imagination: it is changing the conditions of its operation. Much of it concerns history, as whole tracts of past experience silenced by apartheid, by over three centuries of colonialism, are now to be reclaimed, reinvented, reimagined into story. This may be a vital part of the real opposition embodied in South African literature of the future: constantly to oppose the present with a recovered past, in order to open more possibilities for the future.

When the young poet Sandile Dikeni was in prison he began to recite poems through the bars of his cell every night when the inmates bedded down: and at all the barred windows they would cluster, like grapes, like bats, to inhale these words in which their own anger and suffering and loss and loneliness and hope were given shape. They refused to go to sleep unless he had first offered them a poem. Sometimes he would use words they had never heard, strange and disquieting music in their ears. One morning a fellow prisoner accosted him. "This poem you recited last night," he said, "had a word in it I don't know. This *soliloquy:* what does it mean?" Sandile gave him the meaning of the word and then promised he'd never use such strange words again. "Oh no," said the other prisoner, "you must, you must: for now I know a new word."

I come from a literature that still has many new words to learn: and with each new word new possibilities enter the realm of the imagination and extend the prison-house of our language. They offer us new means of contesting — of responding to — the challenges of the real.

And not only the real (the reality of political power; even the reality of democracy) has to be confronted in processes of cultural resistance: language itself, which is the condition of both our affirmations and our oppositions, is to be interrogated and contested. This may seem an impossible task.

And yet! Is this not what it really amounts to in the end? — the opposition posed by literature as an interface of the possible and the impossible. For too long we have concentrated, in South Africa and elsewhere, simply in order to survive, on the *possible:* this is what has made our lives impossible. Only by dreaming and writing the *impossible* can life be made possible once again.

APRIL 1994

A Farm in Africa

We tumble out of bed when the doorbell rings. It is Atwell, the gardener; no one else has quite the same peremptory ring, demanding access very promptly at seven every Wednesday morning. Today, however, he is late — not out of sympathy with the fact that we returned only last night from six weeks in France, taxed with the accumulated fatigues and excitements of travel, but simply because there have been no taxis this morning and the buses are observing a leisurely Sunday schedule.

Atwell is really Jongibandla Bontsa, but in a market ruled by whites he has chosen the English tag to match the persona he has adopted for his job as a gardener. He has a small farm in Transkei, but has been obliged for the past thirty years to work in the Cape, saving up for the day he can go back to run his property; unfortunately his earnings are really just enough to keep him here, and all he can manage is a brief annual visit to his family. Atwell loves to start his day with a good solid conversation, but on this particular morning he doesn't bother to inquire about our trip or to solicit any comment on the immaculate state of the garden left to his care. All he asks, his

Contribution to *S.A. April 27, 1994*, a collection of essays by 45 writers on their impressions of Election Day, April 1994. Published by Queillerie Publishers, Cape Town and Pretoria, 1994.

broad muscular frame pinched in an unusually natty outfit, is, "When are we going to vote?"

I'll check with Marésa, I inform him. Last night's TV preview of the elections has made us reluctant to brave the early-morning queues. Even though the election is the sole reason for our return, there is no need to provoke unnecessary punishment.

When I return to the bedroom with the tea — the joys of being home again — Marésa has already turned on the television. Not an auspicious beginning to the day: the bomb blast at Jan Smuts airport; chaos at polling booths all over the country. The announcers are doing their level best to improve on their own records of vagueness and confusion. (The South African media are sitting on one of the stories of the century, a British journalist commented over the weekend, yet all they can manage is to be dull. There will be stupendous proof of it as the day unfolds.) Filled with dire foreboding, having been informed over the past week of the apocalyptic expectations sweeping the country, we immerse ourselves in the day. Marésa tackles the first bundle of washing and gets a *bredie* going; I venture out into the cold grey gloom of the clouds obscuring Table Mountain.

"When are we going to vote?" asks Atwell as I open the garage door, not yet having made any attempt to exchange his election outfit for his garden gear.

"By midday," I inform him. "The queues are too long right now."

"Is that what Marésa says?" he enquires. He has always been reluctant to take my word for anything; I am not, and he knows it distressingly well, a practical person.

"That is what Marésa says," I confirm. "*And* the television."

Outside the café where I go for the papers and some milk and fruit juice (in defiance of reports over the last fortnight about white South Africans cleaning out supermarkets to stock up for an expected siege, we have made no arrangements to make unusual provision for any but our daily needs), a black man in blue overalls is struggling against the gusty Northwester to get a *stompie* going. "Fukkit," he grumbles after every spent match. "Fukkit, fukkit." It isn't clear whether he is referring to the frustration of his urge to smoke, or the wretched weather, or even the elections.

Inside, the Muslim owner and his family and a gangly bearded white youth are watching images of the bomb blast on the fly-speckled screen of the TV perched on the cold drinks fridge. "It's these Dutch who are doing it," pronounces the young man with great conviction. "That's why I'll never vote for the National Party."

I return home. Both papers have front-page reports on the lowering, at midnight, of the old Union flag and the hoisting of the bold and bright new one. The *Cape Times* carries photographs of both events; *Die Burger,* of course, features only the demise of the old.

I hang out the washing. Atwell appears round the corner. "When are we going?" he asks.

"Later," I assure him. "Have you finished weeding the herb garden?"

There is the accumulated work of six weeks to get to grips with; even on historic days ordinary life goes on. Not without interruption, though. The phone keeps on ringing. Newspapers, radio and television stations from Paris, Helsinki, Copenhagen, London, Rome, Jerusalem, Washington, wanting comments, demanding interviews. I'm sorry, I tell them brightly, Mr. Brink is away, I have no contact number for him. The sorting of the work proceeds in fits and starts. In the background the TV is on automatic pilot, coursing steadily through the day's chaotic progress. (Mandela. De Klerk. Blithe or harassed spokespersons of the Independent Electoral Commission. The First Lady. *I only hope,* says Marike, *that the new South Africa will still have place for the values we have all grown up with.*

A knock on the door. "Is it not time now?" asks Atwell.

"I'll come and tell you," I promise. "Why don't you trim the edges of the lawn?"

He utters an undefinable sound and ambles off.

The weather is getting worse. I remember a Christmas Day when I was five or six: playing outside with my presents, I stopped to gaze up at the fierce blue sky that seemed no different from other days. Surely, I thought, on Christmas Day there ought to be a special look about the sky to *tell* us that it's a special day? Today's leaden skies bear no exceptional message either; and yet this is the hinge where future turns on past, where everything is supposed to change, to change utterly. (On the day after Mandela's release from prison a journalist in Grahamstown took to the streets for comments from ordinary citizens. "And how do *you* feel," he asked a black hawker sitting beside her wares on the pavement in front of OK Bazaars, "about Mandela being free?" The woman looked at him placidly. "I still have trouble selling my vegetables," she said.)

A knock on the door. Atwell presents a pair of broken shears; from a pocket he produces his voluminous white alarm clock. "It is now fifteen minutes past eleven," he says.

I know when I am beaten. "All right, we can go now."

We have consulted with friends on the telephone; the polling station closest to our house is reported to have a shorter queue than most others. With a sense of historical fulfilment we set out. What we do not know is that the shambles in the black township of Khayelitsha, where no ballot papers have been delivered, has resulted in busloads of voters being transported to our suburb of Mowbray. When we arrive there, just as the rain begins to come down, there is a formidable queue, four or five abreast, reaching hundreds of metres to the speedway and halfway back. This is going to take at least two hours, I tell Atwell.

"We wait," he says.

"Not in this rain," says Marésa. "I'll vote tomorrow." She drops off the two of us with a black umbrella, and drives home for raincoats which she delivers ten minutes later. By that time we are already swept up into the waiting crowd and the line behind us is lengthening. The pouring rain turns out to be a great unifier of human souls and bodies. Holding the umbrella over

Atwell's head and mine, I find both my arms pushed heavenward, like those of an ancient Moses blessing the promised land, as two women duck under them for protection; at least four more people huddle against us to find some semblance of protection.

"This is a blessed day," announces a solemn young man behind us, beaming upwards into the rain.

And so begins a memorable wait which is to last for just over six hours.

There are brief let-ups in the rain, but the earth is soggy, everybody is bedraggled and spattered with mud; yet there is a buoyancy, an unrestrained exuberance in the crowd. We are representative of the whole rainbow of South Africa, all shades from shiny bootpolish black via various browns and ochres and beiges to the many shades of pale that pass for white; in the common predicament of the bad weather and the shared experience of waiting — throughout the seemingly interminable day I remind myself that in a language like Spanish the word for *waiting* also means *hoping* — pools of conversation in the long crowd spill into each other to form one moving river of talk: bantering, encouraging, teasing, laughing, sharing, in Xhosa and Sotho and English and Afrikaans. Businessmen and streetsweepers, academics and domestics, society ladies and chars, the affluent and the jobless, all mingle easily, even enthusiastically. (What is going to become of the First Lady's "values"?) From the badges some people are wearing, and the posters and flags on minibuses bringing in ever more people, it is clear that most of the parties contesting the election are also represented among us: yet no one, as far as I can make out, speaks a word of party politics. Instead, we talk about our lives, our jobs, our families, about the long wait. And the tone is mostly lighthearted, easygoing, with laughter constantly hovering just below the surface.

At one o'clock Marésa arrives with coffee for Atwell and me; like the Biblical loaves and fishes the two cups multiply to be shared by seven, eight, ten, a dozen people; the last drops of sugar at the bottom are noisily slurped up by a cherubic black baby waiting on his mother's lap in a minibus.

There are many people with babies or small children: not a very wise idea, I think in the beginning — but as the day wears on I begin to wonder whether they were not more prescient than us. By the time we reach the booths most of these children may well be old enough to vote.

More samaritans appear with buns and fruit and juice and coke to dish out; still others turn up with bundles of black plastic refuse bags to use as cover against the rain. Soon a whole variety of new fashions, all in black plastic, are devised, leading to more banter and laughter.

At one stage we are stuck in the same mudpool for an hour and a half; no one knows what has caused it, yet no one complains. There are no toilet facilities, so from time to time men drop out of the line and cross the broad street to a watertower on the far side.

At irregular intervals Atwell takes out his alarm clock to check the time. "I think we shall still be here at three," he says. Which is when he usually knocks off. But he seems unperturbed by the prospect.

Two o'clock. Half-past. Three o'clock. Half-past. Four o'clock. Marésa returns with more coffee and a hamper of biscuits; this time there is enough for twenty or thirty members of the crowd. "Thank you, Mama. Thank you, Mama," they call out after her.

The solemn black youth behind me turns out to be one of my first-year students. If I don't mind, he proposes at one stage, and since it is obvious we have the time, why don't I give him some notes on a prescribed book he is having some problems with? It becomes a full-fledged lecture.

Half-past four. We are now at the edge of the sports complex which serves as voting center.

Occasionally the conversations falter and subside; people are really getting exhausted now. But what the hell. Every inch one shuffles along is a step closer to that consummation. Here I've been waiting for six hours: some of these people have been waiting for thirty, forty, fifty, sixty *years.* The country has been waiting for centuries.

Five o'clock. We are very close now. And each face emerging from those big doors ahead carries the radiant message of fulfilment, of a joy too great to express in words. New ripples of cheerfulness beset the crowd. We have all become members of one great extended family. Black, brown, white: in the course of this one day a quiet miracle has been taking place. A mere week ago some people have begun to barricade themselves in their homes, expecting a wave of violence to swamp them today. What is happening here is the opposite. We are discovering, through the basic sharing of this experience, that we are all South Africans. It is as simple and as momentous as that. Most of us will return to our separate existences tomorrow. In the commotion of the coming days, months, years, much of this day may fade. But one thing we cannot, ever, forget: the knowledge of having been here together; the awareness of a life, a country, a humanity we share. By achieving what has seemed impossible we have caught a glimpse of the possible.

Half-past five. Atwell and I have reached the threshold. Briefly, we look at each other. We put our hands on each other's shoulders. Then we go in, each on his own, but sharing a small precious moment of history.

It takes only a minute. We return from the cubicles, Jongibandla Bontsa and I. Marésa is waiting to take us home. It is over.

It will never be over.

DECEMBER 1994

Toward a Syncretic Future

CHOICE OF LANGUAGE: THE NGUGI OPTION

The dilemma faced by the African writer in choosing a language is poignantly expressed in a lament by the Kenyan poet Okot p'Bitek:

My husband says
Some of the answers
Cannot be given in Acholi
Which is a primitive language
And is not rich enough
To express deep wisdom
He says the Acholi language
Has very few words
It is not like the white man's language
Which is rich and very beautiful
A language fit for discussing deep thoughts.

It is an attitude corroborated by recent experience in South Africa when a newly established publisher (Kwela) specifically aimed at the indigenous-language market, invited black writers to submit manuscripts in the language of their choice; every single manuscript received was written in English. At the same

Colloquium on the problem of language in African literature, Université Paul Valéry, Montpellier, December 1994.

time Oxford University Press decided to publish a prize-winning volume of short stories by a Zulu writer: but he had written it in English and declined the invitation to translate the volume himself, explaining in an interview that he "felt more at home in English." (I owe these examples to Adriaan van Dis.)

The classic example produced by the long-running debate about writing in the language of the (ex-)coloniser and writing in the vernacular, is of course that of Ngugi wa Thiong'o. His famous choice in favour of the indigenous languages must be admired as a choice against "cultural imperialism" (Ngugi 1981:15), in the belief that "values, cultures, politics and economics are all tied up together" (Ngugi 1981:78) and expressed in language; so that "to choose a language is to choose a world" (Ngugi 1981:53). And if we bear in mind that one of the first philosophical comments from a linguistic point of view on the exploits of the Spanish conquistadores was that "language is the perfect instrument of Empire" (quoted by Barker and Hulme 1985:197), Ngugi's choice appears logical, even inevitable.

Yet the matter is infinitely more complicated. First, let us be brutally realistic: it is significant that Ngugi made his choice in favour of Gikuyu over English only after he had become world-famous as an author, as a result of which his voice had come to carry particular weight internationally. Had he made his decision before the publication of *A Grain of Wheat* (1967) it is not unlikely that he might still have been a largely unknown writer and that his tremendous influence on the rise of the African novel might have remained untapped. His appeal made sense only inasmuch as it advocated a *return* to the vernacular *after* international success in English. Also, in more cynical mood perhaps, one may reflect that Ngugi could opt for Gikuyu because he was sure that as a result of his (deserved) stature his works written in Gikuyu would automatically and immediately be translated into English anyway (and via English into other world languages).

Ideologically even more significant is the fact that his rejection of African literature written in a language like English as "non-African" ("it is Afro-Saxon literature": Ngugi 1981:59) is a denial of Ngugi's own persistent and important claim that languages are not immutable givens but historically determined phenomena. In other words, if Ngugi writes in English his very choice already turns that English into something quite different from the "language of the conqueror" or "the language of the colonizer." If, like all other forms of cultural expression, language can be changed, renewed, reinvented, appropriated, an essentialist view would reduce our arguments to the absurd. Purism is too simplistic to be accepted any longer as an argument in informed academic or cultural debate.

However much one may be prompted by nostalgic or romantic impulses to wish for a return to pre-colonial times, such an urge cannot bear much weight in the kind of discussion we are trying to engage in today. Exposure — and even subjugation — to colonial practice has irrevocably changed the face and fibre of Africa; and the literatures we are faced with have to be approached with that historical consciousness and within that historical context. Oppression, exploitation, dehumanisation, slavery of many kinds, have ravaged the ex-colonial territories of the world. Neo-colonialism may in its own way be as pernicious as full-blown "original" colonialism. But these facts and their effects cannot just be wished away; and so the simple distinction between the indigenous and the imperial can no longer be made.

An analogy: to revert to the abomination of female circumcision in Africa simply because it implies taking a stand against "the West" is as outrageous and myopic as to reject medical science because it is practised by white doctors; or, from the opposite point of view, to reject neighbourly love because *ubuntu* (that unique amalgam of generosity, compassion and understanding) is an African concept. We should try as dispassionately as possible to evaluate the present situation in order to move toward the future: a future which to me seems to make sense only in terms of the embrace of syncretism.

SOUTH AFRICA: SOLIDARITY AND DIVISION

I should like to focus specifically on aspects of the situation in South Africa, inasmuch as these may shed light on the larger problem of language in African literature, but without wishing to suggest for a moment that everything which can be extrapolated from the South African experience must be relevant to the rest of the continent.

As in so many colonial territories, foreign missionaries made an enormous if highly ambivalent contribution to the development of indigenous literatures in the nineteenth century. Ambivalent, because in providing the indigenous languages with forms of written expression and in nudging orature toward literature, they unabashedly loosened the very foundations on which those cultures rested, superimposing on indigenous communities a set of values and beliefs that turned out in many respects to be not only disruptive but destructive. Ambivalent, also, because simultaneously with providing localised and often enclosed indigenous cultures with an international forum and a window to the world, they shook the confidence and self-esteem of indigenous peoples and fostered the insidious belief that there was nothing inherently valuable about these cultures: their languages, and the products of those languages, were portrayed as mere ethnic curiosities.

Even in one of the most remarkable flowerings of black South African literature — the work of the *Drum* generation in the fifties — one discovers not only a positive impulse (the appropriation and reinvention of the American jazz culture), but a negative one as well (a feeling of inadequacy, even of shame, as far as indigenous language and literature were concerned).

An unfortunate byproduct of this development has been an alarming shift in the cultural values embodied in the terms "black" and "African": both of them represent a loss of an earlier holism ("Africa was never dark to us," said Bessie Head). But "black" has become more and more a racialised, i.e. a politically orientated, response to "white," while "African" implies more specifically a response to the cultural-geographic notion of "European" — in certain contexts it may even imply a celebration of "rural" values in opposition to the "urban" values of Europe. And in such a distinction, based on a questionable acceptance of "othering" by the West, many valuable nuances may be lost.

Yet the development has not been altogether negative. Even the English written by the *Drum* generation was something quite different from the "white" English of Europe and America: it was one of the first steps toward the breakdown of the facile relationship between imperial center and colonial margin, which in recent years has led to the ascendancy of literatures produced by the erstwhile "margins" — Africa, Canada, Australia, India, etc. — over those of the metropolis. (The Booker Prize over the last decade bears witness to this trend, and the same is becoming evident in French.)

But the importance of English in the South African socio-culturo-political context goes further than this. By the time the apartheid régime came to power and began to apply in such a devastating manner the old Divide and Rule principle (in order to enable a small white minority to control a massive black majority), English was already in place as a potential forum of opposition. Let us have no illusions about the motives of earlier régimes in imposing the English language on the many different cultures in South Africa: it was just another demonstration of the awareness that "language is the perfect instrument of empire." Yet without this development the apartheid system might well have succeeded in permanently subjugating the fragmented cultures of the country. In conjunction with many other forces, external and internal, it was the fact that all the minorities within the overall majority of the oppressed in South Africa could transcend their historical differences and divergences and meet the threat of divisiveness head-on with the strength of their solidarity, expressed in a *lingua franca,* that finally brought apartheid down.

Through the galvanising effects of poetry recitals, play performances, song festivals (and the exploitation of many other art forms), through the organization of resistance movements in which Xhosa and Zulu and Sotho and Venda and Tswana could fuse their resistance and minimise their differences, it was possible in the long run to triumph. Needless to say, in the process the English language was transformed even more radically than before, broken loose from its moorings, allowed to reinvent itself on African soil, infused by the rhythms and sounds of Africa, expressive of the African experience and of African perceptions and perspectives.

Much of the literature produced by this struggle has been purely pragmatic and unifocal: even so, it dramatically served its purpose. But now, with that part of the struggle behind us, the truly exhilarating discovery is that much of that literature can (still) hold its own in purely literary terms. And the very phrase "in purely literary terms" has become loaded with more, and more shaded, meanings than before: the Western aesthetic tradition, inasmuch as it was conveyed by the English language, has become radically altered through its interaction with the demands and expressions of the experience of struggle. "Aesthetic," in South Africa today, means something startlingly different from what it meant to F. R. Leavis or Gustave Lanson.

But already the South African experience goes beyond the struggle for liberation. For the achievement of that primary object has brought about a new emphasis on the variegated nature of local culture, and on the many indigenous traditions long neglected by the different priorities foregrounded by the period of struggle. It is certainly time, now, more than ever before, for programs fostering the development of literatures in the indigenous languages: for drawing more assiduously on the rich oral traditions of Zulu, Xhosa, Sotho etc.; but also for encouraging written traditions that have already emerged.

Even though much of the writing in indigenous languages has been determined by the market and demands of prescribed books at school — controlled and manipulated and exploited by white initiative, published by white firms, distributed by white organisations, within an education system devised by whites — there has been a persistent trickle of poetry and fiction in the "black" languages; it goes without saying that this should now be systematically encouraged.

Even so, the most formidable obstacle faced by *any* indigenous literature in South Africa, even when written in English, is that of illiteracy. Given that up to 60% of the total South African population may be unable at this moment to read and write, literature becomes something of an élitist concern. Massive programs of education have to be instituted, even on the most basic level, that of mother-tongue primary education, where indigenous literature may find its most valuable initial openings in children's books. Most of us are agreed on this. The only question is whether we are going to face it as a problem — or as a challenge. The present mood in South Africa favors the notion of challenge. And this may point the way for other African societies as well.

THE EXPERIENCE OF AFRIKAANS

The development and the changing function(s) of the Afrikaans language provide a case study to illuminate my argument.

As happened in the case of other European languages (English, French, Portuguese, Spanish, etc.), the Dutch that was brought to the Cape of Good Hope in the seventeenth century soon became deformed and/or revitalized (depending on one's point of view) in the mouths of indigenous speakers; the role of slaves, originating from West and East Africa, Madagascar, and especially Indonesia, was decisive in the shaping of what soon became known as "Afrikaans" (that is, "African"), just as its speakers, many of whom were the products of miscegenation, called themselves "Afrikaners." At least three tiers developed in the linguistic and social stratification at the Cape:

1. The officials of the Dutch East India Company who came and went, retained their ties with Holland (and, it should be mentioned, Batavia) and spoke Dutch.

2. The white and mixed-blood colonists and artisans (including a small but growing component of "Free Blacks," mainly manumitted slaves) who identified themselves more and more with Africa, in opposition to Europe, and who spoke various forms of the developing Afrikaans language; increasing numbers of immigrants from France and Germany were also assimilated into this group.

3. Imported slaves and indigenous Khoisan peoples (followed, since the late eighteenth century, by various Bantu peoples) who spoke their various vernacular languages but adopted Afrikaans as their *lingua franca,* both among themselves and in dealing with the colonisers.

For more than two centuries Afrikaans developed as a quasi-indigenous language *in opposition to* the official European language (first Dutch, later English) of the power establishment. Then, toward the end of the nineteenth century, it became the language of resistance against both the political establishment (associated with English) and the religious and cultural establishment (Dutch): in fact, it became Africa's first language of revolt against the European invader. And it should be mentioned in passing that on several occasions in the nineteenth century white Afrikaner farmers and black Xhosas along the eastern frontier of the Cape Colony joined forces against the English imperial power. The Anglo–Boer War (1899–1902) was lost on the battlefield; but British attempts at cultural domination, including the brutal repression of the Afrikaans language in schools and public places, led to such ferocious resistance that soon after the Second World War Afrikaners finally prevailed and came to power.

Unfortunately, as far as the language was concerned, there were two very negative impulses in this process. First, by consciously promoting Afrikaans as a language of a white ethnic group only, the needs of a large group of "colored" speakers were totally ignored and an opportunity of promoting the aspirations of indigenous oppressed groups as a whole was missed. Secondly, by modelling the Afrikaner renaissance of the twentieth century on the example of the Third Reich, racism became a dominant factor within the culture, and misguided ideals of ethnic and linguistic purity turned Afrikaans into the language of apartheid.

At the same time, however, an "alternative" Afrikaans was kept very much alive — just as English lost its early identification with oppression and exploitation to embody the solidarity of *resistance* to oppression and exploitation. In the case of Afrikaans this happened in a variety of ways.

1. Several writers who associated themselves with the liberation struggle against apartheid used Afrikaans as their medium of resistance. Even at a time when censorship forced me to start writing in English in order to ensure a readership abroad, and in the process to survive as a writer, I never stopped writing in Afrikaans — in order to demonstrate that the language was *not* the exclusive property of the apartheid establishment.

2. The predominantly "colored" University of the Western Cape, where in the wake of the Soweto riots of 1976 more and more Afrikaans-speaking students switched to English, discovered that by 1980 increasing numbers of these same students reverted to Afrikaans, with the argument that this had traditionally been their language and they refused to let it be prised from them by a power group they loathed.

3. The majority of original Afrikaans speakers in the country — those who had been abandoned when Afrikaans became a "white man's language" at the end of the previous century — continued to speak it as their mother tongue, infusing it with a set of values radically different from that of the apartheid régime. By 1990 there were almost three million of these people.

4. Afrikaans had begun to infiltrate a variety of sub-culture black vernaculars in the townships, the mines, and the cities

("flytaal," "tsotsi," "fanagalo," etc.) where it claimed whole new areas of use among speakers in opposition to the exploitative and oppressive minority régime.

5. Lastly, even if this happened for largely deplorable reasons, Afrikaans became a "bridging language" occupying an intermediate territory between the indigenous languages and English. Today Afrikaans is the language understood by more people in South Africa than any other.

Among the many consequences of this situation probably the most significant consideration is the fact that — quite distinct from the "official" status of Afrikaans within the apartheid dispensation — Afrikaans continued to convey, to express, to inform, and to inspire the aspirations of many of the oppressed people in South Africa. And through the more than three centuries of its development it has become impressively adapted to the rhythms, the experiences, the mythology, the needs and yearnings of Africa. It has learned to express its travails and its celebrations, its hardness and its generosity, its determinations and its ecstasies; it is a language of men, and also a language of women; its roots are as much in Africa as in Europe. This being so, it is singularly well equipped to give shape to the *combined* cultural heritage of South Africa and at the same time to face the future, no longer as the exclusive property of this group or that, but as the expression of a new South African identity in the process of being shaped.

A SYNCRETIC FUTURE

I see in this an indication of a possible development in the future. As Afrikaans relinquishes its privileged position as an official language to become one of the eleven most widely spoken languages of South Africa (nine of which are indigenous), it shares the anxieties of others: the fear of isolation, the fear of relegation to the margins, the fear of submergence by English. But it seems to me that these fears are relevant only in a situation of exclusive choices: the very either/or I have questioned at the outset of this paper.

It would be unacceptable for writers, for students at school and university, for ordinary speakers of the language, to be coerced in any way into relinquishing the full exploitation of their mother tongues. (I have seen the distressing consequences of francophone programs in Réunion and cannot accept to see them repeated anywhere else.) The full richness of the vernacular should be allowed — and actively encouraged — to develop and, in conjunction with literacy and education programs, to gain access to larger cultural territories. *But not at the expense of a window to the larger world.* So it would seem to me that increasing interaction should be encouraged.

A year ago I was a jury member in a short story competition sponsored by the Africa service of Radio South Africa: entrants were invited to write in their own language; in the end about eleven thousand entries, in eight languages, from more than a dozen countries, were received. Entrants ranged in age from about ten years to sixty-odd. I am hoping that an in-depth study of narrative forms will still flow from this; but even at this provisional stage I can say that what most impressed me was the way in which narrative traditions from both Europe and Africa merged in the great majority of entries. There was, for me, something wholesome and inspiring about the enterprise, demonstrating as it did the possibility of mutual enrichment, without any need to deny either Europe or Africa.

The greatest poet in South Africa, Mazisi Kunene, continues to write in Zulu and thereby assures the continued flowering of that beautiful language and its impressive literature. But he also continues to translate his own work into English, thereby encouraging a cross-pollination of cultures from which all stand to benefit.

In my own work, I cannot conceive of writing exclusively in Afrikaans any more, nor of writing exclusively in English. And even the interaction between these two is only the starting point, as I turn more and more in my writing toward the great oral traditions of South Africa's indigenous languages: their mythologies, their narrative patterns, their rhythmic structures. Only by acknowledging *all* my roots — not in terms of whiteness or blackness, but as a Euro-African — and by drawing sustenance, through them, from the soil on which I live, can my writing hope to be true both to my past and to the possibilities of my future.

JUNE 1995

Foul Play

I grew up in an environment in which rugby was the very emblem of a system of values specifically associated with the Afrikaner. (My father, whose knowledge and love of English language and literature was impressive, persistently refused throughout his life to listen to any broadcast of religion or rugby in English.) Among the highlights of my schooldays were Fred Allen's All-Black tour of South Africa in 1949 and Hennie Muller's Springbok tour through Britain in 1951–52, and I can remember how pupils and teachers alike grumbled about the presence of the "bloody Englishman" Basil Kenyon and the "bloody Jew" Cecil Moss in "our" teams. Significantly enough no one ever said a word about Okey Geffin's semitic extraction: after single-footedly winning the first test against the All Blacks he was enthusiastically accepted as an honorary Afrikaner. (Years later the Nationalist government declared all Japanese honorary South Africans in order to secure a lucrative coal export deal with Japan.)

But ever since I began to cut my political teeth on the Sharpeville massacre of 1960, the identification of Springbok rugby teams with Afrikaner values became problematic. My admiration for the brilliance of players like Frik du Preez, Jannie Engelbrecht, H. O. de Villiers, Morné du Plessis and others was

First published in the *Guardian*, June 1995.

offset more and more by misgivings about what those teams had come to represent. As a result, for some thirty years I was a fervent supporter of any foreign team the Springboks played against. Even during the transition years since 1991 the chauvinistic arrogance of so many South African teams continued to coincide with that of the political establishment that I was unable unequivocally to root for the Boks.

Then came May 25, of this year and the opening of the World Cup tournament. The way in which President Mandela on that occasion adopted "his boys," and the enthusiasm with which, in front of a TV audience estimated at over two billion, the predominantly white crowd responded with "Nel-son! Nel-son! Nel-son! Nel-son!," as well as the sparkling game itself which ensued, dissolved my last remaining doubts.

But soon afterwards the first round was concluded with that encounter between South Africa and Canada which has now taken its place in the record books as the dirtiest test ever played (once again in front of a public running into millions). And this event has prompted me to re-examine my attitude to the game of rugby, the role of dirty play within it, and its place in the political, cultural and moral framework of South Africa.

Much of the attraction of rugby lies in its extreme physicality. But its full fascination is determined by the way in which brute force and athletic speed are married to quick thinking, the ingenuity and anticipation of a chess player, the absorption of the individual within a larger, fluid motion, the creation of moving patterns and changing rhythms. At its best rugby acquires a poetry of its own, characterized by rapid changes of tempo and unexpected switches of direction, played on many levels simultaneously, and involving the totality of the human person: body, mind and imagination; memory and foresight — all of it pushed to the extreme. Which is why it is balanced on such a precarious knife-edge: if a good game accords physical and emotional delight, a bad one can be awful beyond description. If rugby has the potential to demonstrate the best of which a sportsman is capable, it can also encapsulate the worst.

The way a game turns out may be determined by the players, the coach, the referee, the spectators, the overall cultural context within which it is played. And this is where foul play becomes a marker of larger meanings.

Because the game is so relentless by its very nature, the borders between the permissible and the inadmissible are not always very clear-cut. Both are inherently violent. But surely the distinction between hard play and foul play lies in the resort of the latter to violence of an underhand, malicious, treacherous kind. It is a condition of foul play that it is not supposed to come to light, to be exposed, because it is not directed toward the unfolding of the game but to *private* goals of rage or revenge, to "get at" a specific opponent, to "prove" oneself. It foregrounds the individual, not the team.

In some societies foul play is countered by an ethos that defines the community as a whole (the old-fashioned English concept of "fair play"); in others, the dominant ethos favours and promotes foul play — especially where the community as a whole experiences feelings of insecurity or suspicion, of living under threat, which drive individuals to extreme forms of behaviour in order to compensate for what is perceived — or only vaguely and confusedly sensed — as inadequacies in themselves and their community. The near-destruction of Afrikanerdom in the Anglo–Boer War, following what they perceived as a "century of injustice," created a profound resentment (still evident today after almost a century) that could not be resolved either by open confrontation (which might lead to another humiliation) or by rational discussion (since emotion continued to cloud thinking). The only way to "get at" the enemy (and very soon the enemy came to include *all* manifestations of a threatening Other) was through underhand tactics, comparable perhaps to the strategies of the French Resistance when it was impossible to confront the Nazis outright. This had a pertinent influence on relations with the massive majority of black South Africans whose mere presence instilled in Afrikaners a deep and all-encompassing fear of being submerged. In due course, prompted by a Calvinist conscience, the apartheid régime created the awe-inspiring system of laws in order to sanction the dirty play of race relations; but this very system encouraged an ever more excessive recourse to foul play, as this strategy for survival had by now become part of the Afrikaner psyche. The removal of whole communities was "legal," but this was extended to "illegal" practices of buying, blackmailing, intimidating or murdering leaders in these communities; detention without trial was "legal," but torture became its inevitable illegal extension, etc. And because the systematized foul play of apartheid issued from an ideological mindset, linked to a ferocious survival instinct, the perpetrators of technically illegal practices could rely on the tacit condonation and even collusion of the authorities.

From my student days I recall members of the first rugby team (the name of the team, originally derived from "Theologians," was significantly abbreviated to *Theos*), bragging openly about the number of "kaffirs" they'd beaten up on their way home after every away match. (These return journeys were invariably undertaken on Saturday nights, as travelling by bus on a Sunday was regarded as sinful; and the players were all good Christians.) And on the playing fields themselves foul play came to elicit admiration. South Africa's greatest rugby heroes — Jaap Bekker, Mannetjies Roux, Uli Schmidt and their ilk — tended to be those known to instil terror in their opponents through the violence of their dirty tricks.

In these circumstances foul play is supported by the whole community — so how can it not continue to thrive? The school principals and coaches who regularly go public with their pious commitment to stamping out every sign of foul play in their teams are often themselves past-masters in the game of saying one thing and doing another: after all, hypocrisy is both a condition and a symptom of foul play. It formed the base of the erstwhile Foreign Minister Pik Botha's entire handling of international relations. (In this respect Verwoerd was a more honest man: by legalising foul play, he tried to bring it all out into the open and reconcile it with a good Christian conscience. Only, as I have already pointed out, for every step taken in the legalising process a need was created for foul play to take one step beyond the officially permissible.)

Foul play has by now become a way of life. In sport, the actions of players on the field are replicated by administrators in their offices. Sam Ramsamy, in charge of South Africa's Olympic bid, tries to slip secret clauses into his contracts with the Cape Town City Council; officials in netball, table-tennis, etc. introduce racial quotas, not so much to promote their various sports as to consolidate their own positions in larger political games; and rugby boss Louis Luyt never does openly what can be done clandestinely.

In the broader political context shady deals threaten to become the rule, not the exception. Following the example set by Afrikaners after their access to power in 1948, many new administrators, dizzy with their new experience of wealth and power, have begun to do unto others what once was done to them; even cabinet ministers thrive on kickbacks, perks and well-oiled palms. Most distressing of all was the recent impression created by President Mandela himself when, piqued by Buthelezi's maddening maneuvers, he reneged on pre-election promises about international mediation, thereby creating the impression that those solemn undertakings themselves had been no more than a dirty trick.

Perhaps the crucial question about foul play is the reaction to its disclosure. And this may well be the most alarming aspect of the game between the Springboks and Canada. Almost nowhere in the Afrikaans media was there any hint of an acknowledgement that the Boks were guilty: all the indignation was directed at the referee, the members of the disciplinary committee, the organizers of the World Cup, even at the TV cameramen who had dared to expose the offenders.

The paranoid syndrome of victimology has been developed by Afrikaners to a fine art, ever since the British first set foot in Southern Africa as rulers of the Cape, until and including P. W. Botha's obsession with a "total onslaught." *Everything* is *always* blamed on somebody *else.* God chastises those he loves, and since one dare not openly rebel against him, all manner of projections and surrogates must be found.

The victim syndrome usually manifests itself in oppressed or marginalised minorities; so at first sight it might seem curious that Afrikaners should have constructed their notion of divine election and superiority on their conviction of being victims. But it becomes comprehensible if it is seen as a strongly male-oriented narcissism in which self-centredness and self-righteousness are no more than defence mechanisms contrived by a pathological sensitivity to criticism. It is a collective persecution complex revealing an almost terrifying insecurity.

I'm not suggesting for a moment that the Canadian team was blameless; there was a great deal of persistent provocation. But surely it is time the Springbok camp and the Afrikaans media started pondering the simple fact that our men are always and everywhere involved in foul-play scandals, whether they are playing against Australia, or New Zealand, or Wales, or France, or the Argentine, you name it . . . Of course it takes two to tango; but must the Springboks *always* be one of the dancing partners? In the opening World Cup match between the Boks and the Wallabies it was spectacularly demonstrated how hard a game can be without resorting to foul tactics — and without running, sobbing, to Mum afterwards.

This is what worries me about rugby as a symptom of our larger national game: the inability, for once, to assume responsibility for what happens. Even in the terminology of the obsolescent male chauvinist ethos still largely associated with rugby one might ask the suspended hooker James Dalton who broke into tears on TV, "Aren't you supposed to take this 'like a man'?" I suspect that precisely the nature and definition of "masculinity" constitutes much of the problem confronting the Springboks in particular and Afrikaners in general.

And what I do find alarming is the impression that what used to be "typical of the Afrikaner" is now in the process of becoming "typical of the South African," including those victims of yesterday who now occupy the plush seats of the gravy train. *Because* we were victims, they appear to argue, we are now permitted everything. Because we suffered, it now gives us the right to let others suffer. The mere fact that we were victims gives us a free pass to all forms of foul play.

As long as we're not found out. This was how one of the TV commentators explicitly gave the game away, in discussing the "unjust" punishment meted out to the winger Pieter Hendriks (a reaction which echoed in every way last year's reaction to the ear-biting incident in New Zealand): not that the man had been guilty, but that he'd been the victim of circumstances *because he'd been found out.* As long as South African sports people, and the South African nation, persist in resorting to this dishonest strategy — whether it concerns F. W. de Klerk's disgraceful conduct so devastatingly lambasted by Mandela at the time of the CODESA negotiations, or Mandela's own avoidance of the international mediation he had agreed to prior to last year's elections, or dirty players in rugby, in the economy, in the civil service or wherever — there can be little hope of true progress in human relations, and in terms of morality. What we need is for someone to have the guts at last to stand up and say, "I'm guilty, I acted wrongly, I'm sorry. Let us try again."

FEBRUARY 1996

Reinventing a Continent

"Our continent has just invented another," wrote Montaigne about the discovery of the New World. At the time, of course, *to invent* was a synonym for *to discover;* yet both readings of the word are relevant to a procedure which may well become, increasingly, a preoccupation of the literature produced in post-apartheid South Africa. The need to revisit history has both accompanied and characterized the literature of most of the great "thresholds of change" as Harrow (1994) called them — those periods in which, in Santayana's words, "mankind starts dreaming in a different key." This need speaks as much from the inventive historiography of Herodotus as from the Icelandic sagas, the heroic epics of the Renaissance, the flowering of the historical novel in the wake of the French Revolution, the writings of early modernism (from *Kristin Lavransdatter* to *Finnegan's Wake*), or the postmodernisms of our *fin de siècle,* which cover the spectrum from *A Hundred Years of Solitude* to *The Satanic Verses,* from *Terra Nostra* to *The Name of the Rose,* from John Barth to Italo Calvino, from Kundera to Peter Carey.

In South Africa, the change of direction signalled by the dismantling of apartheid (against the backdrop of the larger watershed marked by the break-up of the former Second World) coincided with the revisions wrought in historical consciousness

Essay written in 1995, and published in *World Literature Today*, Winter 1996.

by postmodernism, which may well have an impact on a novelist's view of history. It is likely to form part of an intensive endeavor in post-apartheid literature to address the silences of the past, and the forms this may assume cannot but be informed by the peculiar concept of history the authors concerned bring to it. In general terms it would involve a choice between two *kinds* of concepts, two ends on a sliding scale, namely "history as fact" and "history as fiction." I know that in my own work I have moved from one notion to the other, not necessarily in a clear linear development, but as part of a continuing dialectic; and it seems to me that this may hold true of the larger territory of the South African historical novel as a whole. This is what I propose to address in the present essay in order to present, at least tentatively, some personal and subjective comments within a larger perspective.

It is important to remember that within historiography itself there has been a move away from the approach of the past as a set of "data," a "reality behind the text," toward the open-ended perception of history itself as text and as narrative. This move has accompanied the shift in the novel, from the realism of the nineteenth century (which, by and large, persisted in South African literature until well after the Second World War) to the constructions and inventions of modernism and postmodernism. Throughout this movement its dynamic has been provided by the underlying tussle between Europe and Africa, and informed by the need to bring under words the invention of a new continent.

In older South African literature, whether written by black or white authors, in English or Afrikaans,[1] the historical novel occupied a very minor place; and as might be expected, the approach was largely traditional — in the form of attempts merely to personalise and dramatise accepted renderings of history. In English, Thomas MacIntosh McCombie wrote *Adriaen van der Stel; or, Two Hundred Years After* in 1885, retelling the struggle of Dutch and Huguenot colonists against an autocratic Cape governor during the early years of Dutch settlement; and the black writer Sol Plaatje presented in *Mhudi* (1930, but written much earlier) the first attempt to retell an epoch from the country's history from the point of view of black experience; for much historical writing in the twentieth century the tone was set by the popular but ideologically suspect novels of Sarah Gertrude Millin (1889–1968) that took the supremacy of the white race as their point of departure. Several other writers, including Stuart Cloete (1897–1976) veered toward an even more sensationalist approach. In Afrikaans, where for the better part of this century the genre has enjoyed considerably more popularity, novels by authors as disparate as J. H. H. de Waal (1871–1937), Elizabeth Vermeulen (1897–1978) and the much more modern F. A. Venter (1916–1997) invariably revisited the great moments of the Afrikaner past — notably the Great Trek and the Anglo–Boer War — to rediscover a divine interest in the trials and tribulations of God's chosen people in darkest Africa. One of the only Afrikaans writers openly to challenge the Eurocentric approach has been Jan Rabie (1920–), who dramatically rewrote Afrikaner history from the point of view of "colored" experience. But not one of these writers revealed any doubt about history as a collection of facts, objectively verifiable; not one of them challenged the underlying ideological assumptions of history as a representation of the real. Even if writers like Plaatje and Rabie do offer an alternative — black or "colored" — view of the past, their acceptance of the *status* of history is identical to that of the other writers concerned, that is, the assumption that interpretations may differ, but that behind the idiosyncrasies of personal perception history exists as an acceptable record of an accessible reality. It is a map drawn of a real, existing land: the lines and contours and place-names may be refined and revised as we move toward ever greater precision, but given the right tools and the right experience, the map at the very least has the potential of becoming a wholly dependable representation of the thing itself.

The problem of this approach, as Hayden White (1978:89) has so convincingly argued, is that it is erroneous for a theorist/critic/reader to presume that the "context" or "historical milieu" of a literary text "has a concreteness and an accessibility" which the text itself lacks, "as if it were easier to perceive the reality of a past world put together from a thousand historical documents than it is to probe the depths of a single literary work that is present to the critic studying it. But the presumed concreteness and accessibility of historical milieux, these contexts of the texts literary scholars study, *are themselves products of the fictive capability of the historians who have studied those contexts*" (my italics).

What is interesting, as a background to postmodernist forages into the historical novel in more recent South African literature, is a small clutch of early fictional writing in which a view of history-as-narrative, history-as-text, is already communicated. It may be significant for future development, as the evolving new South Africa tries to come to grips with its past, that the very first historical novel in the Afrikaans language, S. J. du Toit's *Die Koningin fan Skeba* (*The Queen of Sheba*), first serialized in 1896-1898, offered, in the guise of a factual account of a journey to Great Zimbabwe, a wildly imaginative invention about a distant African past, in the form of ancient documents "discovered" in the famous Zimbabwe ruins and allegedly translated by an expert in the group of travellers. So persuasive was the account that contemporary readers were horrified to learn subsequently that the respected clergyman du Toit had in fact "lied" to them.

Inserting himself — unwittingly, quite probably — in a tradition of the textualization of history at least as old as the *Don Quixote,* the Reverend du Toit may have provided a model for much later postmodernist writing in South Africa.

Another significant forerunner of this trend may be A. C. Jordan's *Imgqumbo Yeminyana* (*The Wrath of the Ancestors,* 1940): although it cannot be regarded as an historical novel in any accepted sense of the term (it deals with a young man from the Mpondomise people who has to abandon his university studies in order to assume the kingship), the way in which the protagonist has to reconcile his progressive ideas with the whole weight of his historical and traditional milieu does problematize the very notion of history. Of particular importance is the way in which any excessive or fanciful usage of history as an ideological tool in the community is persistently branded in the text as "Nongqawuse tales": a reference to that key moment in Xhosa history when, in 1857, the young girl Nongqawuse played a Jeanne d'Arc role in persuading her people that mysterious voices had ordered the slaughtering of all the cattle and the burning of all the possessions of the Xhosa people in anticipation of an apocalypse in which the ancestors would rise from the dead to drive the white race into the sea. Jordan's skilful involution of myth and history, fiction and fact, paves the way for future revisitings of the past in order to evoke it, not as fact, but as metaphor. In this way his text may be read as a dialectic between written history and oral tradition, producing a new form teeming with possibilities for future exploration.

South African fiction began to interrogate history — not just different *versions* of history, but the very notion of its ontology, status and structure — well before the rigorous certainties of apartheid began to crumble. In Afrikaans literature the decisive marker of this change was Etienne Leroux's *Magersfontein, o Magersfontein* (1976; English translation 1983) in which textualization runs riot. The narrative concerns the attempts of a present-day film company from Britain to make a film based on the crucial battle of Magersfontein during the Anglo- Boer War; in the process there is growing confusion between the historical personalities, their fictionalized counterparts in the script, the actors involved in playing these roles, and the "real-life" characters of the actors. One of the consequences for the narrative (which ends in a literal "send-up" in a hot-air balloon) is that all sense of identity is dissipated in the endless postponements and distancings of Derridean *différance,* and the very notion of "historical origins," of an Ur-text, of a reality behind the textualising processes of a self-inventing narrative, is left open-ended.

Once again, as Hayden White (1978:91) formulates it, history itself becomes no more than an extended metaphor: "it tells us in what direction to think about the events and charges our thought about events with different emotional valences. The historical narrative does not *image* the things it indicates; it *calls to mind* images of the things it indicates, in the same way that a metaphor does."[2]

In English South African fiction this process has been demonstrated in quite a variety of novels, including *The Arrowing of the Cane* (1986) and *The Desecration of the Graves* (1990) by John Conyngham, in both of which "real" or "imagined" texts from the past are reinvented in the present. In the narrative world of the first novel (by far the more convincing of the two) the narrator renounces the possibility of physical and emotional fulfilment in a love-relationship with his fiancée to withdraw into a private world where sex is simulated by inserting a manuscript scroll (which represents his own biography and the written record of his white tribe) in a vaginal fissure in the cellar, from which it can be retrieved only in a post-apocalyptic world. By reducing, in this way, his private and collective history to a written text, the narrator reminds the reader that as a character in a novel he *is* no more than text.

Likewise, the driving force behind Mike Nicol's three novels to date is the fictionalisation of history: in *The Powers That Be* (1989) the entire apartheid experience is reduced emblematically to the fantastic story of a small village in the iron grip of Captain Nunes (who, as a construct, is reminiscent of Brecht's Arturo Ui); in *This Day and Age* (1992), crucial battles from the history of the South African racial conflict are reinvented in a curious synchronic relationship (occasionally with a certain strained urge to allegorise) in which disparate incidents are re-textualised to foreground the pervasiveness of evil; in the most allegorical and least successful of the three, *Horseman* (1994), an apocalyptic rider charges through a frightening world that ranges, in time and space, from medieval Europe to present-day Southern Africa to sow terror and confusion. The point is that by turning everything into *story,* and thereby "dehistoricizing"—and defamiliarizing—known events and patterns from European and African tradition, Nicol restores an original violence to the reader's awareness of history. Precisely by shattering the perception of history as "something out there," a record of distant times, people and events, and drawing into the textual here-and-now of a story that exists within the physicality of a book held in the reader's hands, it assumes a new immediacy and in fact a new "reality."

The most impressive demonstration of the textualization of history in recent South African fiction has been the novels of J. M. Coetzee, in which it assumes a dazzling variety of forms. It involves the literal rewriting—and reimagining—of a specific historical sequence of events in *The Narrative of Jacobus Coetzee* (in the diptych novel *Dusklands,* 1974); it also embraces the delineation of the patterns of power in *Waiting for the Barbarians* (1980) in which the experience of empire acquires a heightened urgency precisely because the Empire of the text is not identified exclusively with any historical epoch (ranging from the Roman to the apartheid state) but spans and crystallises them all; elsewhere the process ranges from the recovery of a history already fictionalized by Defoe (*Foe,* 1986), to a history of a possible future already perceptible within the present (*Life and Times of Michael K,* 1983), to the diarising of a personal history in the process of unfolding (*Age of Iron,* 1990), to a reimagined and intensely fictionalized life of Dostoevsky (*The Master of Petersburg,* 1994).

A propos of *Foe,* van Wyk Smith (1990:128) comments on the text and the writing of *Robinson Crusoe* as "the archetypal text of the colonising myth . . . capable of generating endless texts and readings . . . all re-inscriptions of the history of conquest which have powerful "'meanings'" *but no substance in a reality identifiable outside the discourse itself*" (my italics). This, it seems to me, is precisely the point of the endless array of revisitations of history now opening up to the writer of the new South Africa. For a very long time (for eminently understandable reasons, and perhaps not without effect) South African fiction has been intimately tied up with the need to record, to witness, to represent, and to interpret the unfolding of a historical process and its effects on the lives of women, men and children caught up in it. At a time when the media were prevented from fulfilling their basic function of reportage, fiction writers had to assume this burden. But as the Russian writer Victor Erofeyev once said, this activity could be compared to the uses to which furniture might be put in time of war, whether as barricades against the enemy, or as firewood in a winter of deprivation, or as blunt weapons of defence and attack; yet when peace returns, furniture is set free to become once again no more — and no less — than "mere" furniture. Similarly, if in a state of emergency writing assumes functions of representation and persuasion, its "true" function ultimately, always, and already, lies in *being what it is* — a text and a process of textualization; a narrative and a process of narrativisation. And when it turns to history, as it may feel inspired to do in a time when the processes of history are themselves highlighted, it can explore the kinship of story and history precisely by recognising the story nature of history itself. That is: its textual status, and its recourse to the forms and processes of storytelling, emplotment, characterisation, etc. Hayden White once again: "In general there has been a reluctance to consider historical narratives as what they most manifestly are: verbal fictions, the contents of which are as much *invented* as *found* and the forms of which have more in common with their counterparts in literature than they have with those in the sciences" (White 1978:82).

In looking, with the advantage of hindsight, at a few moments in my own writing as a new kind of historical consciousness surfaced, I do not presume to attempt anything more than to clarify for myself, *après coup,* certain issues of which I may not even have been conscious at the time (which is why I am intrigued enough to look at them now), and which may or may not illustrate, in one concrete example, the development of this consciousness at a time when a "threshold of change" — in contemporary South African history, and in the possibility of a new kind of literature emerging within it — is being crossed.

Returning reluctantly to South Africa in 1961 after two years of study in Paris and still enthralled by the world I'd discovered abroad, the last subject that interested me as a writer was this country; my center of gravity was elsewhere. But after spending another year in France, the watershed year of 1968, my second return was different in every respect from the first: this time I *wanted* to come home to "know the place for the first time." What fired my writing was no longer what I had in common with writers in Europe, but what tied me to Africa. For the first time I was possessed by the passionate need to define my roots and invent my subcontinent. And the first form this took was *Looking on Darkness* (1974; first published in Afrikaans in 1973), in which the "colored" narrator attempts to reconstruct his own history (an exercise which, in one way or another, appears to obsess all my other narrators). His sources are twofold: the oral tradition passed on to him by his mother, in which at least some of the original "voices" attempt to find an articulation *within* Joseph Malan's reconstructions; and external, written documentation in books and archives. He inevitably finds that sources are suspect, and so his preoccupation is not primarily with an "accurate" or "objective" report (although at times his conditioning by traditional mind-sets is still evident) but with the appropriation of a personal history through the imagination. (In later novels, like *An Act of Terror,* 1991, the writing of a personal or tribal history would be extended to involve the gradual transition from mythology to historiography.) The suspect nature of the verbal construct is signalled to the "objective" spectator/reader — personified by Joseph's jailers who survey his every move and scrutinise his every word — by the thirteen Shakespeare sonnets he leaves behind as his disguised written testimony. (Whatever else he writes he flushes down the toilet, which means that the text that meets the reader's eye is quite literally an *impossible* text which cannot exist except in the narrator's mind — and he, of course, is dead by the time any outsider can enter the narrative world.) These sonnets are Joseph's "purest" testimony, into which his whole life history has been distilled: and they are literally the words of "someone else" (Shakespeare). Furthermore, even as quotations they are not dependable, as there are erors of transcription in each of them. As an actor, Joseph has a trained memory; it is his only certainty in a world of endless shifts and changes. But the actor's profession is notorious, not only for its "second-hand" quality, but for the futility and unreliability of its sound and fury. And if the sole dimension of existence in which Joseph presents himself as reliable — his ability to memorise the texts of others — is revealed to be dubious, then everything else in his confession, including most notably his narration of his history, is open to question. But this ambiguity remains vested in the role of the *narrator,* rather than the perception of history as such — except if the interposition of the narrator between reader and story is to be read as a demonstration of the opacity of language, which presents language not as an access to history but as a displacement of it, i.e. language not as a transparent sheet of glass but as a stained-glass window (which still requires the light from the "real" world to bring it to life, but which focuses the attention on its intrinsic colors and patterns).

Unreliable narrators of one kind or another recur in *Rumors of Rain* (1978) and *A Dry White Season* (1979). In the first, Martin Mynhardt demonstrates the apartheid mind at work, as he desperately tries to impose a rigorous separation on the different clusters of data that constitute his life, one set surrounding his son, another his best friend, or his father, or his mistress; and this severe ordering of his various worlds — until they are all swept away by a more fluid and chaotic course of events — must inevitably raise questions about his presentation of history as well. In *A Dry White Season* the narrator, a hack writer, is let loose upon an assortment of notes, diaries, press cuttings, etc., and the tension between the attempt to "do justice" to the documents and his professional inclination to sensationalise his material coincides with the tussle between different perceptions of history — even though the novel as a whole, geared toward representation-as-protest, does not radically question the status of history.

An altogether different situation obtains in *An Instant in the Wind* (1976; Afrikaans edition 1975) in which the illusion is created of a "true story" based on authentic archive documents. But these documents do not exist, at least not in the Cape Archives; inasmuch as the story has an original source, it is Sidney Nolan's account of the famous Australian history of Mrs. Frazer, which also formed the Ur-text of Patrick White's *A Fringe of Leaves,* published — by a curious coincidence — simultaneously with the English edition of *An Instant in the Wind.* The novel is presented explicitly as a modern reconstruction and a reimagination of an "original"; but the point is, of course, that this "original" is transposed to a different century and a different continent, which effectively de-authenticates it as a history (even though most of the historical information about the Cape of Good Hope in the eighteenth century is based on travel documents from that time and place).

This differs from *A Chain of Voices* (1982) in which the narrative of a slave revolt in the Cold Bokkeveld in 1825 is indeed inspired by existing documents. What struck me at the time was the way in which the depositions of all the witnesses and accused in the trial had been *transcribed* by court officials (and, in fact, the scribe(s) had left more than one version of his/their transcriptions behind, in various stages of legibility and stylistic competence). Only occasionally, in unguarded moments as it were, could one hear, in an unexpected or ungrammatical turn of phrase, the "original" voice of the speaker sounding through the palimpsest of transcriptions. (And even in these cases it was a mere hunch, a personal opinion, a "feeling": there was no external proof in the documents themselves.) So here I was exposed to history itself; it was the most direct access to "what really happened" I could ever have hoped for. And at the time of writing I was indeed deeply moved by the ring of those voices. Yet upon reflection I must admit today that the most disconcerting aspect of the confrontation was the *un*reliability of historical documentation. (Even on "basic facts," like the ages or names or family relationships of some deponents, the documents turned out to be fairly unreliable.) Moreover, on one absolutely crucial issue the documents were conspicuously silent: toward the end of the proceedings the judge referred to "certain rumors" surrounding the relationship between the slave Galant and the white woman Hester and ordered an *in camera* hearing of evidence in this respect. Nothing further was recorded about the enquiry. Which was enough stimulation for the dirty mind of the novelist to take over in an attempt to "fill in" the blank.

But what is really at issue is that the archival material demonstrated at this point quite dramatically that history, even in the most traditional sense of the word, is not composed only of *texts* (written and otherwise), but strung together from *silences.* And this, it seems to me, is what primarily attracts the novelist (as it originally attracted the historiographer?). Throughout the apartheid years whole territories of silence were created by the nature of the power structures that ordered the country and defined the limits of its articulated experience. Some of these silences were deliberately *imposed,* whether by decree or by the operations of censorship and the security police; but in many cases the silences arose because the urgencies of the situation presented priorities among which certain experiences simply did not figure very highly. (In crude terms, if at a given moment I had to choose between writing a love story and the story of a life disrupted by the machinations of apartheid, I would opt for the latter — not because it was "expected" of me or "imposed" on me, but because in those circumstances I would *choose* to.) In yet other cases the silences had to be discovered *below* the clamor that filled certain gaps: the clamor of "official versions" and "dominant discourses" which caused such a din that one often did not even realise the noise existed, not for its own sake, but purely as a cover-up for the silences below. It is the inverse of what George Eliot intimated in that wonderful line from *Middlemarch:* ". . . there is a great roar on the other side of silence."

A completely different relationship with history informs *The First Life of Adamastor* (1993), originally intended as the first of thirteen chapters in a novel to be entitled *The Lives of Adamastor* (and which was eventually reshaped into Thomas Landman's invention of a family history in *An Act of Terror,* 1991): this was, explicitly, an attempt to counter, from the "inside," two key myths of the dominant historical and ethnographic discourse about Africa: Camoens's version of Europe's early encounter with Africa, personified as a monstrous black giant who resists all attempts to be conquered from abroad, and who is finally punished by Zeus, the god of European patriarchy, for having dared to love the (white) nymph coveted by the Father himself; and, secondly, the persistent European myth about black African sexual potency. In both cases a "send-up" technique of gross exaggeration is used, deliberately couched in the shape of early European narratives, but incorporating stories and story forms from various African oral traditions. This, I hoped, would result in something more complex than a simple refutation of the prevalent discourse, or the positing of a simple alternative: because part of the narrative wealth of Africa lies in moving beyond the simple dichotomies of *either/or,* to arrive at more syncretic and holistic patterns of narrative thinking. And "narrative thinking" is, of course, what writing is about: discovering for the novel, and rediscovering in each new novel, that which, as Kundera said, can be articulated *only* by the novel, and not by any other form of discourse.

In yet another way my involvement with history expressed itself in *On the Contrary* (1983), where the mendacious and imaginative nature of the historical character Estienne Barbier prompted a continuation, in the novel, of the self-inventions Barbier indulged in through the writing of his letters (still available in the Archives) to successive Governors at the Cape of Good Hope. Accompanied by the fictional character of Don Quixote and by a Jeanne d'Arc as much imagined by Barbier as drawn from the popular mythologies surrounding her historical role, the new hidalgo sets out on several journeys (all three of them imagined, by the writer or by the narrator or by both) into the African interior — an interior whose geography is as suspect as its history; it is, in fact, an interior composed not so much of landscapes and climatological conditions as by the *texts* of numerous eighteenth-century travellers through the Cape hinterland. The key figure among them, whose voice is often allowed to speak for itself in the text, is a German of whose very name we are not quite sure: he might be Peter Kolb, or Kolbe, or Kolben, and he apparently spent some time at the Cape at the beginning of that century — but considerable doubt exists about his veracity. Some commentators have even suggested that he wrote his extensive travelogues without ever setting foot beyond the immediate environs of Cape Town. And yet, in his imaginative reconstruction of an African Other without which the self could not come to know itself, Kolb(e)(n) might have ventured closer to grasping an elusive truth about the continent than many others who observed, named and recorded, in meticulous detail, every little plant, insect, animal or human being encountered on their journeys of exploration.

One step further, and one would not even require the pretext (in the most literal sense of a pre-text) of historical "sources" to reinvent the past in order to valorise — and validate — it for the narrative in which the writer is personally implicated. In *Imaginings of Sand* (1996) the compulsively narrating grandmother, mouthpiece of a long line of silent and/or silenced women in South African history, no longer relies on "evidence" or "references" of any kind: her narratives are their own *raison d'être* and derive from the individual's need to insert herself or himself, through storytelling, within the larger contexts of space and (historical) continuity. Where sources are used in recognizable form, they function on at least three levels: sometimes they are

"informal" by nature, like the Great Trek diaries of Sι Smit; on other occasions they are subjected to transferen happens in the case of the well-known seventeenth-centur ure of Krotoa (known as Eva to the Dutch) who acted as i preter between the Dutch and the indigenous Khoikhoi she became the victim of both groups: this chapter from his is transposed in the novel to the fictitious character of woman Kamma,[3] whose involvement in the story is based o particularly illuminating feminist reading of the Adamastor m (cf. Driver 1992:455–7). In other words, the concern of t narrative here is not the "facts" but the *patterns* of alread narrativised history. A third level on which "historical source function in the narrative involves the complete abandonment c that "reality identifiable outside the discourse itself" van Wyl Smith referred to: for instance, one of the instigators of a crucial episode in the grandmother's family history is borrowed, not from historiography, but from another novel, *An Act of Terror.*

In all these instances the importance lies in the recognition of the *need to storify,* not in the specifics of the remedies each individual may bring to the situation. Passing beyond the intertextualities of separate documents, and relying more on images and metaphors than on the grammars of language, the grandmother reverts to pure invention — as an acknowledgement of that primal urge described by Russell Hoban in his famous dictum, "*We make fiction because we* ARE *fiction.*"

And this is, ultimately, the only answer one can give to the inevitable question, "Why?" — *why* resort to fiction, *why* reduce history to storytelling, *why* confront a demanding and turbulent "real" world with the inventions and fabrications of narrative? *Why,* at a time when South Africans are expected to be preparing to face present and future, should one waste time by an *invention,* rather than a strict discovery, of the past? We are moving toward the persistent objection against all postmodernist writing, but most pertinently against its practices within the di-

mensions of history and of morality. For surely, if *anything* may be invented, why should any one particular invention carry more weight than another? If all is text and there is nothing outside the text, how can anything be morally or historically valorised?

The answer, I have already suggested, lies in that leap of the imagination (and, it should be added, of reason) that prompted Hoban to say, "We make fiction because we *are* fiction." Whether one composes a CV for a job application, or reviews a day or week or year or life traversed, or relates a crucial experience to someone else, or writes a letter, or describes an event . . . however one sets about it, it is inevitably turned into narrative, within what Brian Wicker called a "story-shaped world." This, as Hayden White (1978:87) argues, provides a key to psychological analysis as well: "The therapist's problem . . . is not to hold up before the patient the 'real facts' of the matter, the 'truth' as against the 'fantasy' that obsesses him . . . The problem is to get the patient to 're-emplot' his whole life history in such a way as to change the *meaning* of those events for him and the *significance* for the economy of the whole set of events that make up his life." The same process, he indicates, occurs in historiography: "Historians seek to refamiliarize us with events which have been forgotten through either accident, neglect, or repression."

Whether this occurs in therapy, in historiography, or in literature, the powerful act of appropriating the past through imaginative understanding — that is, through the devices of metaphor rather than through a "scientific objectivity" which tries to mask its own uncertainties — is necessary for the sanity of the whole community.

And this is not a random act at all. It is *not* a matter, as critics of postmodernist discourse often pretend, of "any invention will do." What this kind of invention effects is to open a door to *comparative* reading. The new text *has* to be evaluated against the whole spectrum or palimpsest of available texts, and so a polylogue is opened through which versions of the past are

drawn into the present, confronting the reader with the need — and above all with the responsibility — to *choose.*

Since we experience our own lives as a compilation of narrative texts, this approach to historiography within the novel introduces history — or a history — into the whole collection of narratives that constitute us, both as individuals and as a community. And *because* the text is not offered as definitive, final, absolute, but as the exploration of a possibility among others, it invites the reader to keep her or his critical faculties alive by pursuing the processes of imagination in order to arrive at whatever proves more relevant, more meaningful, or simply more useful in any given context. It intensifies the relationship between the individual and her or his spatial and temporal environment. And learning to inhabit the continent of our invention may well be one of the most rewarding challenges facing South Africans — readers and writers alike — in this time of change, knowing that neither its history nor its moral boundaries are fixed and final, but remain constantly to be reinvented and, in the process, revalorized.

Postscript 1997: To the accusation that the (postmodernist) reinvention of history becomes purely subjective, Wetherell and Potter (1992:64) respond: "The constitution of objects is socially organized and highly dependent on our existing forms of discourse and past discursive history. We are not suggesting that if someone thinks New Zealand does not exist then it does not; nor . . . that all there is to reality is ideas. New Zealand is no less real for being constituted discursively — you still die if your plane crashes into a hill whether you think that the hill is the product of a volcanic eruption or the solidified form of a mythical whale. However, material reality is no less discursive for being able to get in the way of planes. How those deaths are understood . . . and what caused them is constituted through our systems of discourse."

Sentimental Journey

Cultivons Notre Jardin — VOLTAIRE

The Jardin du Luxembourg in the rain. It is Thursday April 27, 1995. It is a year later; thirty-five years later. How strange that lines, given enough rope, tend to shape themselves into circles. Always this return to beginnings. Never quite the same; but we seem to need these moments to take stock, to examine ourselves, to rediscover where we were, have been, may be going to. Whether it is reassuring or disquieting is immaterial; what matters is that it is necessary.

These are the gardens I sought refuge in, in the deceptive early spring of 1960, when I needed to try and grasp what was happening in my distant country. I sat down, first on a green metal chair, then on a dark brown bench, surveyed by ponderous statues, on my lap the bright yellow edition of Comte's *Philosophie positive;* but I wasn't reading. I was too numbed by the news of Sharpeville. Those many dead, those wounded, the scattering of the fleeing; the images of young policemen firing madly in all directions. Their faces were marked — I realise now, with hindsight — with the fury and the fear that come

Contribution to *April, 27, One Year Later,* a collection of essays by most of the authors represented in *S.A. April 27, 1994*. Published by Queillerie Publishers, Pretoria and Cape Town, 1995.

from the discovery by a dominant species that it is in fact endangered and may soon be extinct. I was not yet twenty-five; I had grown up in the security of a conservative Afrikaner family, in a succession of small villages in the dry heart of the country where black people had been God's burden and blessing to the chosen white race. As a ten-year-old I myself had explained with great zeal, in a makeshift Sunday school in our garage, to all the servants of the neighborhood, God's curse on Noah's son Ham which meant that his descendants would for ever and ever be the hackers of wood and the carriers of water to the children of the more favored brothers. (And all because Ham had dared to look upon his father's nakedness, like another small boy who discovered that the emperor wore no clothes.) Never in my youth had I encountered a single black person who had not been a servant or a laborer; never had there been occasion to imagine an order different from the one I had been born into. And now, through this one cataclysmic event, the clothes had been ripped from the ruler, and at a distance of eight thousand kilometers I saw with shocking clarity the diseased naked body of the emperor.

It was another eight years before I had fully digested the impact of that discovery: that was in 1968, I was once again in Paris, having returned with the half-formed intention of settling here permanently. Shuttling between two of the centres of the students' revolt of that wild May, the Sorbonne and the Odéon, I would often withdraw into the Luxembourg to meditate for a while on what was happening around me. Resavoring the images — shocking, preposterous, touching or farcical in turn — of the previous days; rereading the tracts and leaflets distributed in the dug-up streets (*There's a beach beneath the paving stones!*); recalling the slogans chanted by the crowd (*Even chamber pots can bloom — Whatever isn't strange is false*). In this green garden I immersed myself in green thoughts; it was both a leap into the imagination and a restoration of sanity, that momentary stay against confusion so cherished by Frost. It was here, more than in the clamor of the streets, that in the course of that watershed year the resolve to return to South Africa was shaped in me. A difficult return to a difficult country. From time to time, through the murky years of the seventies and eighties, there were glimpses of a possible end to the tunnel; but what sane person could really have foreseen February 2, 1990, April 27, 1994?

Last year I was again in France during the month prior to the elections. Of course I had to go back to vote; it was an appointment with history. But it was with a heavy heart that my wife and I headed south, to prospects of endemic violence, mistrust, suspicion, accumulated resentment, hatred, the fruits of centuries of oppression. And then, of course, after the shock of the dawn bomb at Jan Smuts airport on the first morning of the elections, came the miracle. Those hours of queuing in the rain, the small-talk that united academics and streetsweepers and hard-nosed businessmen and municipal workers, Madams and Eves; the simple joy of sharing an umbrella, a plastic mug of coffee from a thermos, a packet of Lemon Creams, a handful of chips; the most basic of all discoveries: our common humanity, common needs, common future, common fate. Yes, it was worth while travelling the eight thousand kilometers to be part of this event. I knew, we knew, that all would not be moonlight and roses, or sunlight and proteas, as we broke into that new land, the future; but we also knew that in darker times we would be able to look back on this day — the essence of its miracle the discovery of the ordinary — and draw strength and faith from it. We had all been marked by a momentous event, and nothing could ever be quite the same again.

Or could it?

Now I am back in the Luxembourg Gardens. I have returned to the place where I was born into the discovery of the world and of my place in it. The rain is coming down in a steady wash, just like last year in Cape Town. The chestnut trees are in full leaf, a deep intense green in the wet, offset against the many other greens of the park; Andrew Marvell would have approved. There are even some scraggly jacarandas in hesitant bloom (memories of Mandela's inauguration in Pretoria, that unforgettable day last year . . .). There are few other people about: a solitary young woman in black, under a black umbrella, beside the leaden pond (is she, too, commemorating something?); a father with two waddling infants in layers of clothing like little Michelin men; a small bunch of tourists from the Far East, relentlessly clicking their battery of cameras in order one distant future day to review what they have missed today. In the flower-beds a few intrepid bobtails are in search of late worms. The statues are crowned with mournful pigeons. The pond is framed in bright flowers: from a distance the yellows and oranges appear like African marigolds, the ones we know as stink afrikaners. (I have a fond memory of a Portuguese friend who innocently insisted on calling them "*nacionalistas.*") Curious and touching to see them survive in all climates, hardy and defiant, amazingly adept at adapting themselves; they may not smell so sweet, yet one cannot but respect their unredeemed and uncompromising color. After some minutes of strained symbolizing I go closer and discover they are not afrikaners after all, but freesias. *Tant pis.*

Defiant in my own way I sit down on an empty green metal chair, opposite the woman in black. Thirty-five years ago my painful thoughts were abruptly interrupted by an authoritarian old crone who insisted on payment for the right of sitting on a green chair; so much for *liberté, egalité, fraternité.* I refused on principle, and after an altercation decamped to the bench where I was then born in a show of blood and guts. Today, in this weather, there are no signs of obtrusive authority. Thoughts are free.

The newspaper I have so foolishly bought at a kiosk in the rue de Rennes is by now soggy with rain, dripping with reports and reviews and assessments of the first round in the French presidential elections, in which the extreme right has secured 20% of the vote. Immigrants must be thrown out, they say; non-whites pose a threat to European integrity; these people who haven't even been able to invent the wheel should be kept out of our industries and schools and cultural palaces. France for the French. *Vive l'apartheid.*

A jogger in red shorts and a white vest comes charging through the rain, head thrust forward, looking down at the mud through which he blunders, arms churning close to his sides; he disappears among the apathetic trees. In 1968 there was a mad jogger like this one who used to run round and round the Luxembourg all day, and probably all night as well. Nothing could stop him. It was funny; and not funny at all. This frenzy of running in circles, with no ulterior cause or aim, running for the sake of running. I have friends like this who ever since the end of the liberation struggle have been unable to change the old habits. Once there is the compulsion to run, in this all-consuming attempt to escape the self, then who can stop it? What we need is to sit down, allow the rains to cleanse us, look into ourselves, find the courage for new beginnings.

Thirty-five years ago. A year ago. Where are we now, where am I?

I know that for many of my compatriots — the majority? — life has not changed very much. They are still poor, homeless, jobless; they still bear the brunt of everything Hamlet bewailed, and more — the oppressor's wrong, the proud man's contumely, the law's delay, the insolence of office, all the misery of their outrageous fortune. There are freedom fighters from the past who restrict the freedom of others in the present; the dispossessed of yesterday who now have yielded to the seductions of power; members of an old master class who act as if they were still in command; victims who carry their scars like trophies, insisting that because they were victims it gives them the right to exploit others (and thereby create new members of this late-twentieth century scourge of the world, victimology). There are those so conditioned by violence, so unaccustomed to the new possibilities of democracy, that they destroy schools, trash university campuses, wreak havoc in hospitals, take hostages, resort to violence when ordinary discussion and negotiation could do the job. There are those whose claims for a better deal are so outrageous that they will rather wreck the economy (and their own chances for a decent future) than bring their demands in line with available resources. There are those so obsessed by yesterday that they are prepared to destroy tomorrow: people who are to politics and to democracy what AIDS is to sex.

The abuse of new-found power and wealth (and the reluctance to act firmly against such abuse), the vacillations of persons in key positions, the apparent inability to deal firmly with escalating crime and violence, the ANC's scandalous dishonoring of written agreements with Inkatha which made last year's elections possible (even if Buthelezi has been acting more like a spoiled brat than a statesman), the impotence of the courts as a result of irresponsible practices of bail and parole, the lies and prevarications and downright incompetence of people who should know better, the continued rape of the environment, the unrealistic and even unscrupulous manipulations of high-sounding phrases like "affirmative action" — all of this has prompted, within a year, serious misgivings about realistic expectations of a new deal and quite simply of effective government.

And yet, and yet . . . How immeasurably worse things could have turned out! Could anyone really have expected us to move forward without making grave mistakes, without fumbling, without suffering or causing pain? We are human; thank heavens.

I stare at Le Pen's face disintegrating on the front page of my desperately wet newspaper; I peer at the gloomy woman in black on the far side of the pond, who has bent over to pick one of the non-afrikaners, an act strictly forbidden on ordinary days; I notice a pigeon shitting on the head of a scowling statue before it takes off into the sky shimmering with hidden light. And I know all is not lost. On the contrary! If I think of where we were a year ago — twelve brief months, three hundred and sixty-five days, a fleeting instant in the long history of my country — it is almost incredible that we should have come so far. In those heady spring days of 1968 one of the key slogans was *L'imagination prend le pouvoir:* the imagination takes power. And I find in it the key to the events of this past year.

True, the government has built only a handful of the millions of new homes envisaged in the program of reconstruction and development. But in the widest sense of the phrase the foundations have been laid, the programs have been mounted, the groundwork done; the schemes are on the point of being implemented. Hundreds of thousands of people who never had such services before now have access to electricity and running water. Pregnant mothers and young children can be hospitalized free. An entire new education system based on equity and non-racism has been introduced. A moribund economy has been kick-started and new investments have begun to trickle in. If violence is still rampant, its nature has changed: it is no longer primarily political, but criminal — which means that by addressing the root causes of socio-economic conditions it can be confronted with a real hope of success. If there is still suspicion, resentment, smouldering anger in many quarters, on the whole relations between different cultural communities have improved immeasurably. The reality of political threats from both the extreme right and the extreme left has practically evaporated. When wrongs come to light, there is an immediate outcry to have them addressed: under the old régime they were kept secret, and openly to denounce the wrongdoers exposed one to the full and fearsome repressive machinery of state security.

Even more important, inspired by the example of the one man who has made it all possible, Nelson Rolihlahla Mandela, there is still a readiness, even an eagerness, on all sides to "make it work." Last year's problems have become this year's challenges. That great reservoir of goodwill that came into view on April 27, 1994 remains a pervasive reality. In spite of our differences — and also *because* of them, since we have discovered our variety as the source of our human wealth — we have embraced a sense of common purpose, an awareness of a larger South African identity in the process of being shaped.

Amid all this, and above all this, there is the daily rediscovery of a precious freedom we did not have before: the freedom to say what we think, to dare think what we think. The freedom to decide for oneself whether to be critical, or supportive, or neutral on any issue, without fear of being blamed or punished in any way.

By any imaginable reckoning we still have very far to go; if there is one thing we have discovered it is that freedom is not utopia. More than anything else it demands the acceptance of ordinary human responsibility for ordinary human situations. Liberation was not — can never be — an end in itself: perhaps we first have to free ourselves from the mentality of liberation before we can start working toward giving democracy a new sense.

We cannot expect too much too soon, or wish to skip any of the tough intermediate stages toward greater fulfilment, individually as well as collectively. We must turn over the old page; but not before we have read every word of it — otherwise we cannot remember. And without memory there can be no real initiative, no bold invention, no leap of the imagination.

The woman in black prepares to go, the bright splash of her illicit flower a shout of unexpected beauty in the greyness of the day. Am I imagining things or is the rain letting up? (In any case, in Africa rain has always been the best of signs.) It is time for me to go too. I drop the soggy paper in a green dustbin. I leave the freesias behind. In a few days I shall be home again, among the bold yellow and orange marigolds of the place where I belong. After the trauma of 1960 I returned; after the ecstasies and agonies of 1968 I once again, and in a sense for the first time, went home. In this severely formal garden to which I owe so much I miss the indiscipline, the untidiness, the messiness, the extravagance of the droughts and the vegetation at home. That is the garden to cultivate, and I must be part of it.

NOVEMBER 1997

Epilogue: Revisiting Dakar

Among recent events which may be regarded as a barometer of the nature and extent of the transition in South Africa was a reunion, ten years almost to the day since a delegation of sixty-odd South Africans, predominantly Afrikaans speaking, clandestinely left the country to meet in discussions with representatives of the exiled ANC in Dakar (Senegal), Ouagadougou (Burkina Faso), and Accra (Ghana).

The low-key reception of the reunion in the South African press was in marked contrast with the veritable hurricane that swept the local media in 1987. Afrikaans newspapers at the time vied to concoct the most outrageous assessments of the excursion. This act of "collective betrayal," as it was gleefully portrayed, fuelled the fires of frustrated politicians and outraged public alike; upon our return white extremists massed at the airport with the intention of tearing the traitors limb from limb. State President P. W. Botha ordered the confiscation of our passports and considered arresting the entire delegation; only the intervention of the Foreign Minister prevented this ignominious showdown.

Today, ten years later, these reactions serve as a useful reminder of just how far we have travelled in such a short time.

A much shorter version of this essay was first published in *Leadership* magazine, September 1997.

Few of us lived through the ensuing months without death threats, brushes with the Security Police, obscene phone calls, and the rest; some lost their jobs; others were subjected to all kinds of overt and covert persecution. Arriving home, I found that all my notes on Dakar had been confiscated by agents unknown in Johannesburg, even though I'd had the foresight to stow them not in my own luggage but in that of my companion, who has since become my wife. Fortunately, ever since my first experience of a security police house-search a decade before Dakar, I had learned never to keep only one copy of notes or manuscripts; and before returning to South Africa I had left a photocopied set in Europe, which was promptly smuggled to me by diplomatic bag. It arrived in time for extensive use in the series of report-back meetings we addressed after our homecoming to ensure that as large a public as possible would be informed about what had happened. For many whites in our audience that was the first occasion ever to hear, at first hand, the case for the ANC. In this way Dakar entered the public consciousness.

It would of course be unwise to exaggerate the importance of that single event in the unfolding scenario of change that has shaken South Africa to the foundations over the last decade: it was, after all, merely one factor among many others, which broke the old molds and created the possibility of inventing a new country. At the same time one should not underestimate the influence of that venture.

Prior to Dakar, Afrikaners had never been involved on such a scale in discussions with a liberation movement demonised by the Nationalist government as a terrorist organization and Public Enemy Number One. And even though a number of us had already established, individually, regular contact with members of the ANC abroad, the sheer magnitude of the encounter turned it into a watershed for the whole process of change. Moreover, precisely the fact that there was nothing "official" about the mission, and that we had neither the mandate nor the wish to enter into "negotiations," created a freedom of engagement without which all the later démarches would have been unthinkable. In our midst were politicians, businessmen, academics, representatives of the media, the arts, religion, sport. In the course of the discussions the two groups soon fused into one, providing an early proof that the notion of a "Rainbow Nation" was not the romantic illusion so many have come to scoff at.

Under the patronage of Mme. Danielle Mitterrand, whose presence lent the meeting an unofficial sanction by one of the Great Powers in Europe, the heady process of mutual discovery, and the mental, political, and moral electricity it created, prepared a climate for the dramatic developments that followed. Only a year after Dakar most of the points elaborated and illuminated in those discussions found their way into the ANC's Lusaka Declaration which, in turn, laid the foundation for the country's present constitution. The urge to understand, the need to embark on a rediscovery of our shared history and to face its worst horrors for the sake of healing the wounds, provided a starting point for the Truth and Reconciliation Commission.

But ultimately, what was gained at Dakar is to be found in matters both less readily defined and, perhaps for that reason, more lasting in their significance: in the fact that it demonstrated, perhaps for the first time, that the impasse in South Africa could be broken, not through violence but through peaceful discussion; and above all, in the acknowledgement of the simple but momentous fact *that we are all South Africans,* that we draw our sustenance from the same soil, the same climate, the same history, and essentially the same hopes and dreams.

One's first impression of the reunion was its confirmation of the long way we had all come. Members of an exiled organization, ten years ago, were now key figures in government, including Deputy President Thabo Mbeki; what had been outlandish and almost unthinkable then had become normal; if in 1987 we had been representatives from two different worlds and mindsets, we were now, in 1997, all involved in the same process of democratisation.

And yet there was also a singular flatness in the encounter compared with the vibrancy of the original meeting. Could it be ascribed, as one delegate suggested, merely to being ten years older than the first time round? Or, as someone in more cynical vein proposed, that the dynamic of the meeting in Dakar had resided in the fact that at the time the ANC needed Afrikaners as much as Afrikaners needed the ANC — whereas today, three years after the elections that had swept the ANC to power, the party no longer had much need of Afrikaner support or understanding? Such a suspicion would be sustained by the fact that of the numerous ANC members in Dakar who had since risen to positions of power, a mere handful found the time, or had the inclination, to attend the reunion.

One major shift which had occurred in the interim was, obviously, the absence of any fault line demarcating an "us" and a "them": today, after all, we are all South Africans in one post-apartheid country. Some of the "internal" delegates of ten years ago actually represent the ANC in parliament today. Yet, sadly, the perception of two blocs was perhaps even stronger this time than in 1987, when almost all of us were swept into a single exhilarating awareness of South Africanness that overrode the obvious differences. This time there was, among many of the Afrikaners, a more narrowly defined, and a more vehemently defended, sense of a beleaguered Afrikanerdom clustered around a language they saw as threatened with relegation to marginality, and perhaps with extinction.

To understand this, one has to consider the drastic changes that had taken place since the original meeting in West Africa. It is doubtful that anyone present at the reunion could have foreseen, ten years ago, either the extent or the pace of those changes: State President P. W. Botha's fall from power and the succession of F. W. de Klerk; the unbanning of the ANC and the liberation of Mandela; a negotiated transition to democracy;

three years of ANC rule, during which de Klerk walked out of the government of national unity before resigning from politics altogether, leaving his party in disarray. One of the consequences was that, by the time of our reunion, the ANC no longer perceived Afrikaners as the redoubtable political force they had seemed a decade earlier.

Among Afrikaners generally, as well as among many of those attending the reunion, the reaction to this shift was, perhaps understandably, a degree of bitterness and viciousness that suggested deep-seated uncertainties and anxieties. This cast something of a pall over the meeting. Considering that most of the Afrikaners concerned represent a cultural and intellectual élite, it was sad, if not downright unsettling, to note how deeply many of them were suffering what one commentator called the pain of a phantom limb. In a few of the most revealing exchanges the passionate concern about *language* was unmasked as, in fact, a concern with lost *power.* In this respect, ironically, Afrikaners today are resembling more and more those white English speakers of the apartheid era who incessantly bemoaned their exclusion from power and used this as an excuse for withholding all involvement in a struggle for change. What the reunion revealed was that we are faced today, among white South Africans and more particularly Afrikaners, with a culture of pure negativity, of incessant sniping at the ANC.

Not that the ANC doesn't have much it deserves to be criticised for. After the euphoria with which the country as a whole reacted to the outcome of the first free elections in 1994, the ANC marked its accession to power with displays of tolerance, generosity, a respect for human dignity, a lack of rancour or vindictiveness, which amazed supporters and opponents alike.

The mood was buoyed by the unveiling of ambitious programs to change irrevocably the face of a country agonising for so long in the grip of colonialism and its wretched consequences: houses would be built on a staggering scale, jobs would be created in their millions, the whole economy would be overhauled, the education system would be reconstructed, health services would be revolutionized, water and electricity would be provided to millions previously deprived of such services. The list went on and on and on. And even in moments of hesitation or doubt, there would be President Mandela's soon-legendary "Madiba Magic" to persuade the faint of heart. Even die-hard Afrikaners from the extreme right, taking part in phone-in radio programs, would refer to Mandela as "our president" in tones of admiration.

But slowly a new tone became evident in private and public discussion. First it was called realism. In due course it gave way to disillusionment. Today, three years later — and all too glaringly in evidence at the Dakar reunion — it is shifting toward resentment, in some quarters toward rage, with undertones of despair. In many ways this change was only to be expected: one has witnessed it in many other societies which have gone through the convulsions of profound social transformation — in the reunited Germany, in the Czech Republic, in Poland, in Russia, in a number of South American countries. Some have already moved on from there; others are still stuck in the mud churned up by the wheels of too-rapid, too-radical change. So the phenomenon as such should not come as any surprise. And there has always been — there is still — the crisp reminder that however dismally many promises may have failed to materialise, however badly many things may have gone wrong, *it could all have been so much worse.* South Africa had really come to the very edge of the precipice when it was drawn away and steered along another route altogether. The apocalyptic disaster so many, both inside the country and abroad, had feared as an ever more imminent outcome had been averted; and in spite of everything a deep and pervasive goodwill, brought to the surface by the elections, had prevailed — encapsulated, for white and black alike, in the often-quoted Xhosa proverb: *Umntu ngumntu ngabanye abantu* (I am a man through other men). This "existing through other" has been, and remains, the essential ingredient of the South African miracle: and I still believe that it is no less than a miracle.

But this does not absolve the ANC from responsibility for the alarming turn for the worse South Africa appears to have taken. It goes far beyond the accusations of promises not kept, the housing and other programs left unrealized, even the unchanged misery in which the majority of the population still struggle to survive. And it goes beyond the astronomical escalation of crime and the machinations and manifestations of corruption to which the newly powerful have proved to be as prone as the old. What is more profoundly alarming is a failure of integrity, a weakness — a rottenness — at the very heart of what used to be perceived as the ANC's main strength: its commitment to transparency and democratic values, the premium it placed on morality, the tolerance it demonstrated toward a diversity of opinions, the regard it had for human dignity. On all these scores the present government in South Africa has become suspect, demonstrating all too often an arrogance, obtuseness, mendacity, and callousness dramatically at variance with its historical image.

Over the last eighteen months or so many events have pointed in this direction, of which I single out only a few random examples:

• In the notorious *Sarafina 2* debacle the Minister of Health, Dr. Nkosazana Zuma, blithely bypassing all regulations and prescribed procedures, paid a preposterous amount to the playwright Mbongeni Ngema to write and produce a play which could be performed to spread AIDS awareness — seemingly unaware of the fact that a number of other plays on AIDS were already being performed throughout the country, with spectacular success and at a fraction of the cost, to vast school and township audiences. Ngema, co-author with Percy Mtwa and Barney Simon of the world-wide stage hit *Woza Albert!* proceeded to slap up a sequel to his Broadway success *Sarafina*. Unfortunately, written all too obviously with a glitzy international market in mind and with little or no concern for AIDS, *Sarafina*

2 played only to a number of élitist audiences before it disappeared. The venture, coming at such vast expense at a time when many hospitals had to be closed down for lack of funds and doctors and nurses resigned in droves because of bad pay, was scandalous enough; but the way in which the ANC, faced with a barrage of criticism, closed ranks around the minister and contemptuously refused to acknowledge any hint of culpability did not augur well for the future of transparency in government. The same reaction followed a seemingly endless series of further blunders by Dr. Zuma, whose stubborn arrogance has come to resemble more and more that of her predecessors from the apartheid era.

• In the run-up to the elections of 1994 the borders of several of the country's newly proclaimed provinces were drawn rather hastily. Among the most vociferously unhappy of the provinces was Mpumalanga in the north-eastern region of the country; but the dissatisfied electorate was placated when Thabo Mbeki, now Deputy President, personally gave his solemn assurance that a referendum would be held as soon as possible after the elections to ensure that the demarcation would respect the wishes of the majority. Three years later, after several violent demonstrations in the area, it has become clear that no referendum will be called and that governmental decree, rather than the will of the people, will settle the matter in this case as in several others. What is alarming is the way in which the ANC is here repeating the same mistakes of early colonial masters who blithely ignored cultural, ethnic, political, historical, and geographical considerations in drawing their random maps of power; it would seem as if the bitterness and divisions suffered by the whole continent as a result have still not been heeded.

• Patrick Lekota, the hugely popular premier of the Free State Province and one of the rare leaders who has the total confidence of his black *and* white electorate, was sacked against the express will of the majority of ANC supporters in the province, and a candidate of the party's National Executive Committee was imposed on the region. Not only did this fly in the face of the most basic notions of democracy but it would seem that the new premier, who did not even live in the province, had been chosen largely because her presence could no longer be tolerated in the South African Broadcasting Corporation, which she had headed for a short and disastrous spell. The same rule-by-*diktat* approach has become apparent in other provinces, as well as in the run-up to the 1997 election of new office-bearers within the ANC, where less and less scope is allowed for democratic electioneering and freedom of choice. Shortly before the event, President Mandela simply announced that a top candidate for the position of Deputy President, Matthews Phosa of Mpumalanga, was withdrawing: the first Phosa himself allegedly learned about it was when he read about it in the newspapers.

• While one appreciates the urgent need for affirmative action to redress the iniquitous imbalances of the past, this has led to staggering excesses. In one publishing company, to name a single example, the entire white management was made redundant (with huge severance packages) and replaced by black executives; immediately after the restructuring, all the dismissed white executives were re-employed as "consultants," at roughly double their previous salaries, to provide in-job training for their replacements. This happens throughout the civil service as well, at crippling cost to the country — which makes it less and less likely that the vast housing, welfare, and education programs South Africa so desperately needs can be implemented. And any criticism of such practices is very rapidly, and very effectively, smothered by branding the critics as "racist." (The deplorable fact that much of this criticism is indeed racist, emanating from whites who cannot adapt to the loss of the privileges they used to take for granted at the expense of blacks, does not make it any easier.)

• Much of the devastation of white colonial and neocolonial rule in South Africa has taken place through the exploitation of cheap black labor. The shameful consequences of this exploitation (linked to "Bantu education" which was explicitly geared to keeping blacks subservient and near-illiterate) are only too evident. With the gulf between rich and poor deepening by the day, it is obvious that the entire approach to labor in the country needs an overhaul. Also, it was only understandable that a strong trade union movement (which had already gathered momentum during the last decade or so of the apartheid era) is indispensable. The problem is that at present the unions are holding the ANC to ransom; far beyond the need for radical reconstruction — and far beyond what the economy can afford — the costs of production in South Africa have risen so alarmingly that would-be foreign investors are being scared off. Basic common sense has skulked out through the back door as exorbitant demands for wage increases, *without any commensurate increase in productivity,* threaten the growth of the new economy at the very moment when it most needs to flourish. Of course there are sectors where wages are still disgraceful by any standards; but when a sweeper or cleaner earns more than an individual with a post-graduate qualification and five years' experience in teaching at a university, surely there is occasion for concern. Yet anxious to placate a sizeable section of the electorate on which it relies to be returned to power with a two-thirds majority at the next elections in 1999, the ANC is willing to sacrifice some of its most urgently needed projects (in education, for example). It is, of course, expedient. But was it really naïve to expect of an organization with the background of the ANC to be just a little more than merely expedient?

• One of the most prominent leaders of the Mass Democratic Movement of the eighties, when the ANC was a banned organization, now faces charges of stealing the equivalent of hundreds of thousands of US dollars donated by governments, NGOs, and charities all over the world specifically to alleviate the plight of the poor. Once a rallying force against apartheid, inspiring the oppressed masses in their years of suffering, this individual now turns out to have lived a life of luxury — on the money he received, as a man of God, on behalf of the poor. This may be bad enough, but it is, perhaps, no more than a revelation of human frailty. However, it does become unsettling when representatives of the government use their official positions to raise money for his defence, and when the Minister of Justice personally endorses the accused as a hero of the people. Of course anybody is innocent until found guilty; but when the state itself goes out of its way to make a spectacle of its support for one side in a case still to be tried, justice becomes a farce. One has seen this happen, at the opposite end of the political spectrum, in the heyday of the Ku Klux Klan in the US; it is not edifying to see it repeated in the new context. And in a sense this is worse, because if it is something perhaps to be "expected" of the extreme right, it is less so when it occurs within an organization which has for so long been justifiably proud of its moral high ground. If such disrespect toward the law is demonstrated even within the Ministry of Justice, no wonder that crime is rampant in the country.

• The government, commendably, overhauls the education system and opens all schools to all races. Just as commendably it decides to break down the discrepancies between education for the privileged and the underprivileged (which under apartheid coincided with "whites" and "blacks"). As one of the consequences, it is decided that the ratio between teachers and pupils should be the same in all schools. But in implementing the policy, thousands of teachers from "privileged" schools (including, for obvious reasons, many of the best qualified teachers in the country) are sacked — at staggering expense — in order to bring these schools down to the level of those with the worst ratios, rather than the other way round. Because that alternative is deemed too expensive, presumably because mismanagement, corruption, nepotism, unrealistic extremes of affirmative action, and the like have so depleted the state coffers that there is nothing left when it comes to the truly significant contents of transformation.

The process of restructuring education in this manner also involves the possibility for the state to "redeploy" teachers in underprivileged schools (as an alternative to retrenchment), and indeed it seems a noble cause, even if it appears obtuse in the light of the disruption this may cause to families, the careers of spouses, etc.; but it does remove from schools and their governing bodies the right to appoint the teachers of their choice, as they are obliged to accept whatever teacher the Department of Education designates to fill a post. And so, in the praiseworthy attempt to redress past evils, democracy once again becomes the first victim. When some schools resisted this plan, and won their battle in court, the government responded in exactly the way the apartheid régime used to solve similar dilemmas: it passed a new law to reverse the effects of the court decision.

• One of the gains of the new dispensation has been the fact that the Afrikaans language, perceived for so long as "the language of apartheid," has finally been set free from its political cage to return to its roots as the language of people born in Africa, many of them slaves and oppressed and humiliated at the time but now free to assume their full destiny as Africans. And many of the ANC leaders, including most notably President Mandela, have expressed their recognition of the language as inextricably part of the South African cultural weave: no longer privileged — and suspect — as one of two "white," official languages, but as one among many others, splendidly equal. Yet at least one minister has in recent months been overheard saying that the Afrikaans language is the ultimate price the ANC will exact for their suffering under apartheid. Again, this may be an understandable human reaction (especially if "human" is to be read at its lowest and most vindictive level). But after so much inspiring talk, for so long, about *ubuntu,* and generosity, and forgiveness, and understanding: is this really all it comes down to again? A tooth for a tooth and an eye for an eye. One had expected more than this. I believe one had *reason* to expect more.

It may seem curious, if not foolish and pigheaded, after this list of grievances — and many more could have been added! — to assert that I still have faith in the future of the ANC; that I still believe it capable of demonstrating to the world not just the operations of a new dispensation but a new *kind* of dispensation: a dispensation which indeed falls far short of its ideals of democracy and transparency and morality, but which nevertheless remains committed to them, *as ideals.* Perhaps my position is something like that of Boccaccio's Jew from Paris who resisted all attempts to get him converted to Catholicism, until at last, to please his persistent Christian friend, he went to Rome and returned a convert. Not because he had been overwhelmed by the religious qualities of the Church, but rather the opposite: he had seen in Rome, he said, no sanctity, no devotion, no good works or examples among any of the clergy, only lechery, avarice, gluttony, and a proliferation of other sins, as if the pope and all his followers were doing their level best to destroy every vestige of Christianity. Yet, "since I perceive that what they endeavor to achieve does not occur, but that your religion continually increases and becomes brighter and more illustrious, I justly am of the opinion that the Holy Spirit is its support and foundation." And I think the ANC, as illuminated — above all — by the example of Mandela, remains the only hope, however tenuous at times, for showing the country, and perhaps the world, a way out of the millennial morass of racism, self-interest, inequality, and indignity. Provided it can return to an affirmation of those political and moral qualities that earned it respect during the almost eighty years that preceded its accession to power.

There is no excuse for any of these actions. But they are not free-floating or absolute: they exist within a very specific social and historical framework, and the briefest glance at Russia should confirm that such convulsions, even if unpardonable, are not exceptional and may to a large extent have been historically unavoidable. Most whites, their middle class still safely ensconced in the comfort and privilege they have constructed on the exploitation and denial of others, have no conception of the odds against which the ANC has been battling: a civil service bureaucracy inherited from the apartheid era and bent on frustrating almost every attempt at introducing change; a security establishment which has, at least partly, gone underground with the express intention of fomenting unrest and making the situation unmanageable and the country ungovernable; the staggering burden of illiteracy or near-illiteracy; the increasing gulf between haves and have-nots; the persistence of mindsets that are the co-products of privilege on the one hand and victimhood on the other; the unrealistic scope of expectations kindled by the transition (and which may occasionally appear amusing if witnessed from within the relative affluence of a white suburban home but assumes dire proportions when placed in context); the staggering cost of meeting the challenges of this *fin de siècle* in addition to redressing the legacy of wrongs from the past.

It is, at best, dangerous to justify any set of means in terms of its end: yet it does not seem outrageous to argue that at least in *some* situations a measure of coercion may be required in order to *move toward* democracy in a context where a vast electorate (black and white) has had no exposure to democracy before, with the result that many clamor for its fruits while as yet unprepared to shoulder its weighty responsibilities.

And so I would suggest that, given the circumstances, one can understand, even if no one in his senses can condone, some aspects of the abuse of power evident from the instances I have referred to. At the same time I would like to think that such instances, prolific as they may be, are only the ugly flotsam and jetsam on the surface of the stream: down below, the current is still running deep and strong, and in the right direction.

Informed criticism, even head-on attack, is a vital part of true democracy. But a purely negative stance denies two immensely important dimensions of the transformation over the last decade. There is, first, the simple *extent* of the actual change South Africa has lived through, the undeniable distance it has travelled since the dark days of torture and power-politics and lies and manipulation, toward the *possibility* of free speech and of co-operation which we experience today. A cardinal feature of the new South African society is the fact that every time a scandal breaks (and with the increased freedom of the press it is bound to happen sooner rather than later) there is a huge public outcry, which would have been unthinkable under the previous régime. Second, if one compares the actual situation in the country, warts and running sores and all, with any alternative that might have obtained had the changes *not* taken place, it is immediately evident that the difference is, by any standards, amazing.

There is a larger framework of thinking which may be obscured by the kind of purely destructive complaining that surfaced at the Dakar reunion, and which has dominated so much of public debate over the last year or so, not just among Afrikaners but among whites generally. Underlying this sniping is, in almost every instance, the hurt caused by the loss of power. And as one ANC spokesperson pointed out at the reunion, we should distinguish very clearly between the pain caused by the loss of privilege and the suffering of real deprivation.

It seems to me an abdication of moral integrity to wage a struggle for the protection and/or maintenance of the Afrikaans language unless it is inserted within the much larger problematic of a *multicultural society,* or of a *spectrum of minority languages.* Similarly, sniping at the ANC for eroding white culture or exacerbating white fears invariably means turning a blind eye to the much more comprehensive problem of *minorities* in a variegated country. For as long as people persist in this kind of compartmentalized group thinking, ignoring the larger, and more challenging, frameworks of intellectual and cultural enterprise, we shall perpetuate the fracturings of the past and fail in any attempt to realize what the first Dakar meeting so dramatically demonstrated: the possibility of coming, and acting, and working, and living together in a country which is still one of almost boundless opportunity.

How depressing, one thought so often during the day of reunion, that speaker after speaker bemoaned the dangers threatening Afrikaans or the exclusion of Afrikaners from power.

Because ultimately this is the attitude of people who threaten to exclude *themselves* from any meaningful part in the amazing adventure the new country has embarked on, by making themselves irrelevant to the larger process. By harping only on group issues, by acting only within a framework of narrow oppositionality, defining themselves uniquely in terms of what they are *against* rather than of what they can share, they deprive not only themselves of a role in shaping the future but the country as a whole of benefit from their often quite formidable talents. This kind of abdication of responsibility is surely a warning signal that cannot be ignored.

It translates into an absence of vigorous debate in South Africa about the fundamental issues facing our fledgling democracy. There may be many reasons for it: the loss of power which inhibits whites; the reluctance among blacks to interrogate the machinations of the government they had for so long struggled to put in place. But whatever the reasons, the renunciation of moral and intellectual responsibility can have dire consequences for the values of our new society. And unless the real energies and talents and the imagination and intellectual effort demonstrated at Dakar ten years ago can be recovered and activated within the new enlarged context, the country as a whole will pay the price.

Bibliography

Atwood, Margaret 1972: *Surfacing. A Thematic Guide to Canadian Literature.* Toronto, Anansi.

Barker, Francis, and Hulme, Peter 1985: "Nymphs and Reapers Heavily Vanish: the discursive con-texts of *The Tempest.*" In Drakakis, John (ed): *Alternative Shakespeares.* London, Methuen.

Barthes, Roland 1976 (1975): *The Pleasure of the Text.* London, Jonathan Cape.

— 1979: *A Lover's Discourse.* London, Jonathan Cape.

— 1968 (1953): *Writing Degree Zero.* New York, Hill & Wang.

Coetzee, J. M. 1988: *White Writing. On the Culture of Letters in South Africa.* New Haven and London, Yale University Press.

DeLillo, Don 1991: *Mao II.* London, Jonathan Cape.

Driver, Dorothy 1992: "Women and Nature, Women as Objects of Exchange. Toward a Feminist Analysis of South African Literature." In Chapman, Michael, *et al.*: *Perspectives on South African Literature.* Parklands (Johannesburg), Ad Donker.

Gordimer, Nadine 1988: *The Essential Gesture.* Cape Town and Johannesburg, David Philip/Taurus.

Harrow, Kenneth W. 1994: *Threshholds of Change in African Literature. The Emergence of a Tradition.* Portsmouth and London, Heinemann.

Kermode, Frank 1997 (1966): *The Sense of an Ending. Studies in the Theory of Fiction.* London etc., Oxford University Press.

de Kock, Ingrid, and Press, Karen 1990: *Spring is Rebellious. Arguments about Freedom by Albie Sachs and Respondents.* Cape Town, Buchu Books.

Kundera, Milan 1983: *The Joke.* London, Faber & Faber.

Massie, Robert Kinloch 1997: *Loosing the Bonds. The United States and South Africa in the Apartheid Years.* New York etc., Nan A. Talese, Doubleday.

Morgan, Thaïs E. 1994: *Men Writing the Feminine. Literature, Theory, and the Question of Genders.* Albany, State University of New York Press.

Moyana, T. T. 1976: "Problems of a Creative Writer in South Africa." In Heywood, C. (ed): *Aspects of South African Literature.* London, Heinemann.

Musil, Robert 1988 (1930): *The Man Without Qualities,* Vol. 1. London, Picador.

Ndebele, Njabulo S. 1991: *Rediscovering the Ordinary. Essays on South African Literature and Culture.* Johannesburg, COSAW.

Ngugi wa Thiong'o 1981: "Return to the Roots." In *Writers in Politics.* London, Heinemann.

— 1986: *Decolonising the Mind.* London, James Currey; Nairobi, Heinemann.

Nicol, Mike 1991: *A Good-Looking Corpse.* London, Secker & Warburg.

Okot p'Bitek 1972: *Song of Lawino and Song of Ocol.* Nairobi, Heinemann.

Rive, Richard 1981: *Writing Black.* Cape Town, David Philip.

Rufin, Jean-Christophe 1991: *L'Empire et les nouveaux Barbares.* Paris, Clattès.

Smyth, Malvern van Wyk 1990: *Grounds of Conquest. A Survey of South African English Literature.* Kenwyn (Cape Town), Jutalit.

Visser, Nicholas 1990: "Beyond the Interregnum: a Note on the ending of *July's People.*" In Trump, Martin (ed): *Rendering Things Visible.* Johannesburg, Ravan Press.

Wetherell, Margaret, and Potter, Jonathan 1992: *Mapping the Language of Racism. Discourse and the Legitimation of Exploitation.* New York etc., Harvester Wheatsheaf.

White, Hayden 1978: *Tropics of Discourse.* Baltimore and London, Johns Hopkins University Press.

Notes

Reimagining the Real (pp. 144–163)

1. Cf. Kundera's introduction to *The Joke* (1983:xii) in which he welcomes (tongue in cheek?) the changed historical circumstances in which "the novel [can] ultimately be what it has always meant to be: *merely* a novel."

2. Occasional references to short stories by black writers are prompted by the consideration that, largely for social and economic reasons, South African black fiction has shown a preference for this genre.

3. In texts by black authors, on the contrary, with *Woza Albert!* foremost among them, the destruction of present misery is merely the means through which the utopia of liberation can be achieved.

4. Cf. notably Visser 1990.

5. Even if the novel was initially banned, it was soon released in the watershed period of 1989–1990 when censorship of literature in South Africa was dramatically reformed — presumably because the banning of an Afrikaans work, *Magersfontein o Magersfontein* by an author close to the power establishment, had embarrassed the régime.

6. Once again there is a link, here, with the larger experience of decolonization. Cf. Ngugi 1986:108: "Struggle. Struggle makes history. Struggle makes us. In struggle is our history, our language and our being."

7. This comes close to Barthes's description of revolutionary writing in France as "the one and only grand gesture commensurate with the daily presence of the guillotine. What today appears turgid was then no more than life-size." (Barthes 1968:22)
8. Once again it is useful to be reminded that this is not a problem peculiar to South Africa. With the disappearance of the "Second World" from the global scene the First seems suddenly bewildered in its own attempts at finding new descriptions of itself. There is a need for the Empire, as Rufin (1991) argues, to find a new set of "Barbarians." And especially if these new barbarians are to be found in the "south," as Rufin believes, this may have profound implications for South African culture, among others.

Reinventing a Continent (pp. 229–245)

1. For equivalents of "historical novels" in Zulu, Xhosa, Sotho and other indigenous literatures one would have to explore oral tradition. The influence of this tradition on a novel like A. C. Jordan's *Ingqumbo Yeminyana* (*The Wrath of the Ancestors*) is discussed elsewhere in this essay.
2. This functioning of metaphor White explains by referring to the familiar metaphorical equation of "my love" and "rose": it does not suggest, he points out, that the beloved is *actually* a rose; nor does it suggest that the loved one has the specific attributes of a rose, i.e. that she or he is red, or yellow, is a plant, has thorns, needs sunlight, "should be sprayed regularly with insecticide" etc.: "it is meant to be understood as indicating that the beloved shares the *qualities* which the rose has come to *symbolize* in the customary linguistic usages of Western culture . . . The metaphor does not *image* the thing it seeks to characterize, *it gives directions* for finding the set of images that are intended to be associated with that thing." (White 1978:91)
3. The Khoikhoi word *kamma* means *water,* which refers to a creation myth in which the first woman (in Africa) emerged from water; in Afrikaans it refers to the realm of the imagination, of illusion, and of fiction.